IMAGES
of America

Gennett Records and Starr Piano

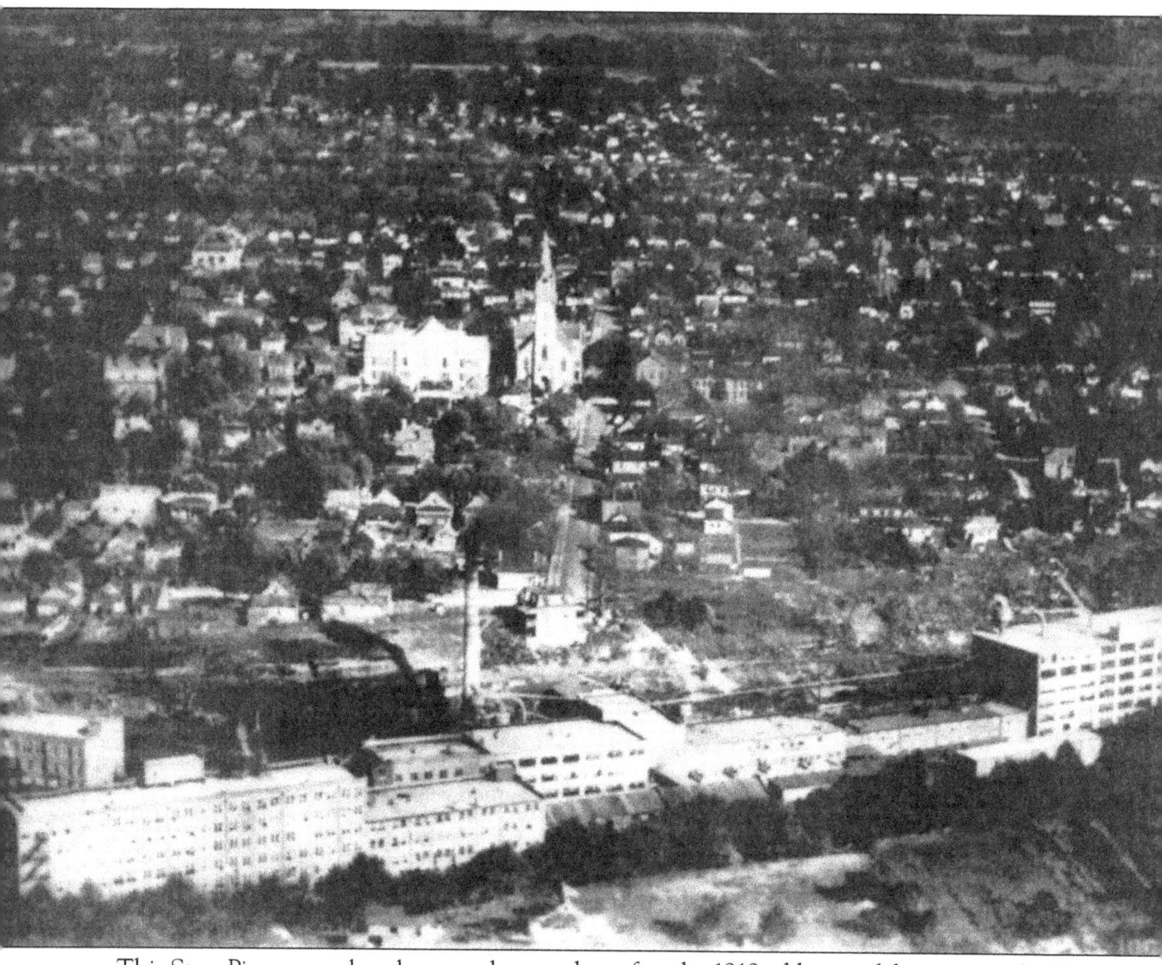

This Starr Piano complex photograph was taken after the 1919 addition of the concrete building on the far right. Starr Piano added the six-story building to accommodate its expansion into manufacturing phonographs and pressing records. From 1919 to 1920, a very profitable time for Starr, the annual production of manufactured goods included 35,000 spring-driven phonographs and more than three million records, all recorded in its Gennett studios. This photograph appears in a 1991 edition of the *Pal-Item* newspaper. (Stephanie Gennett Beach.)

On the Cover: In 1923, Art Landry and His Call of the North Orchestra first recorded at Gennett's New York City studio in the spring before they headed to Richmond, Indiana. Gennett took this photograph of Landry with his orchestra during the June 2 session, where Gennett rejected most of the recordings. The outfit returned two weeks later for a productive session that included "Rip Saw Blues" and "Melody in F." This photograph also shows the drapery used by Gennett to deaden the recording room and how they arranged the musicians to maximize a balanced mix in the acoustic recording era. (Linda Gennett Irmscher.)

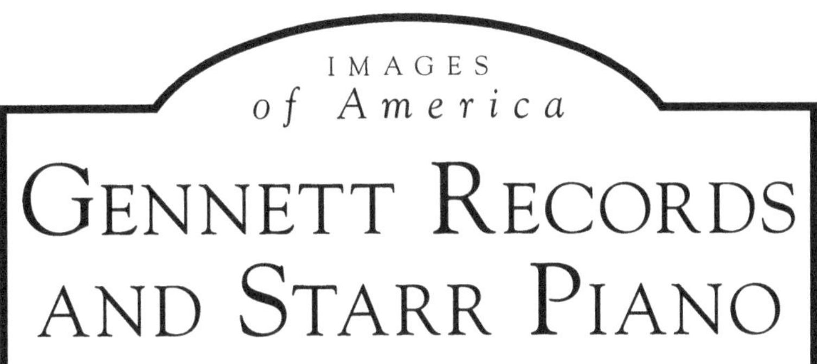

Charlie B. Dahan and
Linda Gennett Irmscher

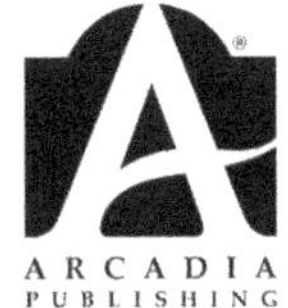

ISBN 978-1-4671-1725-8

Published by Arcadia Publishing
Charleston, South Carolina

Library of Congress Control Number: 2016936950

For all general information, please contact Arcadia Publishing:
Telephone 843-853-2070
Fax 843-853-0044
E-mail sales@arcadiapublishing.com
For customer service and orders:
Toll-Free 1-888-313-2665

Visit us on the Internet at www.arcadiapublishing.com

This book is dedicated to the loving memories of Bonnie Babbitt Dahan and Harry Gennett Jr.

Contents

ACKNOWLEDGMENTS

Charlie B. Dahan (CBD) and Linda Gennett Irmscher (LGI) thank the following people and organizations for their support and willingness to share so much great information and photographs with them: Stephanie Gennett Beach; Brian Henry Martin; Rosanne Karlebach; Mike Gennett; Laurel Martin; Brenda Starr Duckworth; Steve Gennett; Carvin Rinehart and Infinit Print Solutions; Bob Jacobsen, David Fulton, and Lynn Johnstone at the Starr-Gennett Foundation; Jim Harlan at the Wayne County Historical Museum; Sue King at the Morrisson-Reeves Library; Millie Martin and the *Pal-Item*; Olivia Beaudry, Martin Fisher, Rachel Morris, and Greg Reish at the Center for Popular Music at Middle Tennessee State University (MTSU); Dave Lewis at the Birthplace of Country Music Museum; Rick Kennedy; Elizabeth Surles at the Institute for Jazz Studies; Richard Nevins; Marc Dahan; Dino Gankendorff; T. Malcolm Rockwell; Uncle David Lewis; Rebecca Forste; Tony Russell; Marshall Wyatt at Old Hat Records; John Dougan, Susan Myers-Shirk, Rebecca Conard, Beverly Keel, Brenden Martin, and Carroll Van West at Middle Tennessee State University; Sharon Mitchell, Harry Rice, and Rachel Vagts at Berea College Special Collections and Archives; the Indiana Historical Society; Donna and Bob Geddes; Joe Bussard; Sherwin Dunner; Roger Misiewicz; Peter Whelan; Tom Irmscher; Melissa Dahan; and Juliana Dahan.

INTRODUCTION

On October 3, 1993, the local newspaper *Palladium-Item* asked the citizens of Richmond, Indiana, to clip a coupon and answer a pressing question: Should we "Save or Raze" it? The remaining buildings in the Whitewater Gorge, better known as Starr Valley, were the "it" in question. The *Palladium-Item* asked its readers to consider both the financial and historical cost of saving or razing the buildings. So much history occurred on that 35-acre lot. Starr Valley holds significant familial, industrial, economic, cultural, musical, political, and even military history—basically Starr Valley is a site of American history.

In 1884, Nashville residents Henry Gennett and his father-in-law John Lumsden became equal partners with Jesse French and Oscar Field in the St. Louis, Missouri, Jesse French Piano Company. By 1891, Gennett relocated to St. Louis and served as the piano retailer's vice president and sought to purchase an established and reputable piano manufacturing company.

Richmond, Indiana, businessmen James Starr and Richard Jackson encouraged Trayser Piano to move to Richmond in 1872 and establish a piano factory. By 1878, they purchased 23 acres along the Whitewater River and constructed a four-story factory building. The piano was the centerpiece of American homes, as it provided both entertainment and cultural expression. On April 7, 1893, Henry Gennett and John Lumsden purchased a 50 percent ownership stake in Starr Piano.

Henry Gennett and his entrepreneurial and visionary skills provided Starr Piano a much-needed boost from his St. Louis office. In January 1894, a huge fire destroyed much of the Richmond factory complex. Rumors persisted of Starr moving its headquarters to St. Louis. However, John Lumsden stated that he did not believe in "crying over spilled milk" and confirmed Starr Piano's commitment to rebuild and expand in Richmond. Henry Gennett moved to Richmond, as he believed Starr Piano possessed more profit potential with its skilled craftsmen and labor and supervised the rebuilding and expansion of the factory complex. With Gennett's focused leadership, Starr Piano grew its market share, and by 1903, he assumed control of Starr Piano after the deaths of his partners.

As the company expanded, Henry Gennett looked to his three sons—Harry, Clarence, and Fred—to help run the factory and retail operations. While the Gennetts succeeded in the piano business, the subsequent growth of the burgeoning phonograph industry threatened the piano's market share.

The phonograph industry changed from a tight oligopoly to a free market when Henry Gennett's three sons decided to expand into the sound recording field in 1915. The phonograph industry was both a natural fit for Starr Piano's capabilities and retail network and a serious threat for market share in the home entertainment industry. Starr Piano's entry into the recording industry caused a paradigm shift that led to "the birth of the modern recording industry and the introduction of American music and culture to the world."

On December 10, 1918, one of the two lateral record patents expired, and Fred Gennett believed the remaining one held by Victor was duplicitous and not valid. In April 1919, Starr Piano's newly christened Gennett Records placed a full-page advertisement in *Talking Machine World* that announced its records were now available as lateral discs. Victor immediately sued for patent infringement and lost. Starr Piano's victory in the *Victor Talking Machine Company v. Starr Piano* lawsuit acted as a catalyst for the rapid growth of new record companies. However, these new companies faced an uphill battle in the popular and highbrow music marketplace from the larger Victor and Columbia. The new record labels needed to take advantage of vacuums of music Victor and Columbia ignored from the outset—American vernacular music.

In 1921, Starr Piano opened a recording studio in its Richmond, Indiana, industrial complex. This was the only permanent recording facility between New York City and San Francisco with the exception of Chicago. The new studio placed Gennett Records in the unique position to record the popular and vernacular music emanating from Chicago, Cincinnati, Indianapolis, and Kentucky. Fred Gennett realized there was little to no competition with regional and local music and that a significant population possessed both the finances and technology to consume these records. It existed and was untapped.

Starr Piano's Chicago store manager, Fred Wiggins, scouted and recommended several hot jazz artists popular at the Lincoln Gardens and the Friar's Inn nightclubs. Such groundbreaking jazz pioneers as the New Orleans Rhythm Kings, King Oliver's Creole Jazz Band featuring Louis Armstrong, and Jelly Roll Morton headed down the line to record in the newly opened Richmond studio. When word spread of the great jazz records made in Richmond, several Indiana residents ventured to Starr Valley to record, including Bix Beiderbecke and Hoagy Carmichael, who released his first version of "Stardust" on Gennett. Rick Kennedy in *Jelly Roll, Bix, and Hoagy: Gennett Records and the Rise of America's Musical Grassroots* observes, "Despite its location in rural Indiana, the Richmond studio produced some of the first significant jazz recordings and exerted an impact on the music scene that was immediate, widespread, and lasting."

The Chicago connection also brought several acoustic blues artists to Richmond, including Georgia Tom Dorsey, Big Bill Broonzy, and Scrapper Blackwell. In 1929, Paramount Records leased Gennett's studio and sent some of its groundbreaking blues artists—Charley Patton, Blind Lemon Jefferson, and Blind Blake—to record in Richmond. Gennett also developed relationships with rural Kentucky music talent scouts Dennis Taylor and Doc Roberts. These connections to rural music established Gennett as a leader in the burgeoning hillbilly music market. Charles Wolfe in *Kentucky Country* observes, "From 1925 to 1933, Gennett recorded more country music from Kentucky than from any other state, and preserved many rare examples of the variety of traditional music in Kentucky."

For as quickly as Starr Piano's recording division arose, it just as quickly crashed. After several years of strong growth, Starr Piano suffered greatly after the 1929 stock market crash and the subsequent Great Depression. Increased competition from radio and motion pictures also aided in its collapse and eventual decision to close the plant and the business in 1952. Harry Alpert of J. Solotken Company purchased a majority ownership and sold the pressing plant to Decca Records. Decca operated a record manufacturing concern in the Starr Valley complex through 1956 when Mercury Records took over the facility through 1969.

Throughout the 1970s, most of the buildings in Starr Valley remained abandoned. Unable to attract new tenants and plagued by ongoing vandalism, Alpert auctioned Starr Valley to the highest bidder on October 28, 1976. Frank Robinson of Richmond purchased the site for $84,000. The vandalism and deterioration led Robinson to tear down all but two of the remaining buildings.

Perhaps Robinson's demolition served as either a wake-up call or the last straw for several of Richmond's citizens. In the 1980s, these concerned citizens explored ways to preserve and commemorate the historic site. Some eventually formed a not-for-profit organization, the Starr-Gennett Foundation, and worked in concert with local and state governments to both gain control of the site and develop ways to preserve and interpret it. They arrived at a plan and received various grants that repurposed the remaining building into an events venue and turned the 35-acre site into a greenway in the early 2000s. Additionally, the foundation installed historic interpretative markers and a Gennett Records Walk of Fame in the sidewalk along the river in 2007. Each September, the foundation inducts new musicians into the Gennett Records Walk of Fame and promotes several concerts and community events to celebrate and acknowledge this story throughout the year. "Once there was music here" proclaims an interpretive sign that now resides in Starr Valley at the site where the Starr Piano buildings once stood; but now there is a place to commemorate and celebrate its history and continuing influence on American music and culture.

One

The Rise of Starr Piano 1872–1915

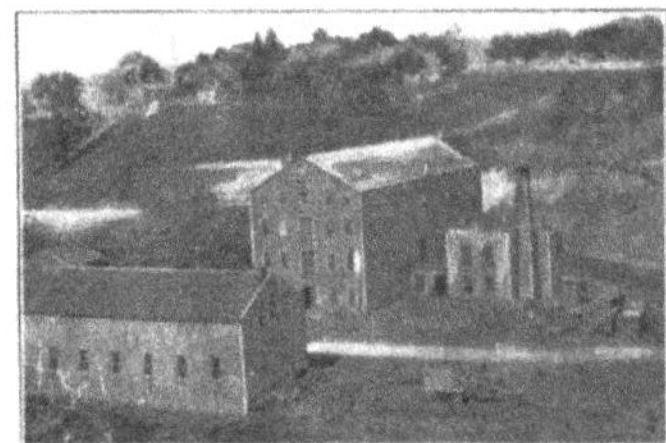

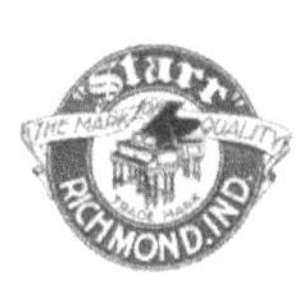

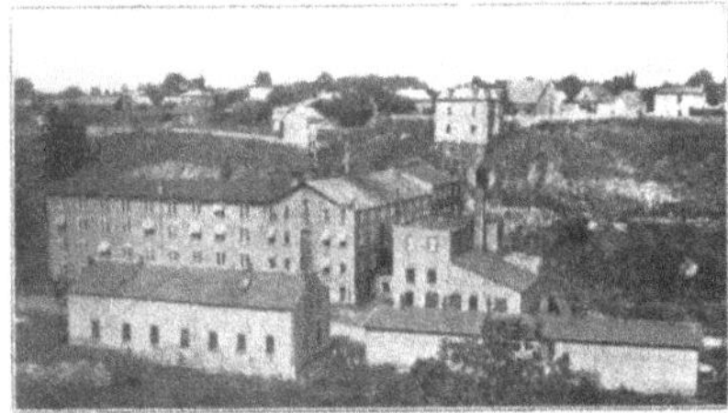

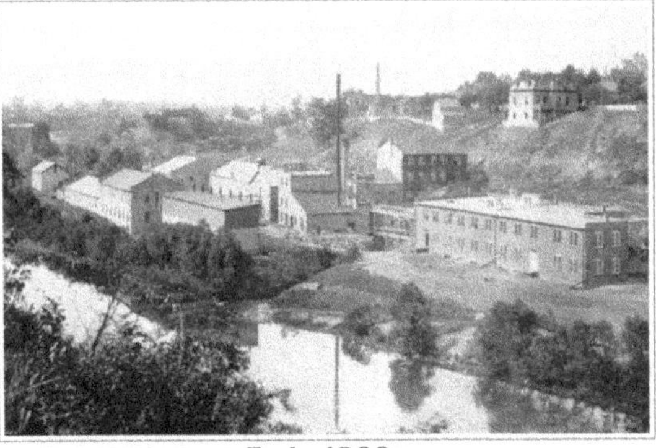

The Starr Piano Company began in Richmond, Indiana, as a single building near the railroad depot in 1872. The company made two to three pianos a week. In 1878, the owners purchased 23 acres along the Whitewater River and constructed a four-story building. The Starr Piano Company incorporated in 1893 and rapidly expanded into the next century. By 1915, the complex covered 35 acres, employed 750 people, and produced 15,000 pianos a year. Starr Piano then decided to enter the recording field. (LGI.)

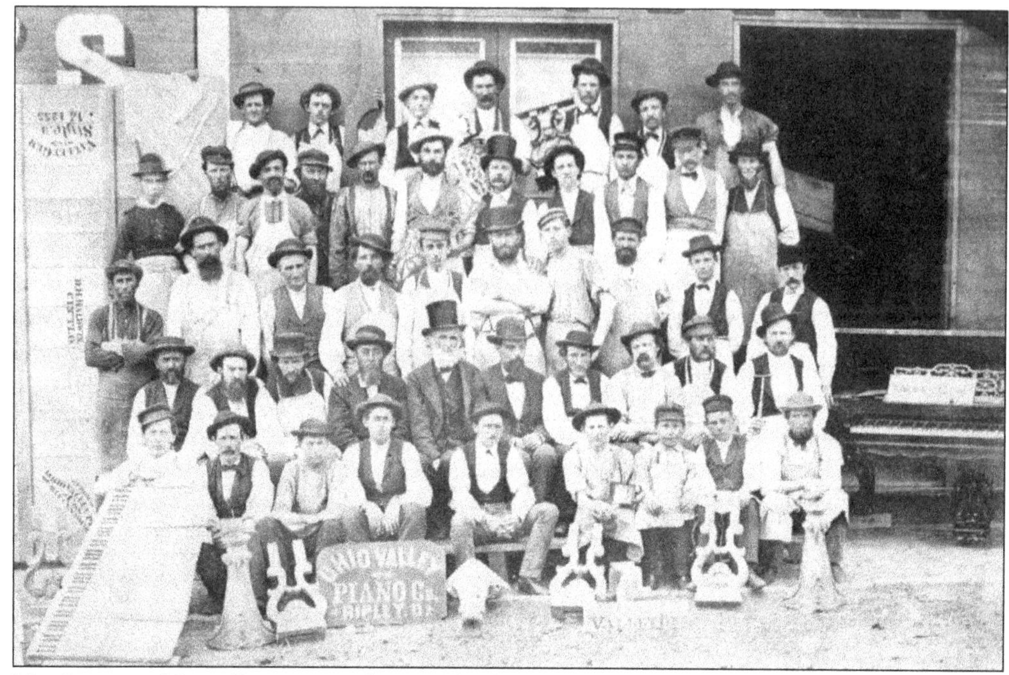

The history of Starr Piano started in 1865, when George Trayser (1808–1881) began building pianos in Ripley, Ohio. Four years later, Trayser incorporated the Ohio Valley Piano Forte Company. Its pianos were sold under the name Valley Gem by D.H. Baldwin. In 1872, Trayser's successful piano company moved to Richmond after it came to the attention of residents James Starr and Richard Jackson. The owners constructed a three-story building at North Eighth and Elm Streets. (LGI.)

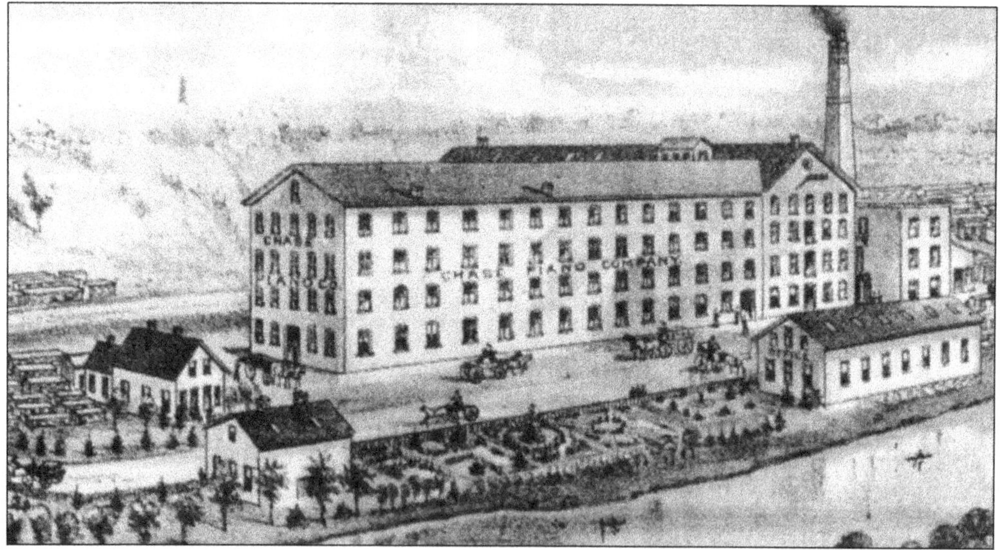

In 1877, the Valley Gem Company merged into the Trayser Piano Company, which now included Milo Chase. Trayser retired in 1878 and sold his interest in the company to Chase. In 1878, Trayser Piano Forte was incorporated and renamed Chase Piano Company. The owners then bought 23 acres along the Whitewater River and built their first four-story building. Business was flourishing and 10 to 15 pianos were produced each week. (LGI.)

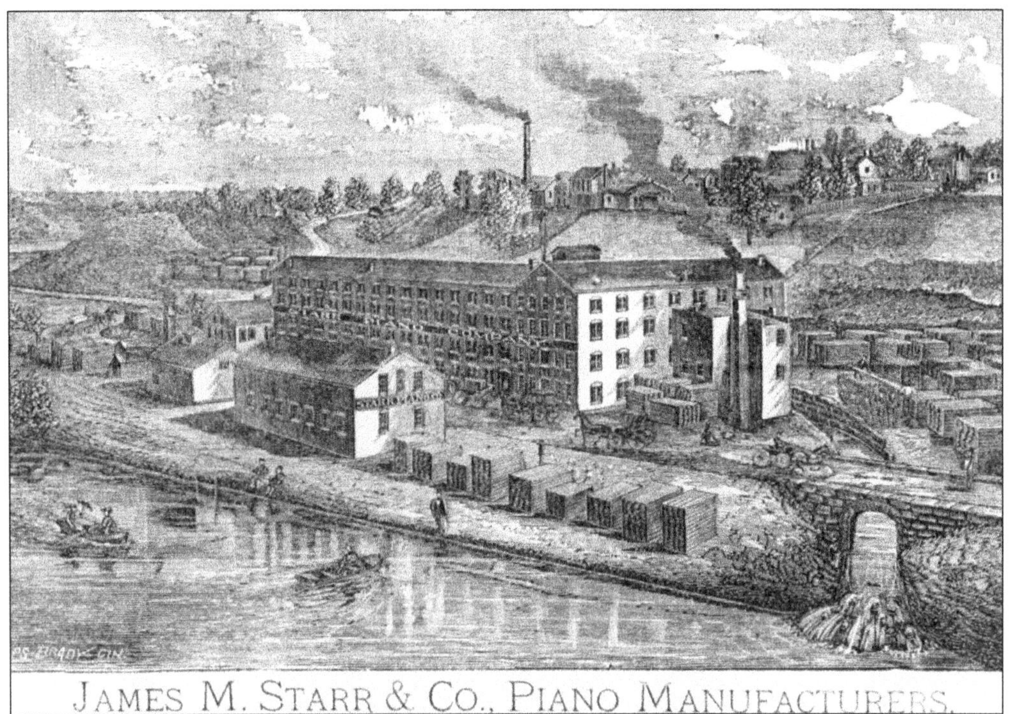

James and Benjamin Starr were involved financially as soon as Trayser moved his piano company to Richmond in 1872. The brothers were sons of Charles Starr, a business leader who was instrumental in the early growth of Richmond. Today, Richmond's historic Starr District is listed in the National Register of Historic Places. By 1883, Chase Piano Company employed 150 people. Milo Chase left in 1884, and James Starr took over the entire plant, which consisted of the four-story building where all the woodwork was done, a small one-story structure used as a storehouse, and several lumber sheds. The name was changed from Chase Piano to the James M. Starr Piano Company. James Starr became president and his brother Benjamin ran the expanding factory, which was now producing 20 pianos each week. The photograph below was taken around 1900. (Above, Morrisson-Reeves Library; below, LGI.)

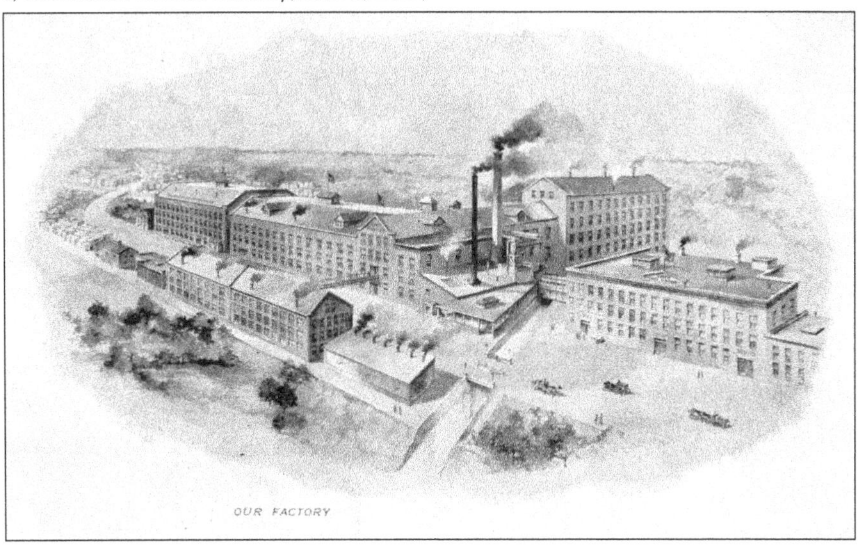

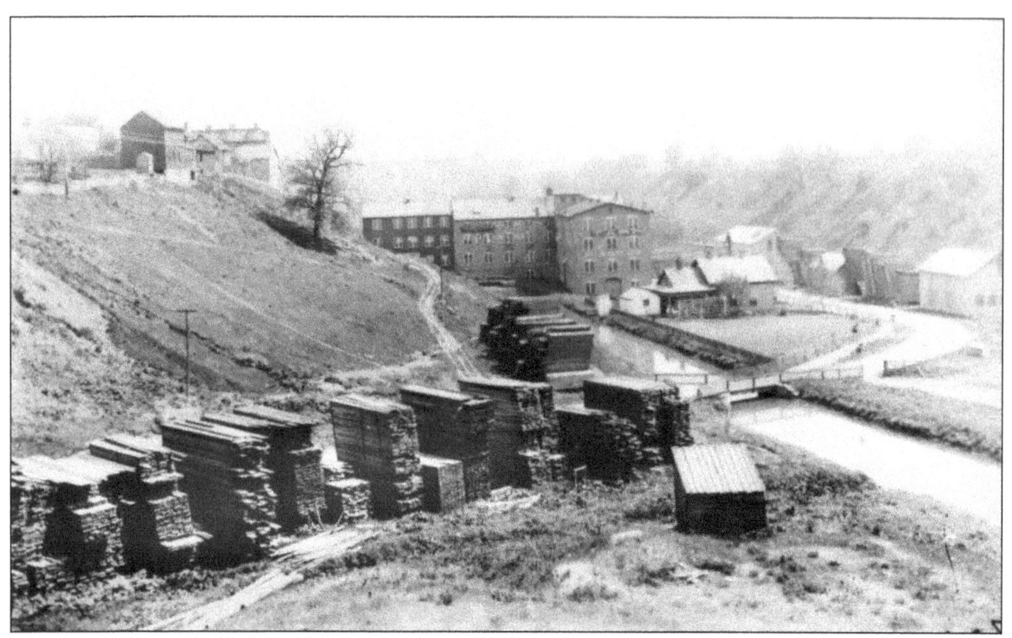

This 1892 photograph shows lumberyards containing no less than a million-and-a-half board feet, with every foot thoroughly air dried and seasoned for a long time before it was moved to the large dry kilns. There, it was further treated with the "common sense" process of hot-air blasts and condensation and evaporation, and then sent to the mill department. The result was the "most reliable lumber to be obtained," according to a 1900 Starr Piano catalog. (LGI.)

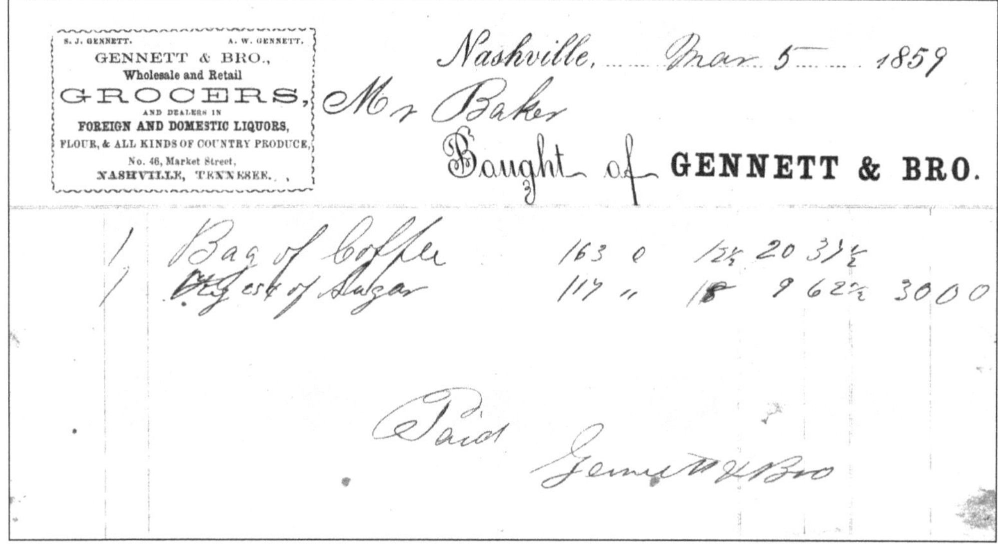

S. J. GENNETT. A. W. GENNETT.
GENNETT & BRO.,
Wholesale and Retail
GROCERS,
AND DEALERS IN
FOREIGN AND DOMESTIC LIQUORS,
FLOUR, & ALL KINDS OF COUNTRY PRODUCE,
No. 46, Market Street,
NASHVILLE, TENNESSEE.

Nashville, Mar 5 1859

Mr Baker

Bought of GENNETT & BRO.

1 Bag of Coffee 163 0 12½ 20 37½
1 ... of Sugar 117 " 18 9 62½ 30 00

Paid
Gennett & Bro

Gennett and Brothers, a family wholesale and retail grocery business, began in Nashville, Tennessee, in 1833. Henry Gennett's father, Andrew, died in 1858 when he was six. This 1859 grocery receipt shows Henry's older brothers, James and Anthony, were running the business. Around 1872, Gennett & Brothers switched from a crowded grocery business and became the only wholesale peanut commission merchant. Henry then entered the business as a bookkeeper and three years later was listed as a member of Gennett and Company. (LGI.)

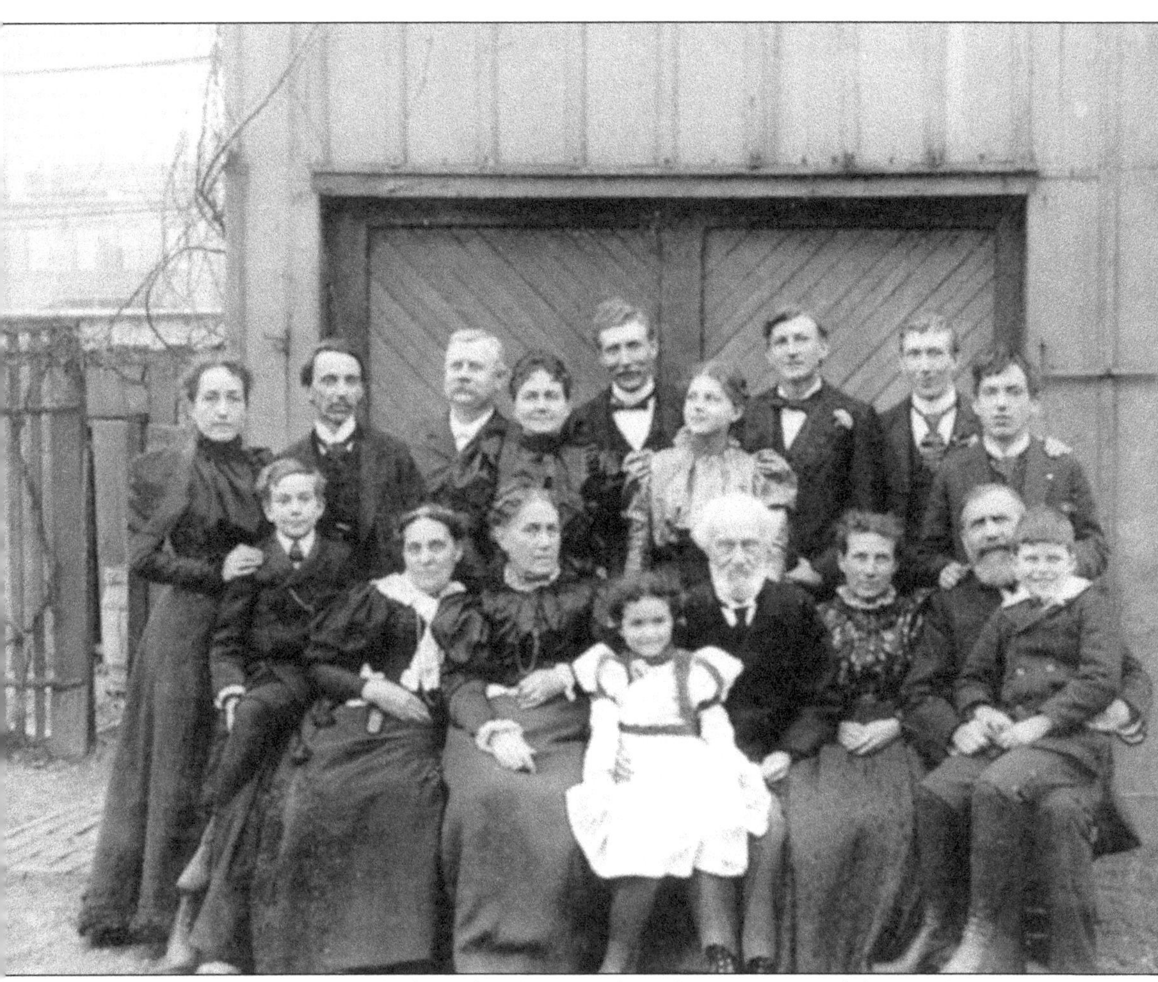

Three prominent families of Nashville—the John Lumsdens, the Gennetts, and the Frenches—were well acquainted since they were all doing business within a block of each other on South Market Street before and after the Civil War. The business ties between the families became even closer through the marriages of Lumsden's three daughters. The eldest, Caroline or "Callie," married Jesse French in 1872, and the youngest, Alice, married Henry Gennett in 1876. Jesse French became the first in the extended families to enter the music business when in 1873 he bought a Nashville music business and renamed it the Jesse French Piano Company. It is thought that Oscar Field joined French in this business in 1875 and later married the third Lumsden daughter, Maria, in 1882. Oscar and Maria moved to St. Louis in 1883, where he worked as a piano manufacturer representative. Jesse French soon joined his brother-in-law in business, and together they formed Field, French and Company, which later became the Field-French Piano Company. In 1884, Henry Gennett paid $15,000 and, with Field, French, and Lumsden, became an equal partner. (Jesse French family.)

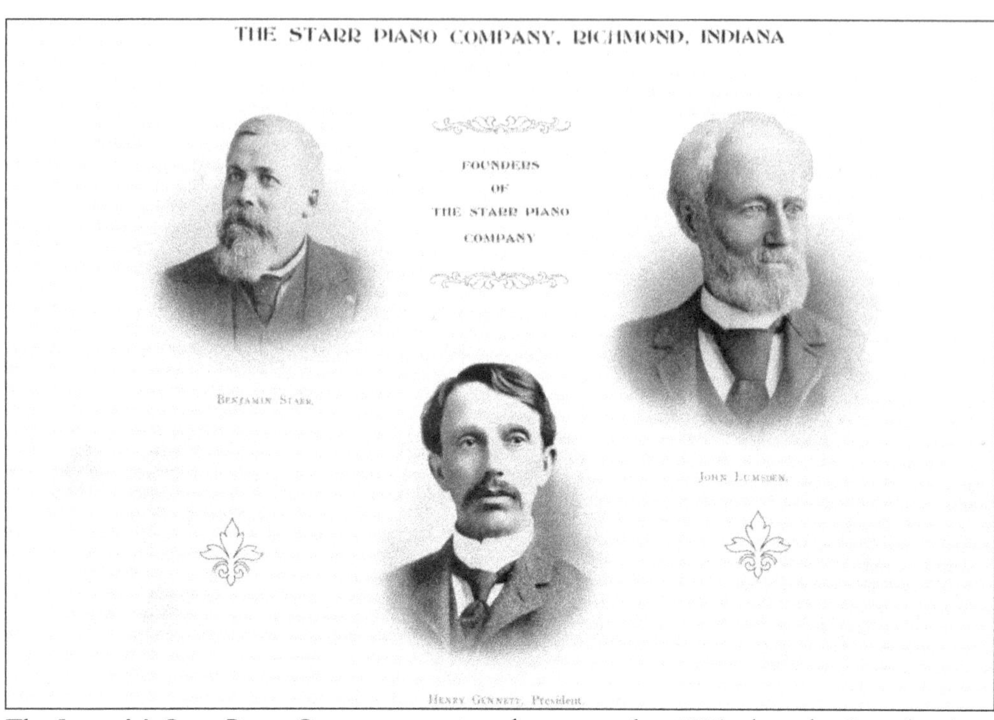

The James M. Starr Piano Company continued to grow after 1885 when the Starr brothers took control. Great numbers of Starr pianos were being shipped to Jesse French retail outlets throughout the South, and the companies were well acquainted. In 1892, merger negotiations began between John Lumsden, his son-in-law Henry Gennett, and the Starr brothers. On April 7, 1893, the new Starr Piano Company was organized and significantly recapitalized with a $100,000 stock issuance. Gennett and Lumsden owned 50 percent and, along with French, joined the Starr brothers on the company board of directors. John Lumsden died in 1898, James Starr died in 1900, and Benjamin Starr died three years later. From left to right are (first row) Henry Gennett, Benjamin Starr, James M. Starr, John Lumsden, and Jesse French; (second row) Harry Gennett, factory superintendent W.C. Bosenberry, John Lumsden French, Harry Nolder, and the unidentified office manager. (Both, LGI.)

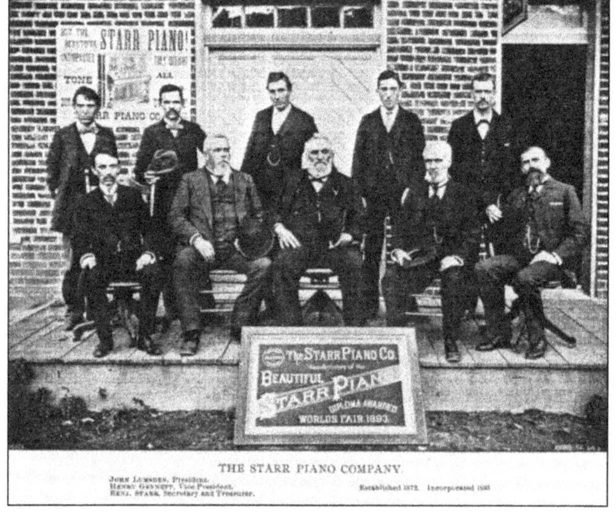

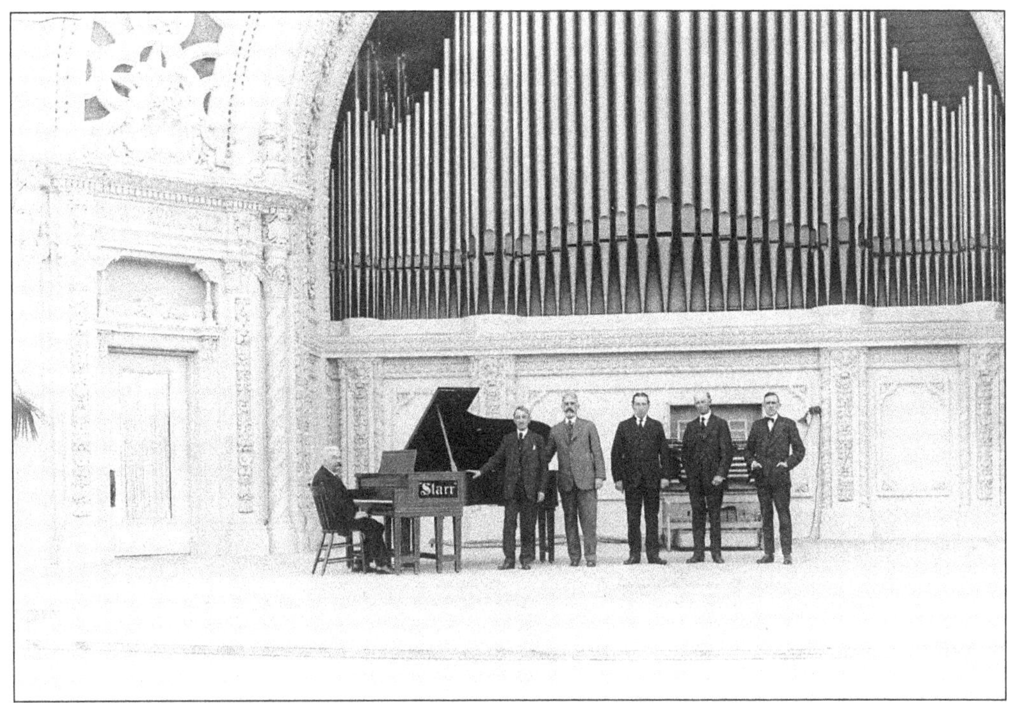

At the 1893 Chicago World's Columbian Exposition, celebrating the 400th anniversary of Columbus's landing in the New World, Starr Piano exhibited five upright pianos for judging. Henry Gennett is onstage, second from the left with his hand on a Starr Concert piano. Starr Piano Company, Richmond, Indiana, received the highest award for tone quality, well sustained; for evenly balanced scale; for well-regulated action, good touch, and repeating qualities; and also for carefully selected material and good workmanship. (Roseanne Karlebach.)

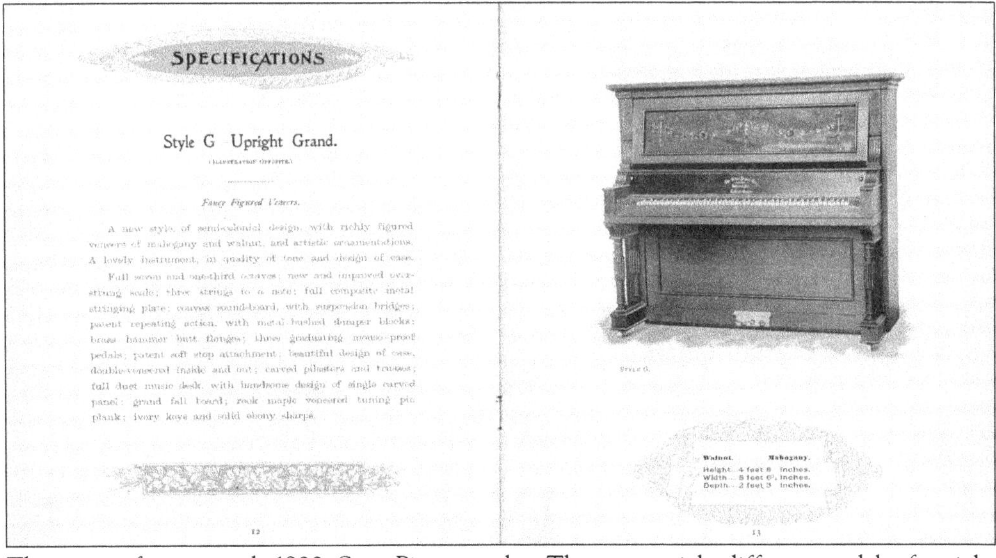

SPECIFICATIONS

Style G Upright Grand.

(ILLUSTRATION OPPOSITE.)

Fancy Figured Veneers.

A new style of semi-colonial design, with richly figured veneers of mahogany and walnut, and artistic ornamentations. A lovely instrument, in quality of tone and design of case.

Full seven and one-third octaves; new and improved overstrung scale; three strings to a note; full composite metal stringing plate; convex sound-board, with suspension bridges; patent repeating action, with metal bushed damper blocks; brass hammer butt flanges; three graduating mouse-proof pedals; patent soft stop attachment; beautiful design of case, double-veneered inside and out; carved pilasters and trusses; full duet music desk, with handsome design of single carved panel; grand fall board; rock maple veneered tuning pin plank; ivory keys and solid ebony sharps.

12

STYLE G.

Walnut. Mahogany.

Height 4 feet 8 inches.
Width 5 feet 6½ inches.
Depth 2 feet 3 inches.

13

This page is from an early-1900s Starr Piano catalog. There were eight different models of upright Grand Starr pianos presented, each as delicately ornate as the one pictured. A press notice in the catalog states that "the Starr Piano has advanced with remarkable strides, in appearance, in finish and in the development of musical quality of tone and a delicate touch." (LGI.)

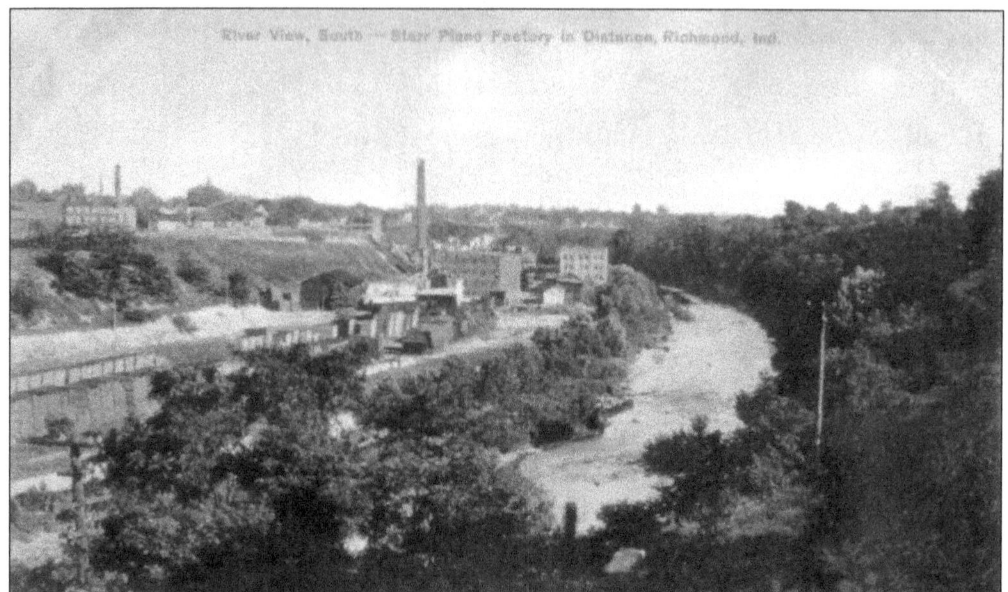

The piano manufacturing business was a booming industry and Starr Piano was ready to take advantage. The company had been adding new and improved machinery and was rapidly expanding due to money that the owners had invested. The rate of piano production in the United States was several times greater than the rate of population growth. In 1897, the capital stock of Starr Piano was doubled, to $200,000. The output of pianos was 5,000 pianos a year and 100 pianos were being shipped each week. These pianos were being hauled out of Starr Valley in large wooden crates, each on an individual horse-drawn cart. The crate was stenciled with the destination city and style of piano that it contained. Transportation was not easy. A December 1901 paper, the *Review*, states that the Starr Piano Company of Richmond, Indiana, had the distinction of receiving the first carload of lumber that had ever been shipped over the Cincinnati, Richmond & Muncie Railroad. The consignment was from a lumber dealer in College Corner, Ohio. The image below dates from around 1909. (Above, CBD; below, Wayne County Historical Museum.)

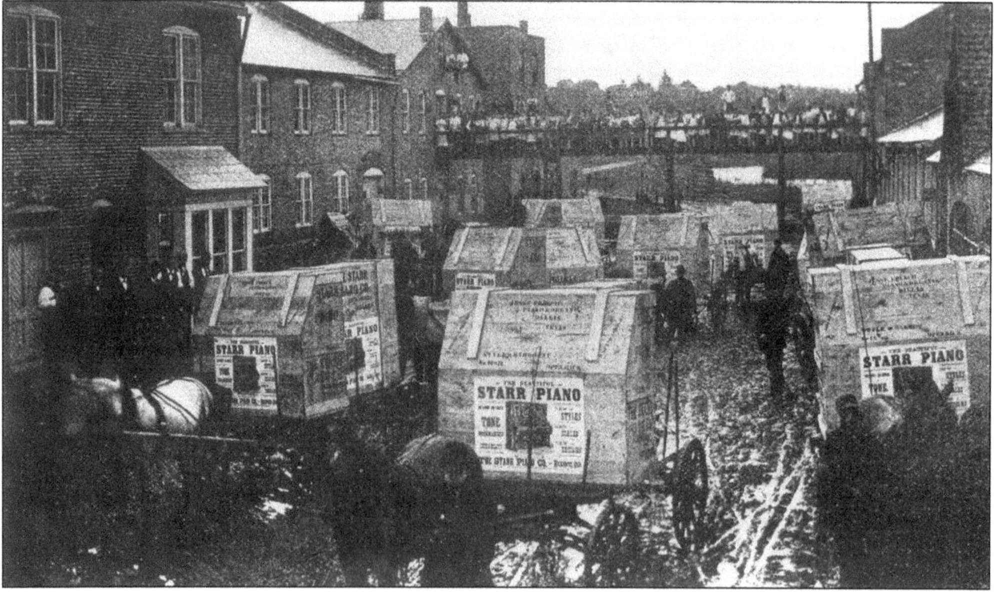

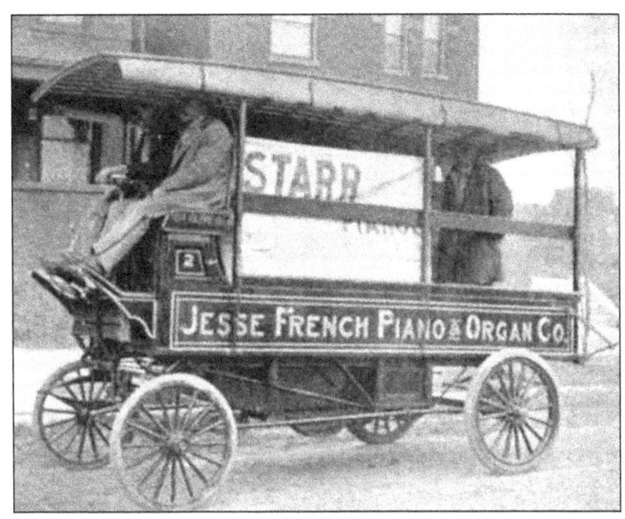

This 1901 picture shows the Jesse French and Organ Company St. Louis delivery truck, complete with a Starr Piano banner. The Jesse French Piano and Organ Company was incorporated in 1884 with equal partners John Lumsden and his three sons-in-law—Jesse French, Henry Gennett, and Oscar Field. St. Louis was home to the families until Henry Gennett moved to Richmond, Indiana, in 1894, to run the Starr Piano Company. (Royal Feltner.)

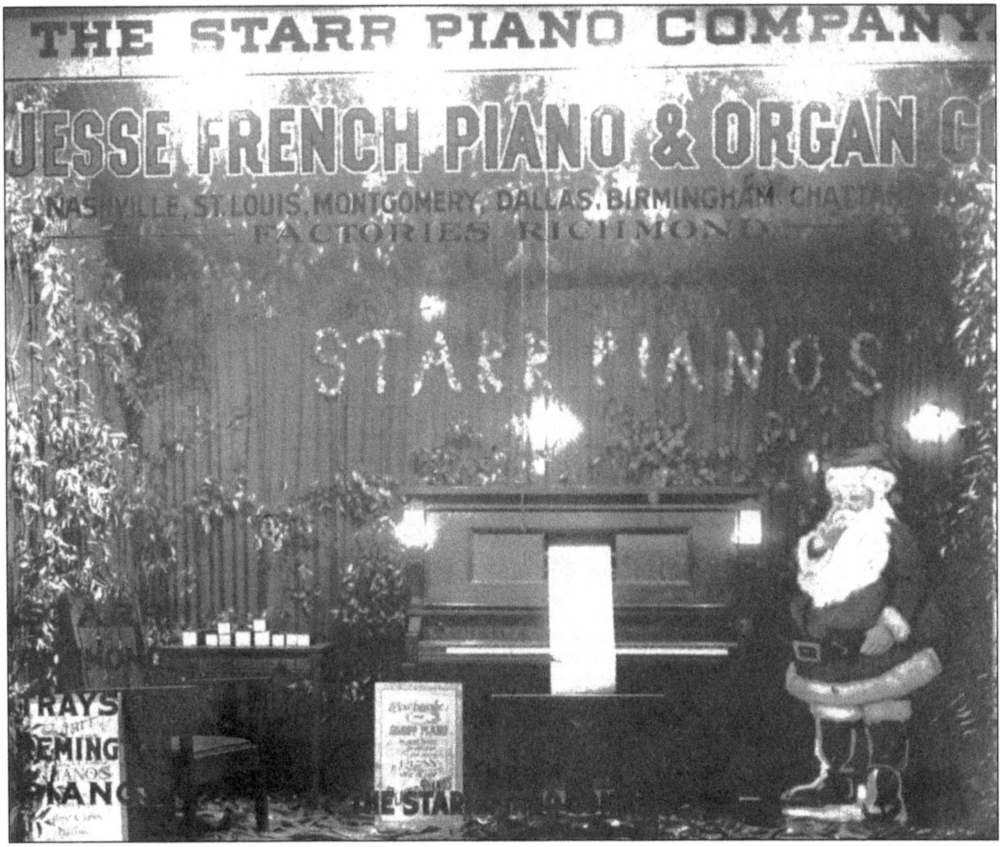

In this image, it is Christmastime at a Jesse French Piano and Organ Company retail storefront advertising Starr Pianos. There were Jesse French retail outlets throughout the South, including Nashville, St. Louis, Montgomery, Dallas, Birmingham, and Chattanooga. The company provided the strong distribution network necessary to put the Starr product in homes throughout the country. Even though Jesse French was on the board of directors of Starr Piano for several years, he was never actively involved. (Morrisson-Reeves Library.)

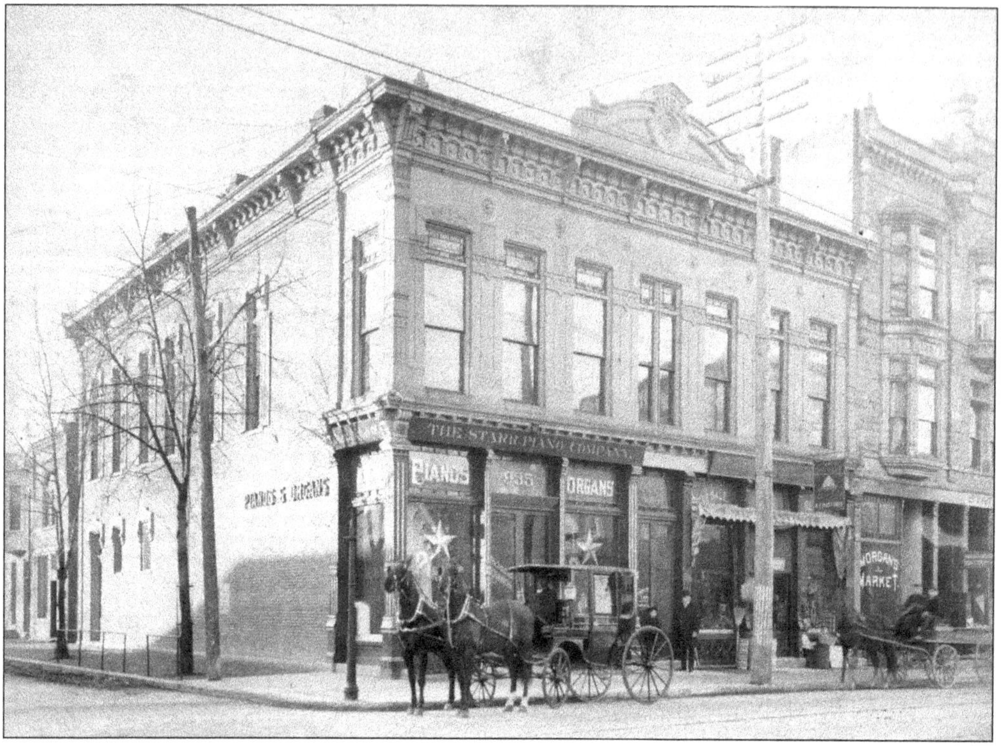

Around 1893, Starr Pianos and some organs were on display at the spacious showroom located at the southwest corner of Tenth and Main Streets. The address was 935 Main Street, Richmond, Indiana. Melodious sounds were often heard as people passed by the open door of the showroom. The early founders were expert piano makers because many had served an apprenticeship to piano makers in Germany. That early product was considered an excellent one, embodying the best in the art of piano construction. An early-1900s Starr Piano catalog states that "it was then and is still now recognized as a fine art with the greatest attention to the smallest detail during the assembly." The 1898 photograph below shows Henry Gennett (left) and his eldest son, Harry, in front of the Richmond Starr Piano showroom. (Above, Wayne County Historical Museum; below, LGI.)

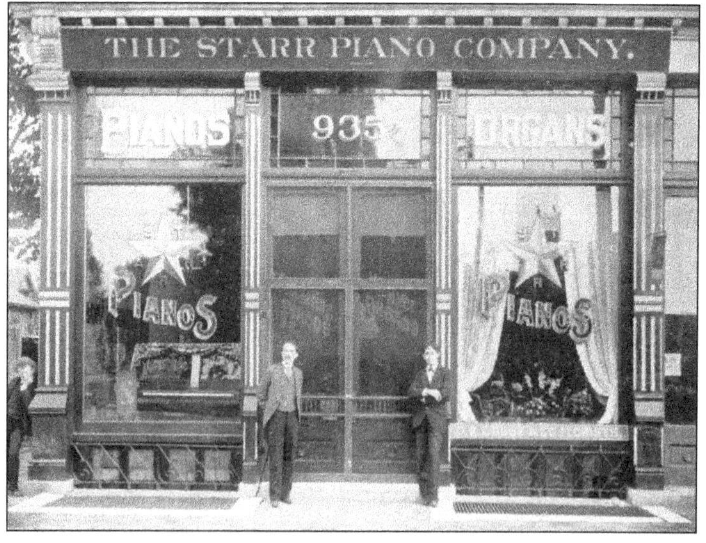

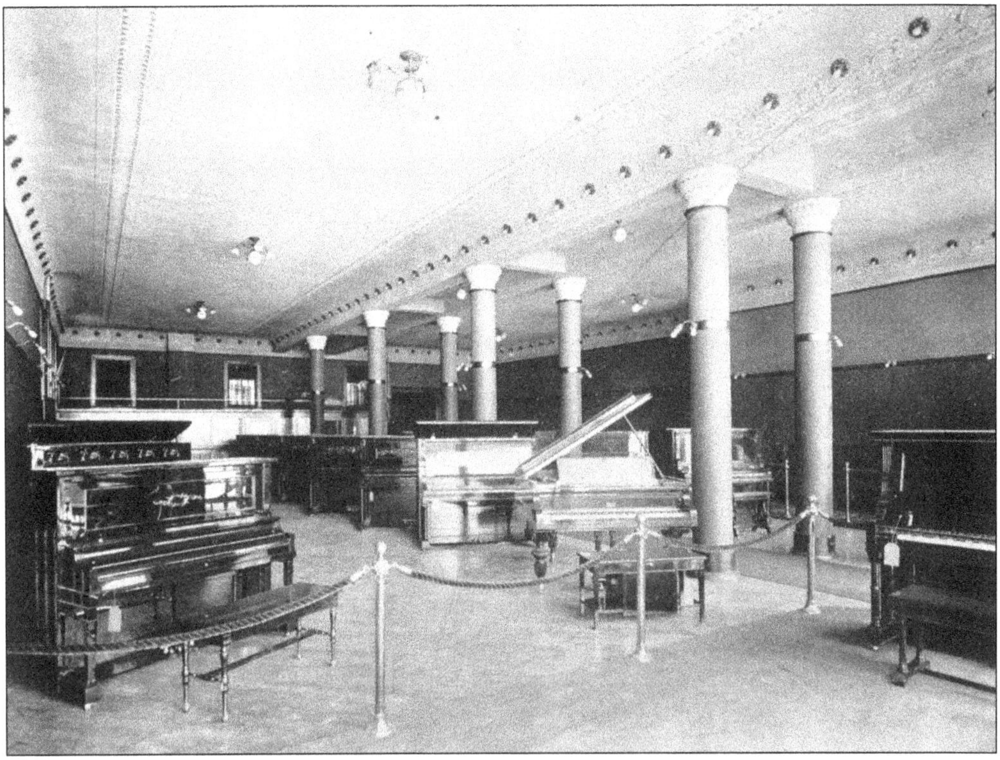

The spacious interior of the Richmond, Indiana, Starr Piano showroom displays just a few of the many styles of pianos the company made. The Starr Piano Company was the manufacturer of Starr, Richmond, Trayser, Remington, Grand, Upright, and Player pianos. Only experienced woodworkers, many from Europe, were hired to make the master patterns for Starr products. (LGI.)

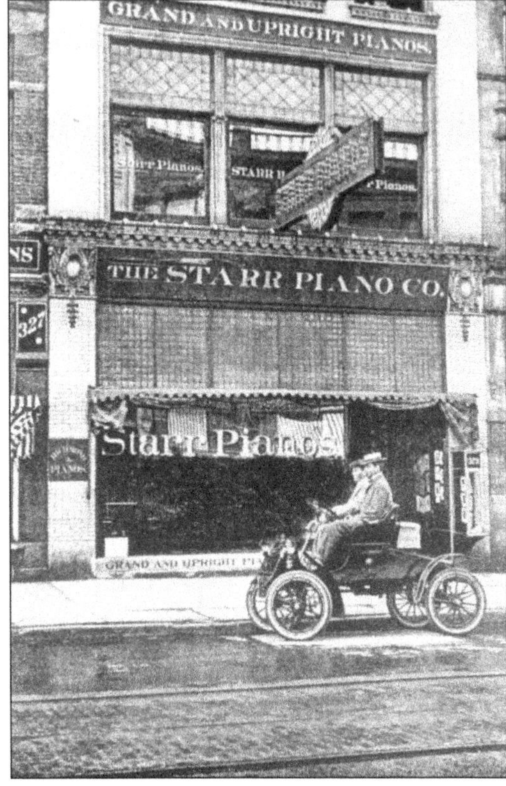

Clarence Gennett, the secretary and treasurer of the Starr Piano Company, is inspecting the Starr Piano showroom in Toledo, Ohio, on August 22, 1904. Gennett, wearing the cap, and a Mr. Pierce are in a Ford two-cylinder automobile with 10–12 horsepower. Gennett traveled from Richmond to Dayton, Piqua, Toledo, and then to Cleveland. These were all locations for Starr Piano branch stores. (LGI.)

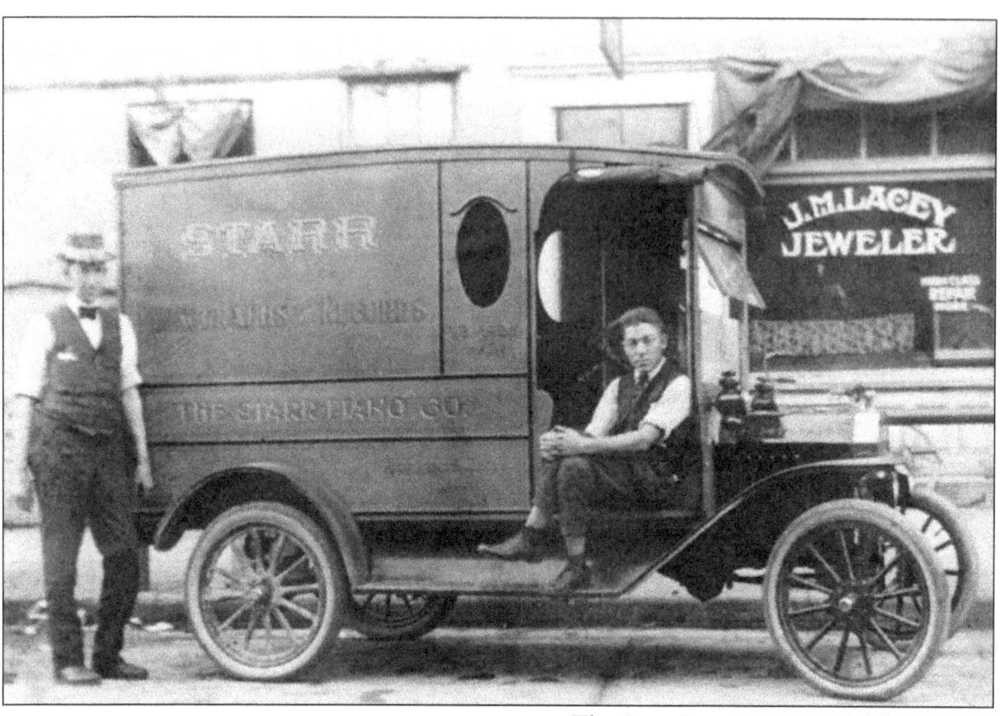

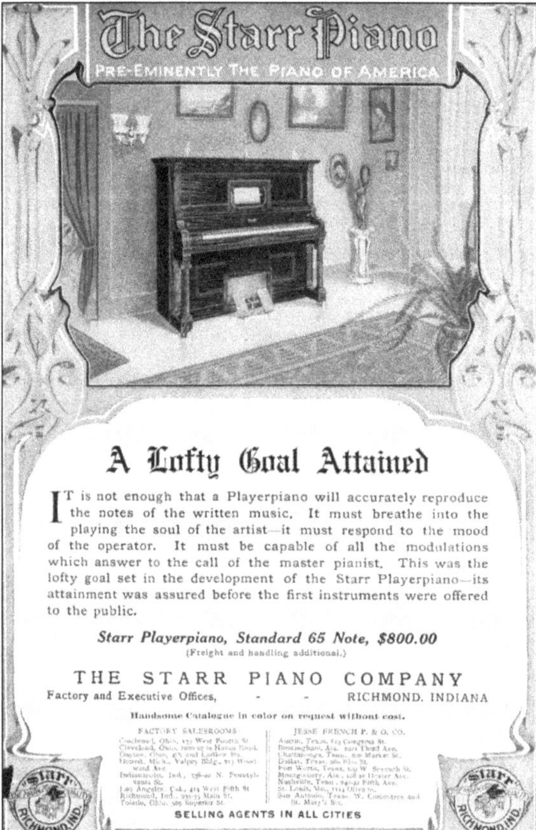

The Starr Piano motorized delivery wagon in Richmond, Indiana, was progress from the horse-drawn carts taking pianos out of Starr Valley. After 1915, Starr Piano added the manufacture of phonographs and pressing records to its list of products. (LGI.)

In 1906, the Starr Piano Company began producing the Starr Player piano, which appealed to the family in which no one played the piano but still wanted to enjoy the "live" feel of playing the piano. The player piano could accurately reproduce the notes of the written music or it could be played as a piano. Retail sales were handled through Starr Piano factory salesrooms or through Jesse French Piano and Organ Company outlets. (LGI.)

The Nashville, Tennessee, Starr Piano showroom was located in the Jesse French Piano Building. The address was 240–242 Fifth Street North. Nashville was always closely linked to Starr Piano since it was the birthplace and home for many years of both Henry Gennett and his father-in-law, John Lumsden. The building is still standing. (Mike Gennett.)

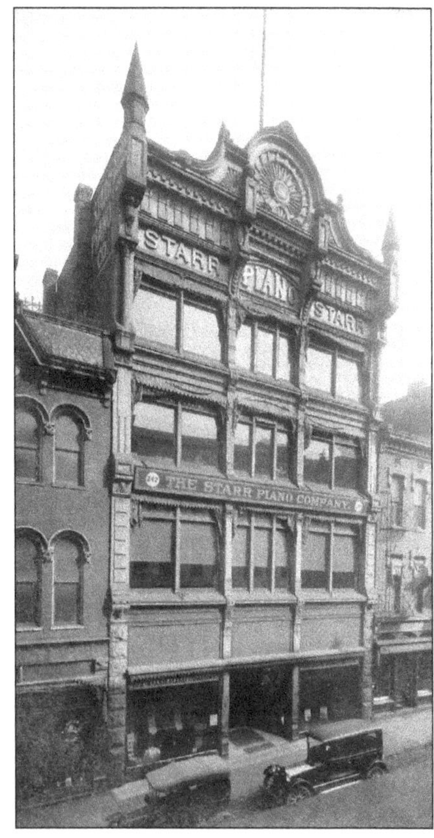

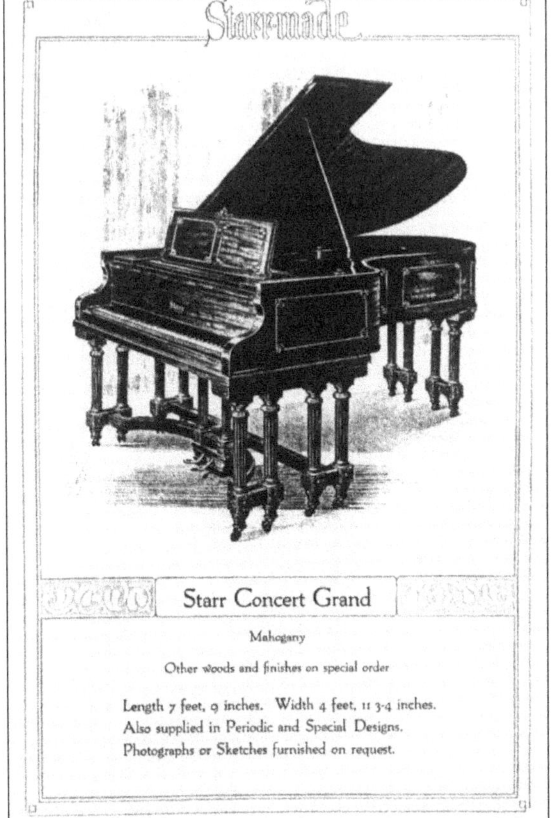

The Starr Concert Grand piano was available in mahogany and other woods and finishes by special order. The wood for each piano was carefully selected and seasoned for months and sometimes years. Every part was finished separately, numbered, and then put together. It took many months to make a Starr piano. (Morrisson-Reeves Library.)

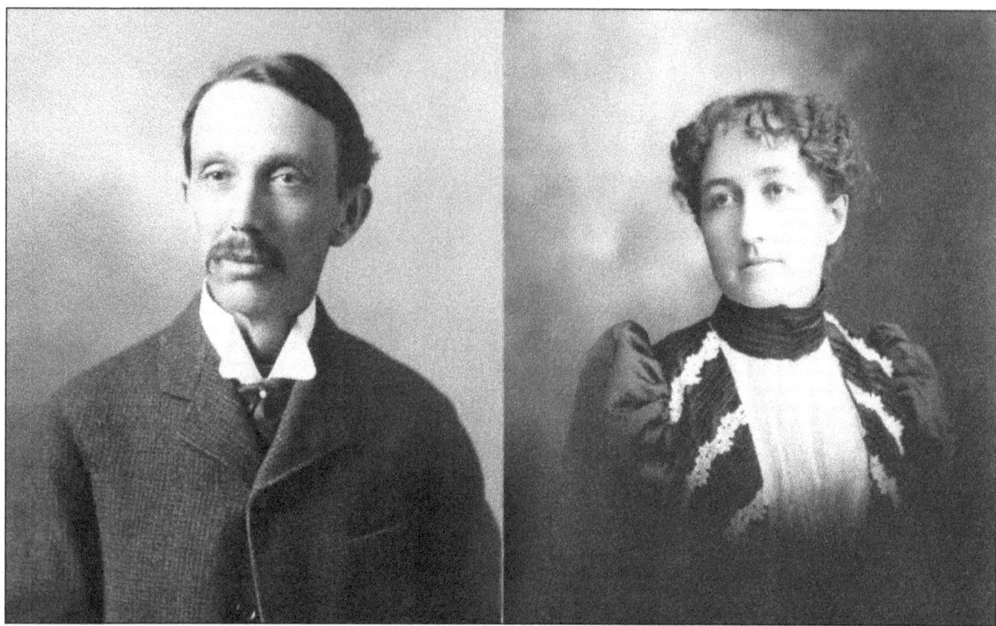

Henry Gennett (1852–1922) and Alice Lumsden (1859–1952) were both born in Nashville, Tennessee, and married there in 1876. They had four children—Harry, Clarence, Fred, and Rose. After Rose's birth in 1891, the family moved to St. Louis where Henry was a partner in the Field-French Piano Company. In 1893, Henry and his father-in-law bought a 50 percent share of the Starr Piano Company in Richmond, Indiana. A disastrous fire the next year nearly destroyed the complex. Gennett and his family moved to Richmond in 1894, and he was in charge of rebuilding and expanding the piano factory. Members of the family pictured below are, from left to right, (first row) Rose, Alice, Henry, and Fred; (second row) Harry and Clarence. (Both, Laurel Martin.)

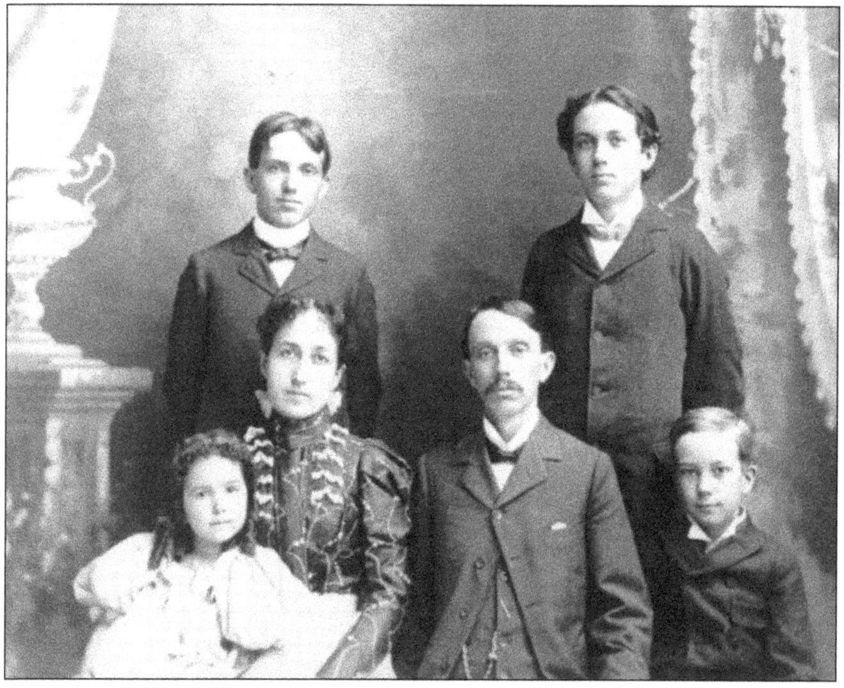

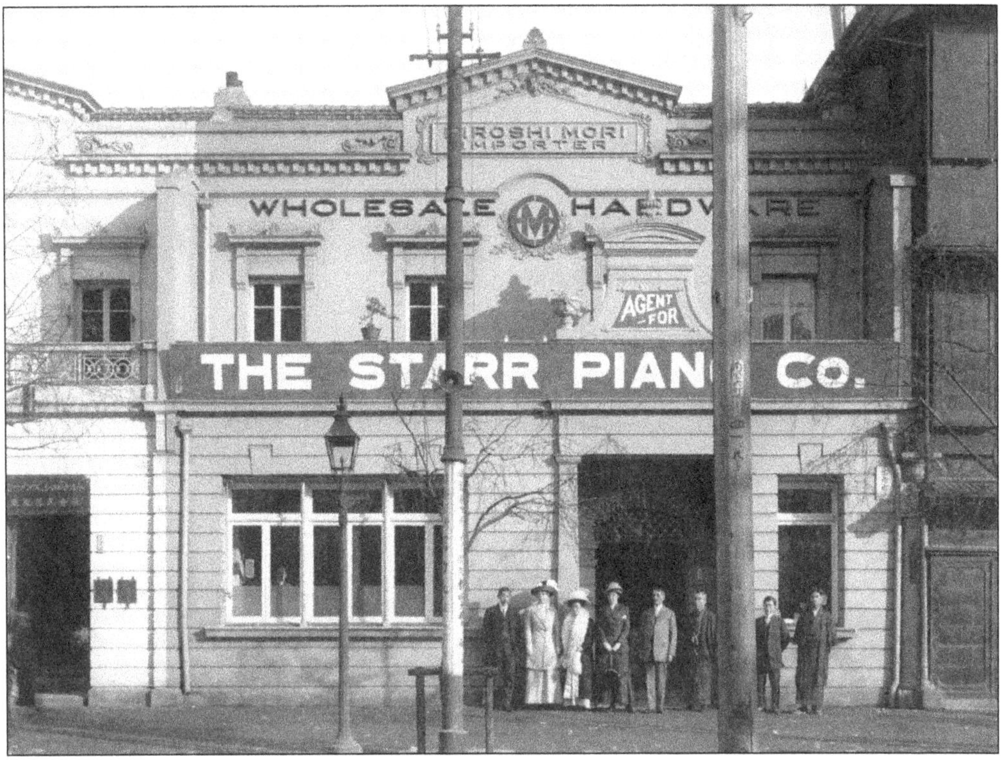

Henry and Alice Gennett took Rose when they toured the world by steamship in 1911. Henry made a business stop in Yokohama, Japan. Other destinations included Paris, Cairo, Hong Kong, and Algiers. Henry was a true visionary and had great entrepreneurial skills. Alice was a classical matriarch. She had a regal presence and strong character, combined with true leadership qualities. After Henry's death in 1922, her wisdom in family and business matters was always accepted. Alice lived with her daughter Rose in California until her death in 1952 at age 92. The 1910 photograph at right shows Henry with his grandson Harry Jr. (Above, Rosanne Karlebach; right, Mike Gennett.)

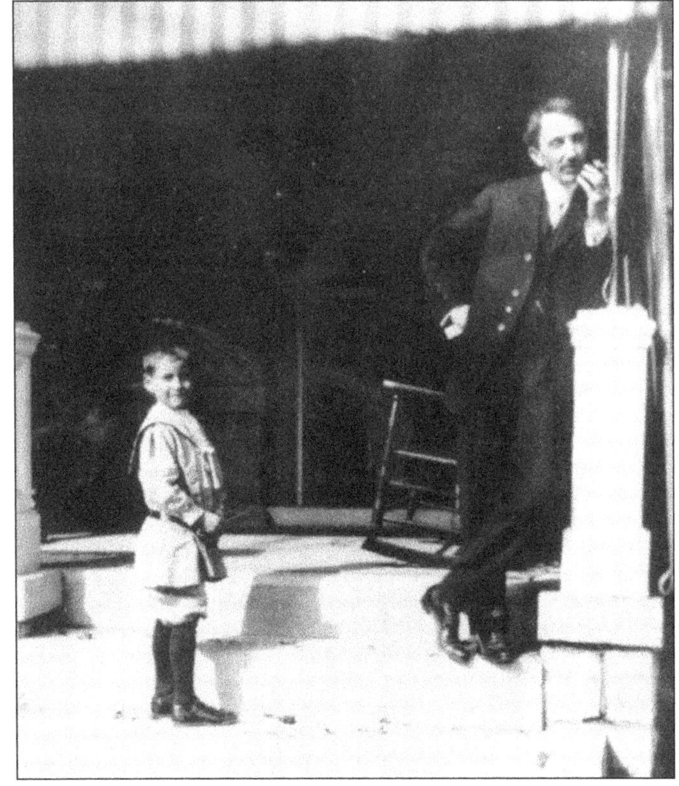

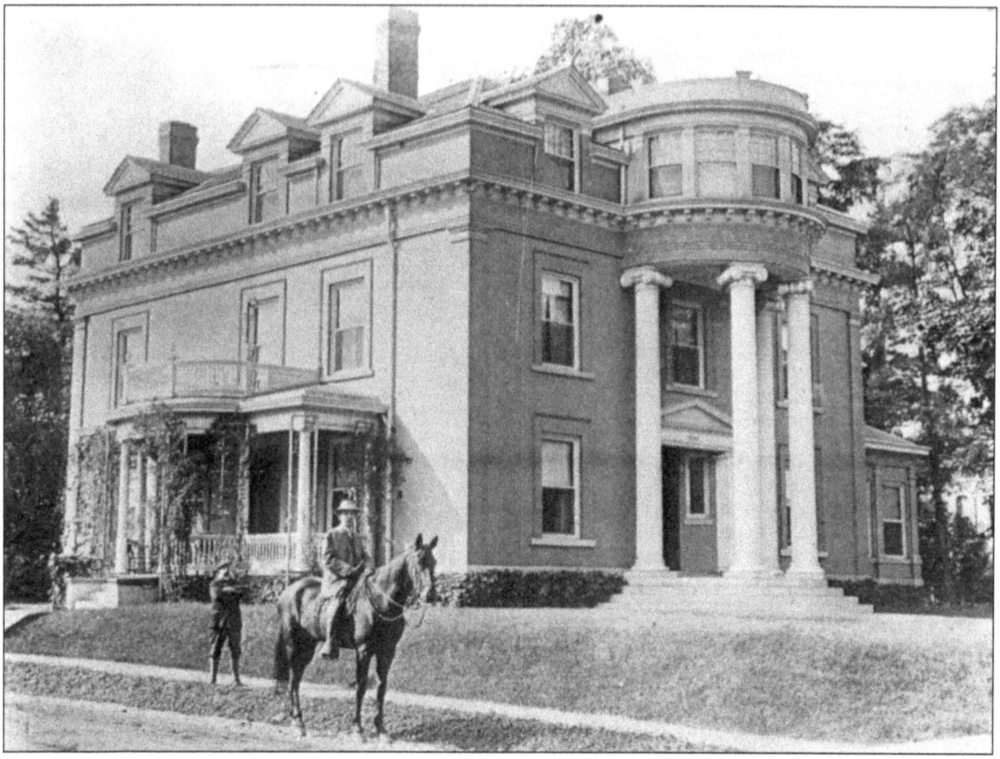

Henry Gennett is in front of the family mansion at 1829 Main Street, Richmond, Indiana, built in 1898 at a cost of $18,000. He would sometimes ride his horse Jim the 19 blocks through Richmond to work at the Starr factory. In 1922, Gennett's memorial service was held in the front hall of the mansion. The doors were opened to the street so that his friends and many of the 2,500 Starr employees could be included. (Laurel Martin.)

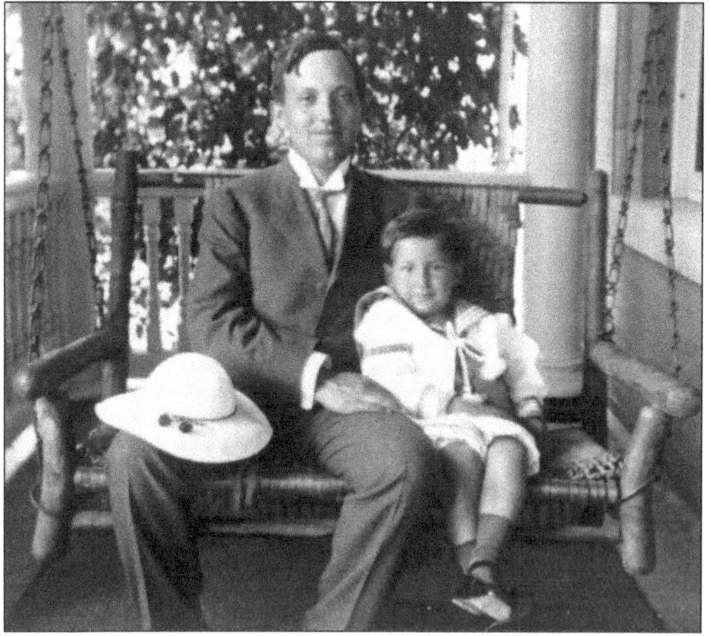

Harry Gennett (1877–1952) and Grace Robinson (1879–1958) were married on December 28, 1898, in Richmond. Her father owned Swayne and Robinson. Harry and Grace had four children—Margery, Alice, Harry Jr., and Ruth. Harry began working at Starr in 1895 and became a skilled piano maker. His first love was always making pianos. The picture of Harry and his son was taken in 1910 on the porch of the mansion. (Mike Gennett.)

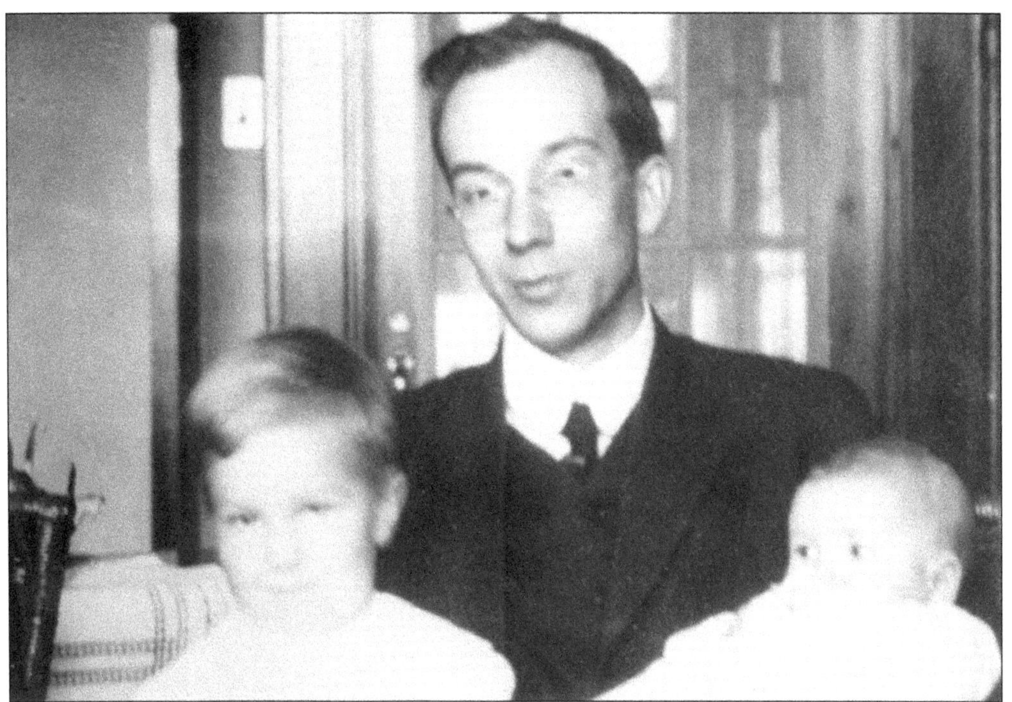

Frederick Gennett (1885–1965) and Hazel Reid (1886–1959) were married in Richmond on December 1907. They had four sons—Robert (left) and Richard (pictured with their father) and Fred Jr. and Henry. Fred started working at Starr Piano in 1905 and supervised the record division. (Mike Gennett.)

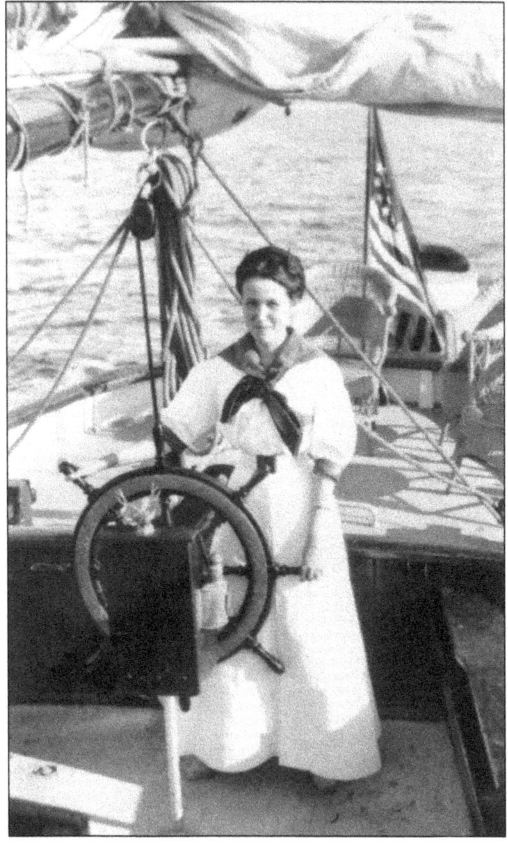

Rose Gennett (1891–1994) was a widow when she married Robert Martin in 1920. They had two children, Henry and Alice. Rose's father, Henry, died in Dayton, Ohio, in 1922. Alice Lumsden Gennett, Rose, and her family moved to Los Angeles in 1936, and Alice took charge of the Pacific Division of the Starr Piano Company. Rose became the fourth president in 1945. She was still driving to work in her 90s. Rose is pictured at the helm at Catalina in 1912. (Laurel Martin.)

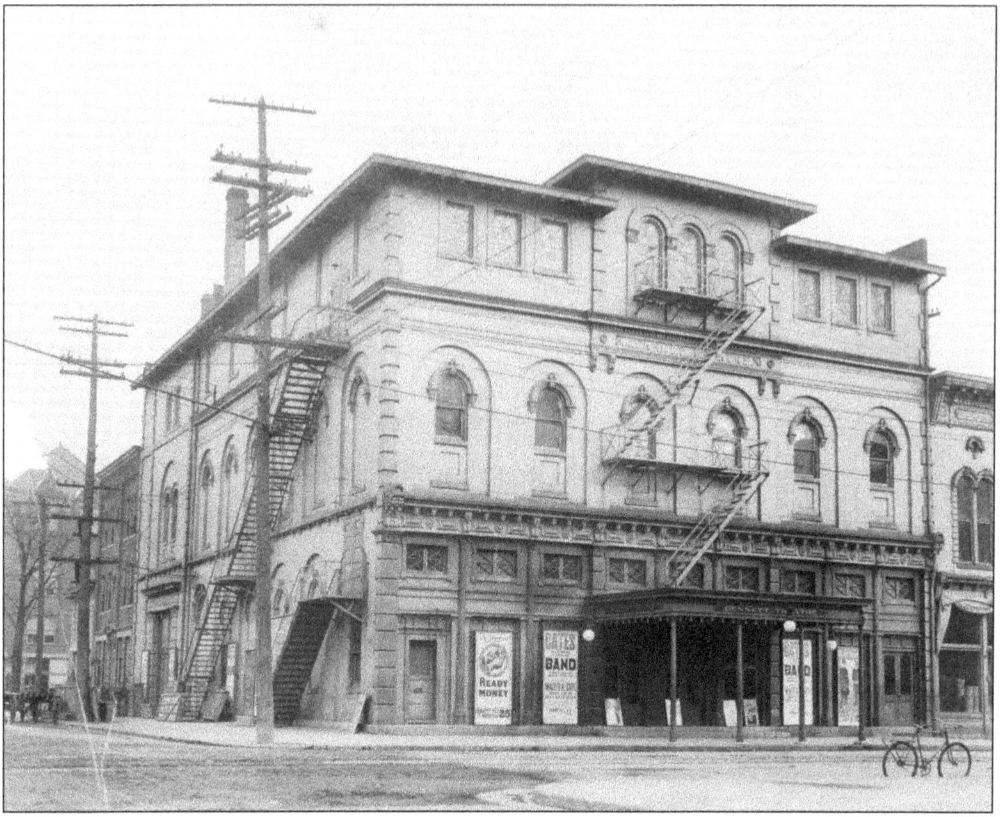

The Gennett Theater was on the southeast corner of Eighth and North A Streets. Clarence Gennett purchased a vacant property in 1898 and had the new theater built in only 92 days. It opened on December 22, 1899. The theater was expanded and remodeled in 1904. A three-story building named the Gennett Flats was added and is still standing. (Wayne County Historical Museum.)

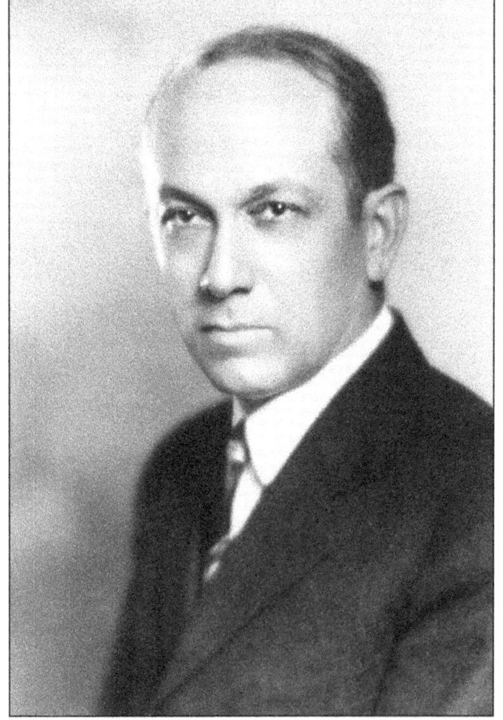

Clarence Gennett (1879–1953) married Ruby Hasecoster (1874–1972) in Richmond on February 28, 1905. Ruby was the daughter of John Hasecoster, who was the architect for the Gennett mansion. They had four children—Augusta, Martha, Ruby, and Clarence. Clarence began working at Starr in 1896. Henry Gennett and his family had become an important part of Richmond's cultural community and were very involved in the Gennett Theater. This image was taken around 1905. (Mike Gennett.)

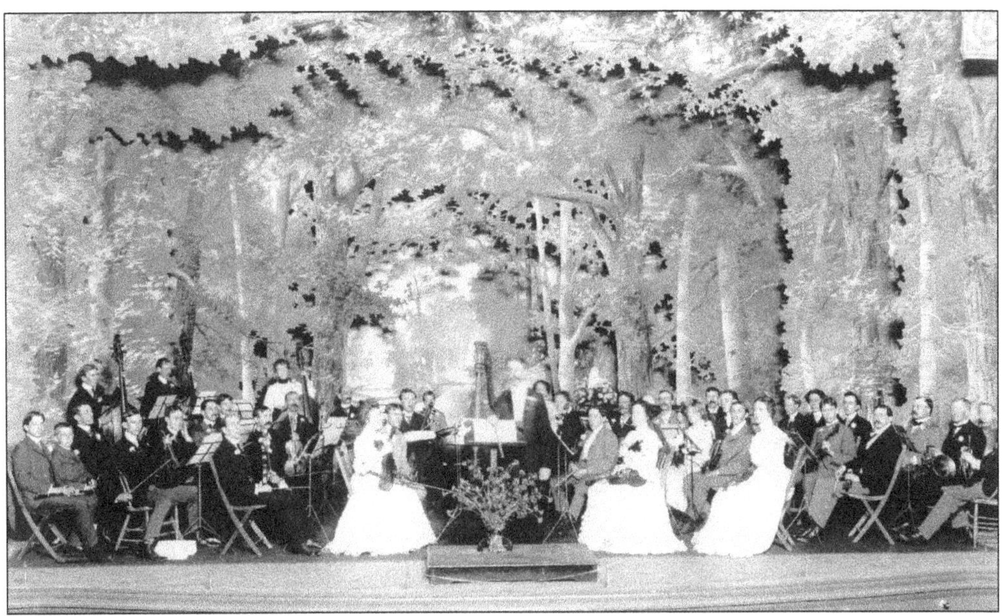

Four Gennett family members were onstage for the Richmond Orchestra concert in the Gennett Theater around 1902. Alice Gennett was president of the Richmond Orchestra Association and played the piano. Harry Gennett played the cello, Clarence Gennett played the cornet, and Fred Gennett played the tympani-tambour petite (drums). In 1916, the theater was converted to a movie theater and then was torn down in 1935 to make way for a filling station. (Rosanne Karlebach.)

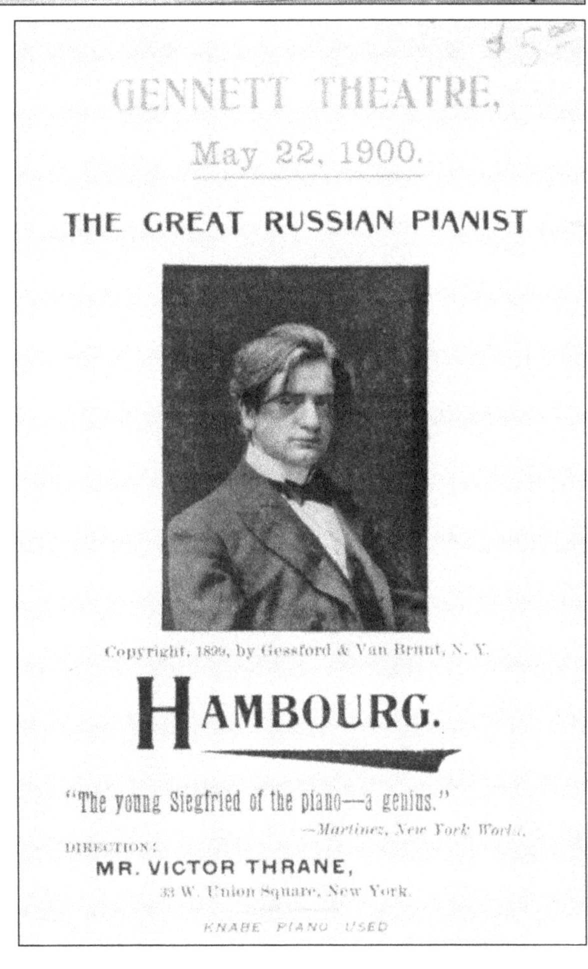

The great Russian pianist Mark Hamborg began his world tour in 1895 at the age of 16. The first stop was Australia. He returned to London and then appeared in Paris in 1896. From there, he went to Brussels and Berlin. Hamborg performed in New York in late 1898 and continued to tour the United States. His performance in Richmond, at the Gennett Theater, was on May 22, 1900. (Morrisson-Reeves Library.)

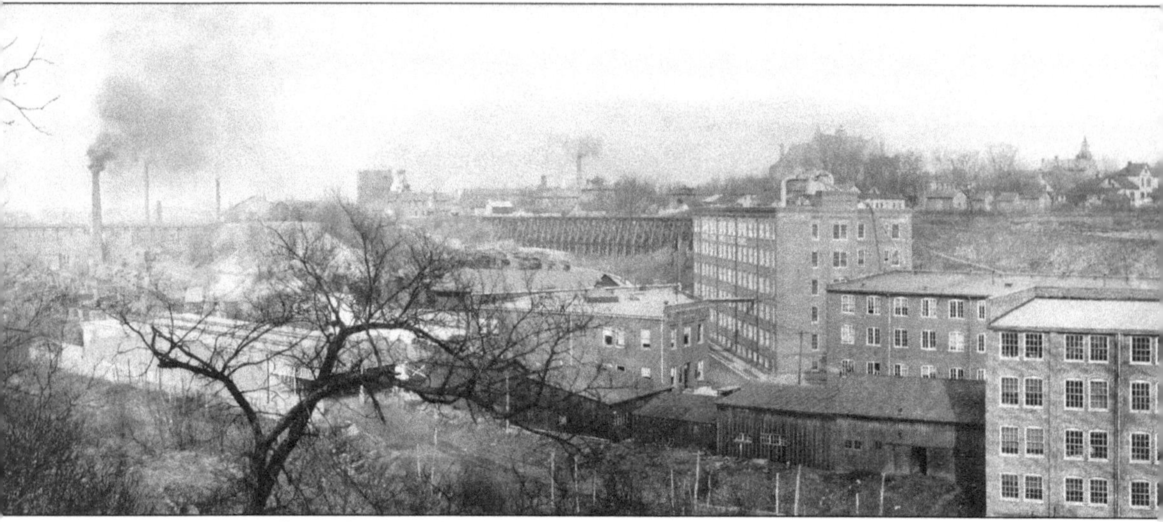

This panorama shows the many buildings of the Starr Piano Company in 1910. The Starr Upright of 1910 rivaled the upright pianos made by Baldwin and Steinway. In addition to the prestigious award at the 1893 Chicago World's Columbian Exposition, Starr Piano received the highest award at the 1897 Tennessee Centennial Exposition in Nashville, the 1904 St. Louis World's Fair, the 1909 Alaska–Yukon Pacific Exposition, and the 1915 Panama-Pacific Exposition. Fifty-two models of pianos were being made at the factory. The company viewbook stated that Starr Piano Company was the largest and most complete factory in the world devoted exclusively to the manufacture of high-grade musical instruments. "The Starr Piano Company and the cultural life of the

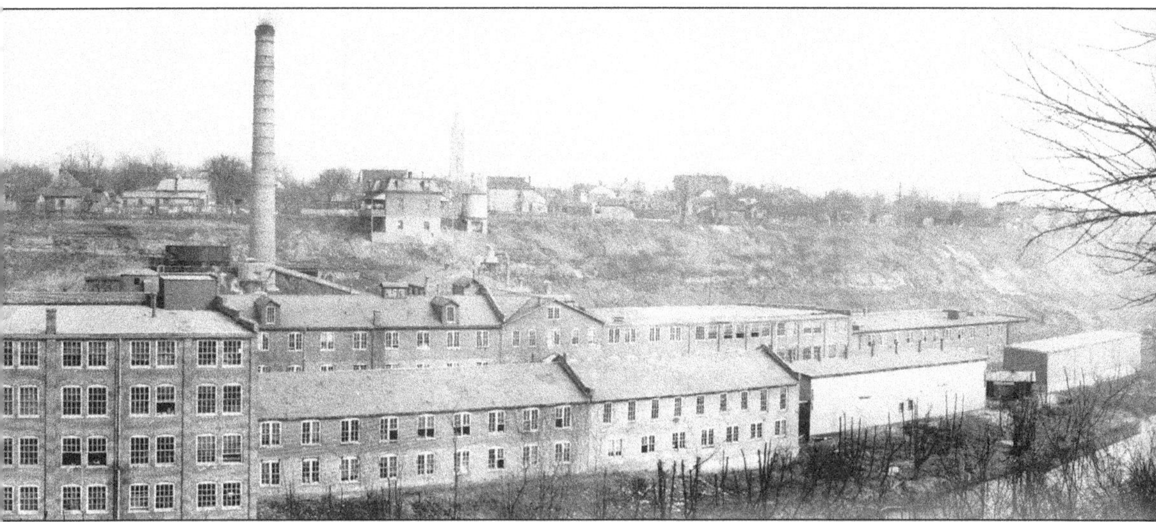

community, in the latter's musical phases have been inextricably interwoven from the beginning of the company's existence and are drawn closer with each succeeding year," according to a 1913 article in the *Richmond Palladium*. By 1915, the Starr Piano factory was producing pianos at peak production and had Starr Piano stores throughout the country. An amazing fact was that Starr Piano had its own power plant, which generated the plant's entire gigantic supply of electricity, heat, and power. Fifty tons of coal were consumed daily. The famous Gennett Recording studio with the railroad spur running beside it is on the lower right side of the photograph. (LGI.)

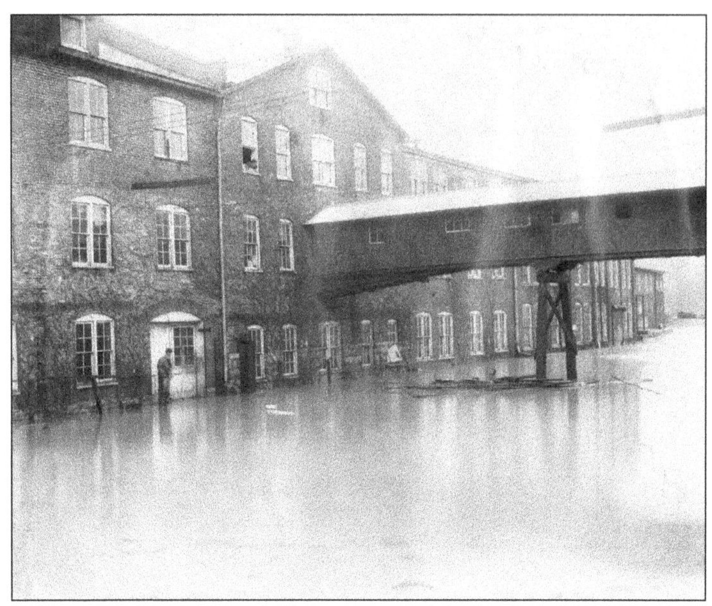

The Starr Piano Company was built along the Whitewater River in a floodplain. There were previous floods in the 1890s and a disastrous fire in 1894, which nearly destroyed the entire complex. According to a local newspaper, the fire was caused by the dynamos (early electrical generators), which had malfunctioned. The March 1913 flood is mentioned in the company director's minutes. (LGI.)

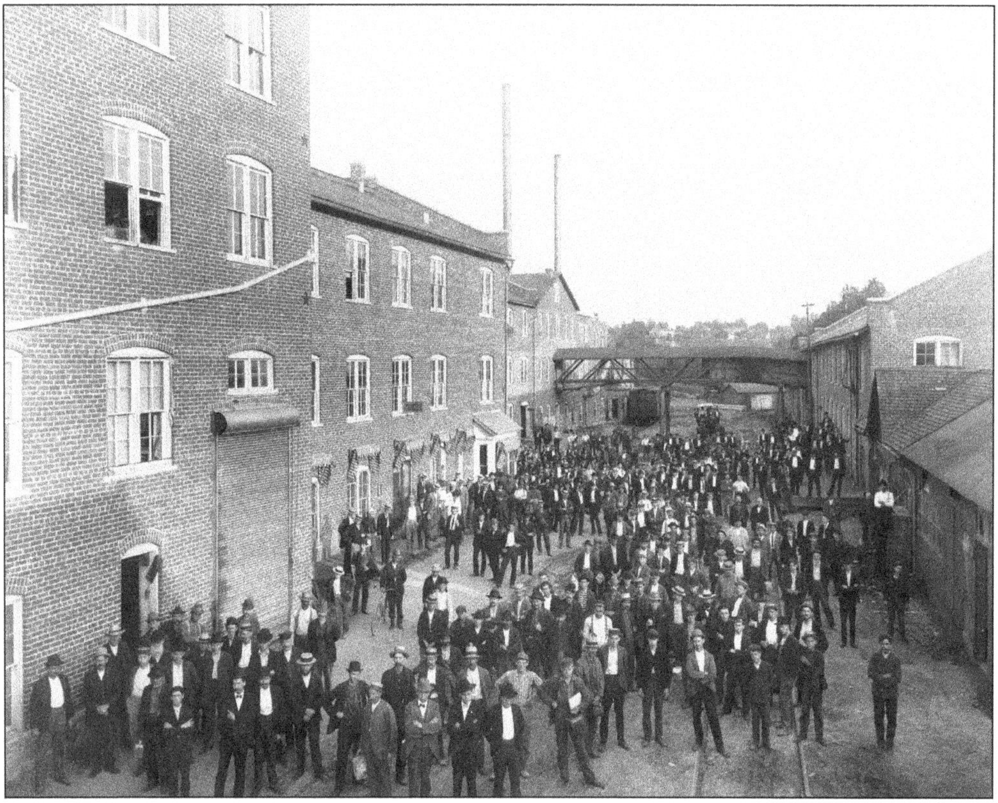

Work at Starr was six days a week, 10 hours a day for a total of 60 hours a week. Saturday was a short day since the whistle blew at 4:45 p.m. instead of 5:45 p.m. Regular hours started at 6:30 a.m. The work week later changed to five days. Starr employees were dedicated to their work. Before 1915, it was estimated that 10 percent of the Richmond population worked at the factory, many from boyhood. (Morrisson-Reeves Library.)

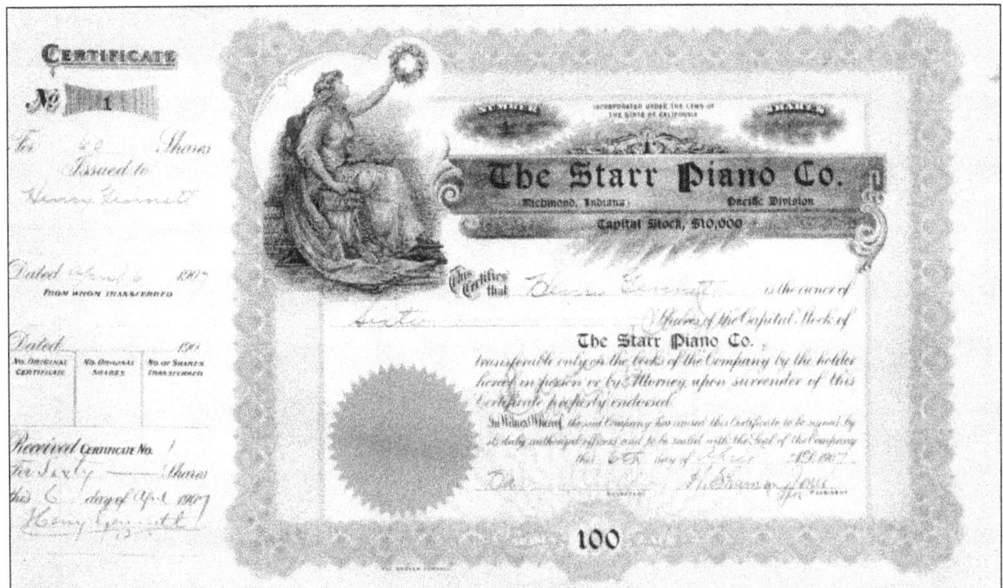

Certificate

No 1

For 60 Shares
Issued to
Henry Gennett

Dated April 6 1907
From whom transferred

Dated 190
No. Original Certificate	No. Original Shares	No. of Shares Transferred

Received Certificate No. 1
For Sixty Shares
this 6 day of April 1907
Henry Gennett

Incorporated under the laws of the State of California

The Starr Piano Co.

Richmond, Indiana — Pacific Division

Capital Stock, $10,000

This Certifies that Henry Gennett is the owner of Sixty Shares of the Capital Stock of The Starr Piano Co. transferable only on the books of the Company by the holder hereof in person or by Attorney upon surrender of this Certificate properly endorsed.

In Witness Whereof, the said Company has caused this Certificate to be signed by its duly authorized officers and to be sealed with the Seal of the Company this 6th day of April A.D. 1907.

Secretary — President

100

The Starr Piano Company, Pacific Division, was incorporated in the state of California in 1907 by Henry Gennett for the purpose of distributing the manufactured products of Starr Piano. After his death in 1922 and the settlement of his will in 1936, Alice and her daughter Rose and family moved to Los Angeles. Alice became president of the Pacific Division and her children, Harry and Rose, were partners. They both held her business sense in high esteem. (Brian Henry Martin.)

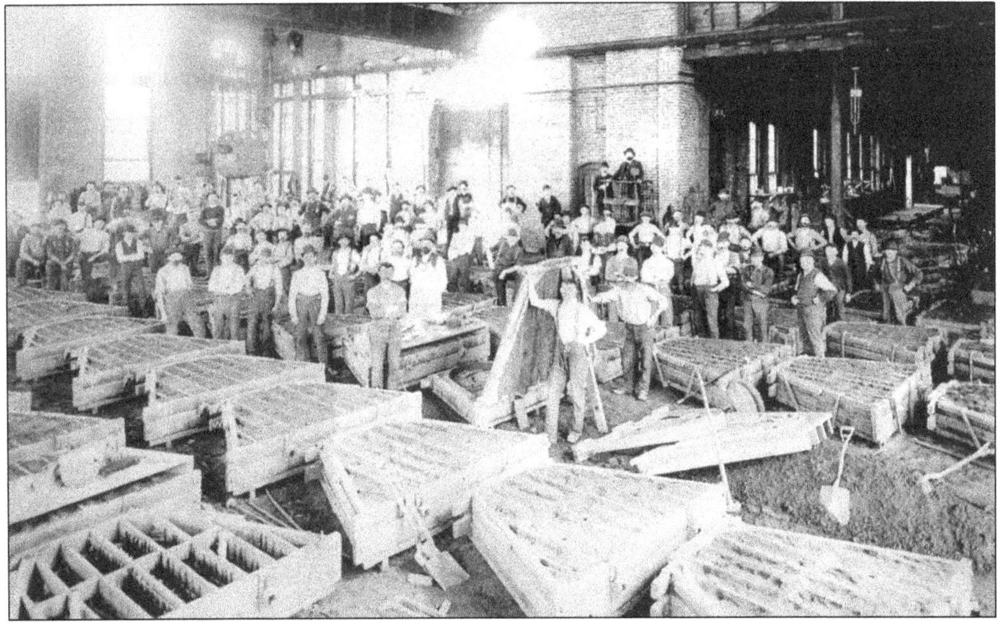

Swayne, Robinson and Company, a Richmond ironwork manufacturer, made the only two parts of a Starr piano that were not manufactured at the massive Starr Piano complex. Grace Robinson married Henry Gennett's eldest son, Harry. This photograph shows the Swayne, Robinson and Company warehouse filled with casting soundboards and the workers involved. The other part the company made was the piano sound frame. (LGI.)

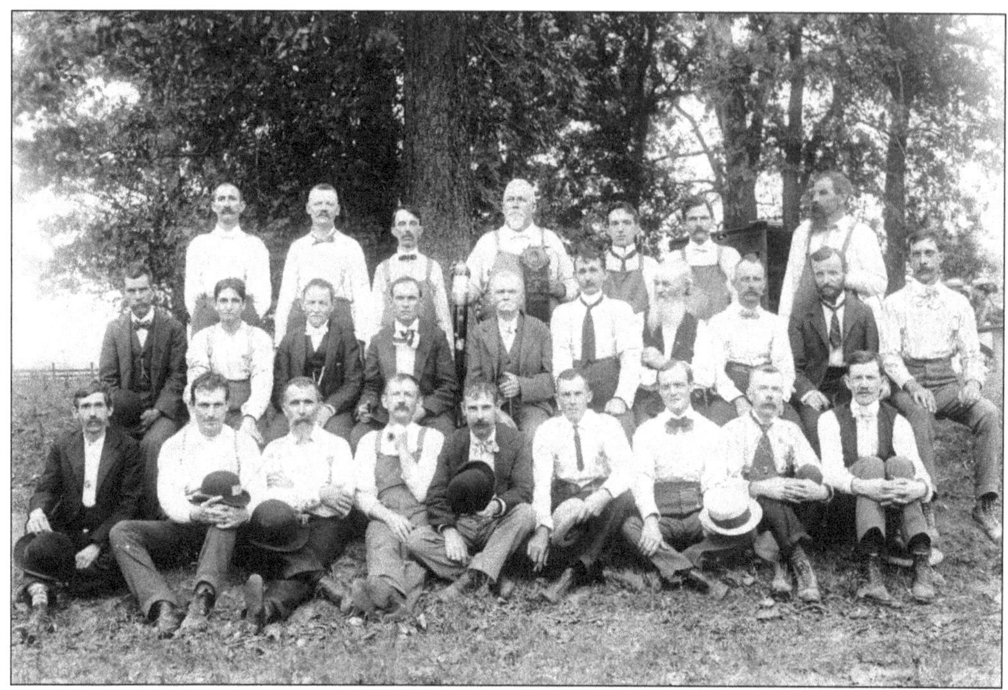

An outdoor gathering for Starr Piano employees was held on August 20, 1901. In the back row are Henry Gennett (third from left), Benjamin Starr (fourth from left), and Harry Gennett (fifth from left). The rest are unidentified. (Wayne County Historical Museum.)

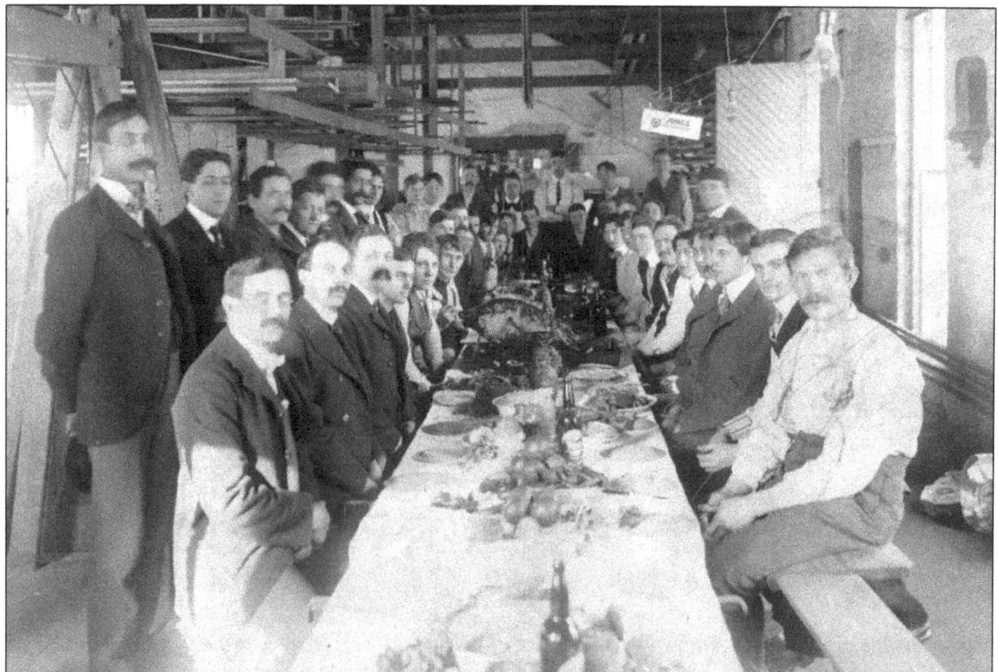

In 1903, a banquet table was set up for a feast inside one of the Starr Piano buildings. Henry Gennett is seated second on the left side of the table, and his son Harry is seated third on the right side. (Wayne County Historical Museum.)

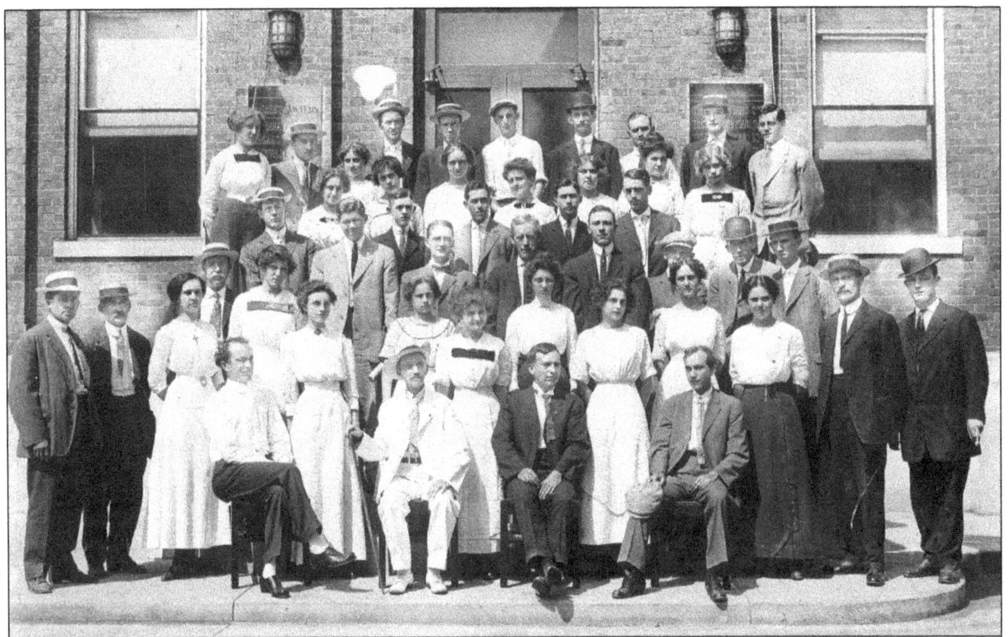

On September 20, 1912, a picture of the office workers was taken in front of the Starr Piano administration building. The building was complete with a beautiful wood grand staircase. In the first row are, from left to right, Clarence Gennett, treasurer; Henry Gennett, president; Harry Gennett, vice president; and Fred Gennett, secretary. Grouped around them are all but three of the 51 executive office employees. (Morrisson-Reeves Library.)

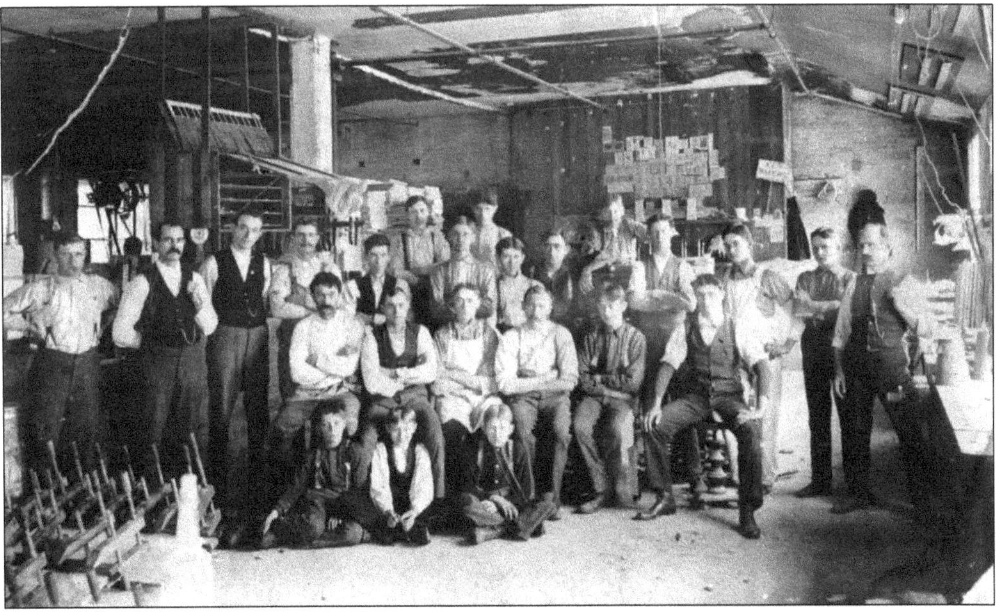

Dick Bennett, far right, was the early foreman of the sixth-floor key room. Fred Kauper began working for Starr Piano in 1893 at the age of 19 and was the key room foreman from 1911 to 1936. He earned $4 a week when he first began working at Starr Piano. Kauper retired from the piano company in 1952 after 59 years. His brother William worked there for 52 years. (Wayne County Historical Museum.)

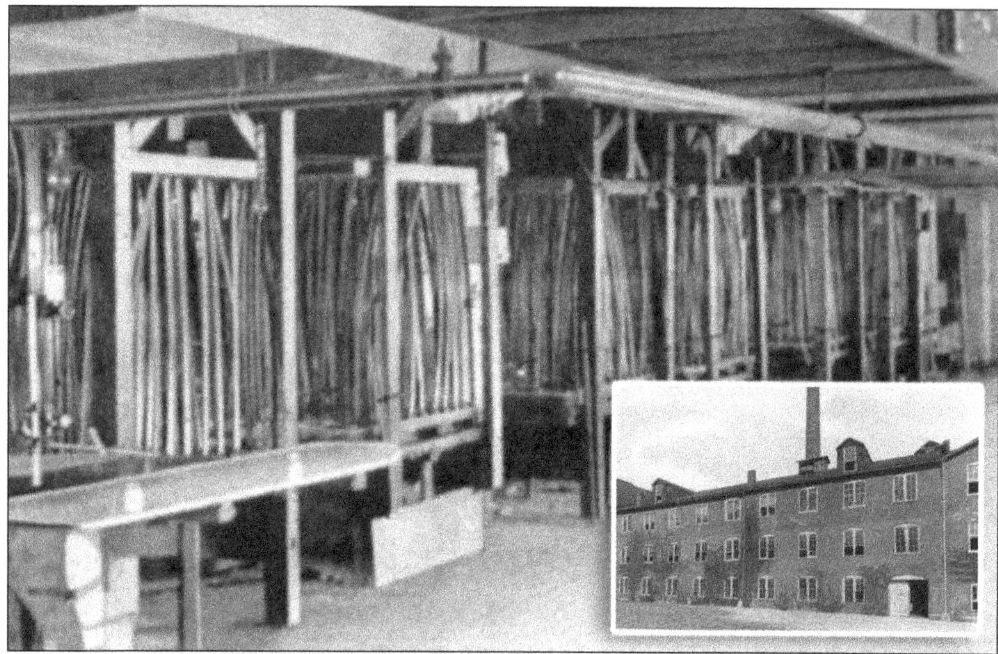

The lumber was taken from the drying kiln to the mill where it was planed, cut to specific dimensions, and sent to various departments. Many steps were involved in the process. This picture shows the manner in which the ribs were made to stick to the soundboards. The vertical sticks exerted pressure to the freshly glued ribs until they set. (LGI.)

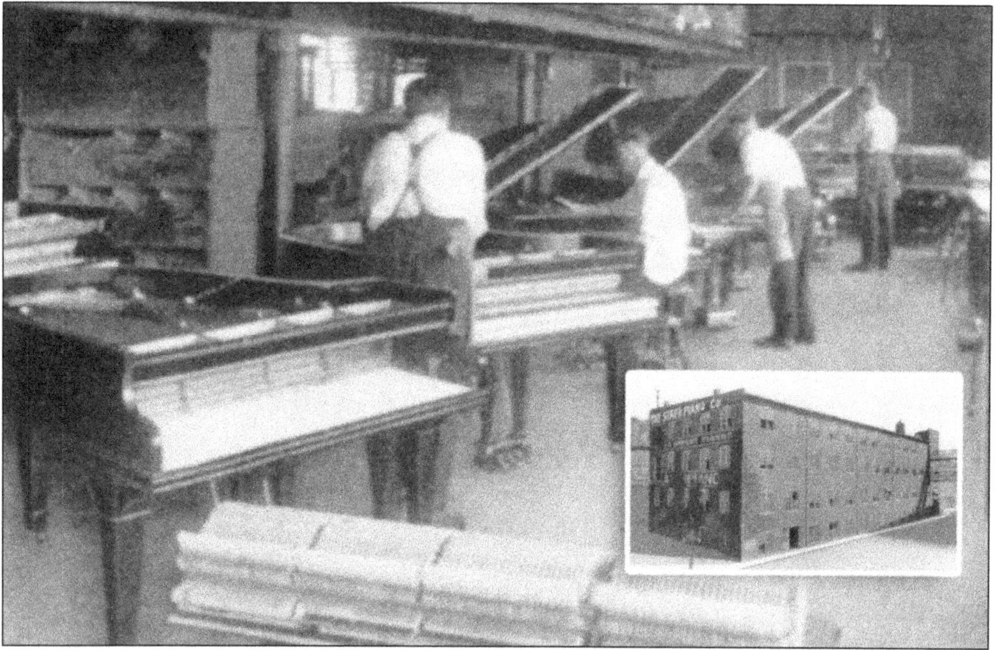

After the piano soundboards were fastened to the backs, metal plates were attached and then drilled for the string pegs. A great deal of the varnishing was done in this building. This photograph details the area of the Grand Piano case construction where the grand pianos were taken for completion by installing action, regulating, and tuning. (LGI.)

A great amount of effort went into each piano after it was varnished. Each part was hand-rubbed and polished and before shipping was oiled off and polished again. The photograph was taken in the polishing building, which also had a section for piano and player piano action regulating. (LGI.)

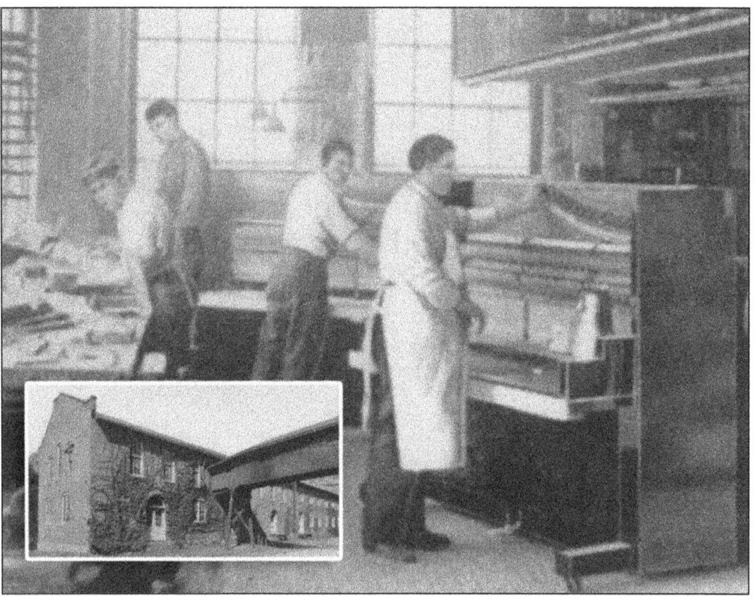

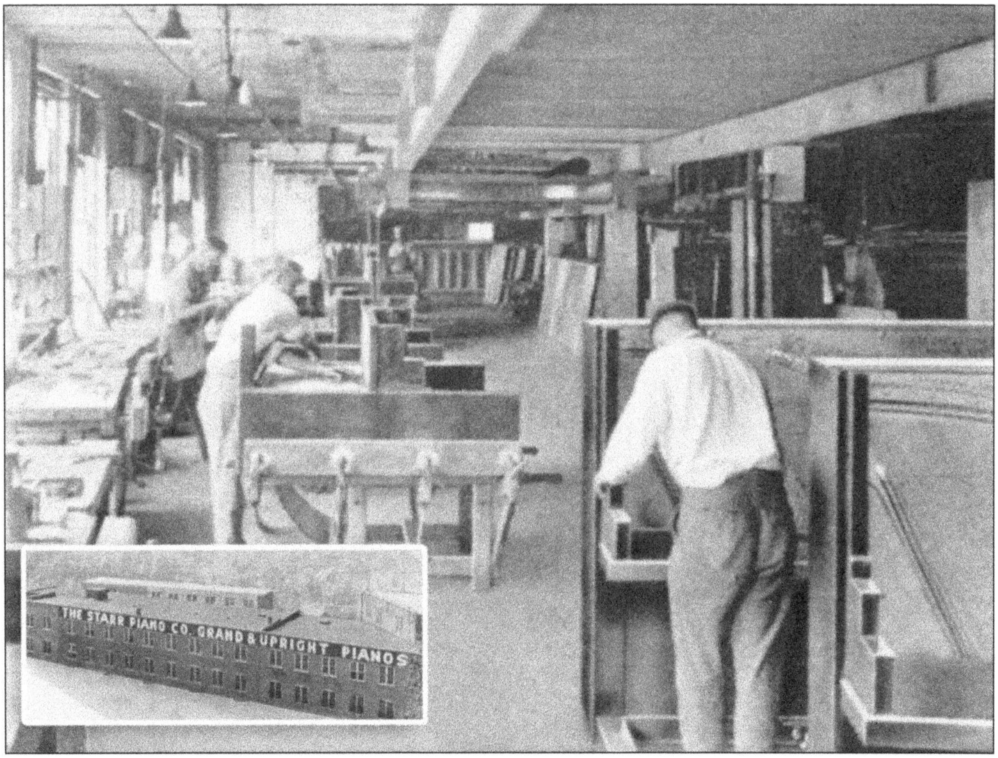

There were hundreds of backs, sides, tops, and so forth in this building waiting for assembly. After each plate was attached to the back and strung, the various parts for the upright and player cases were brought together here. The shipping department was one of the busiest areas in the entire plant. Thousands of Starr-made instruments were shipped to all parts of the world. Railroad tracks were parallel to each shipping platform. (LGI.)

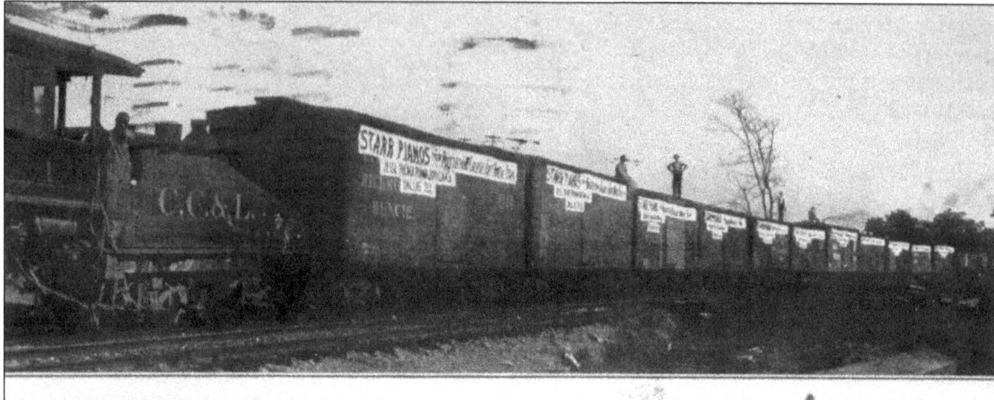

This postcard, dated April 15, 1909, shows 11 cars of the Chicago, Cincinnati & Louisville (CC&L) Railroad full of Starr pianos. A sign on the first car read, "Dallas, TEX." The CC&L was the shortest railroad route between Cincinnati, Ohio, and Chicago, Illinois, and passed through Richmond, Indiana. It was started in 1903 and operated until 1910 when it was taken over by the Chesapeake & Ohio Railway of Indiana. (LGI.)

2 VIOLETS

To any one sending

THE STARR PIANO CO.

RICHMOND, INDIANA

the name of a prospective piano purchaser on the reverse side of this card, we will mail an artistically mounted enlargement of this picture suitable for passepartouting

Starr Piano used many methods of advertising. The 1909 postcard of a "Starr Girl" features Violet. If one wrote the name of a prospective piano purchaser on the back side of the postcard and sent it to Starr, that person received an enlargement of the picture. Some of the other marketing items included playing cards, pamphlets with party toasts, instructions for drawing animals, a card that explained palmistry, and candy recipes. (LGI.)

This 1904 campaign dollar for Theodore Roosevelt states, "Cast your political ballot as you will, but when casting about for a Piano don't forget the "STARR" stands on the Platform of Honest Workmanship, reliable dealings, and one PRICE to all." If one desired, there was a dollar for the other party. (LGI.)

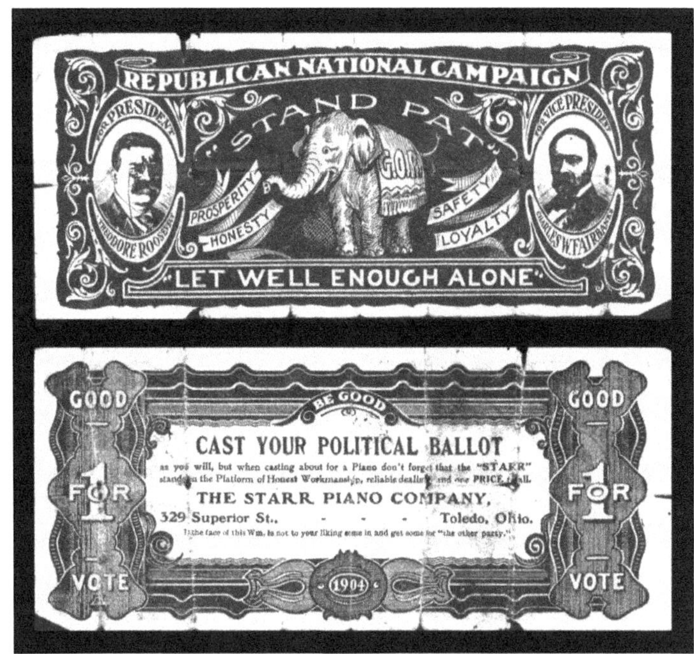

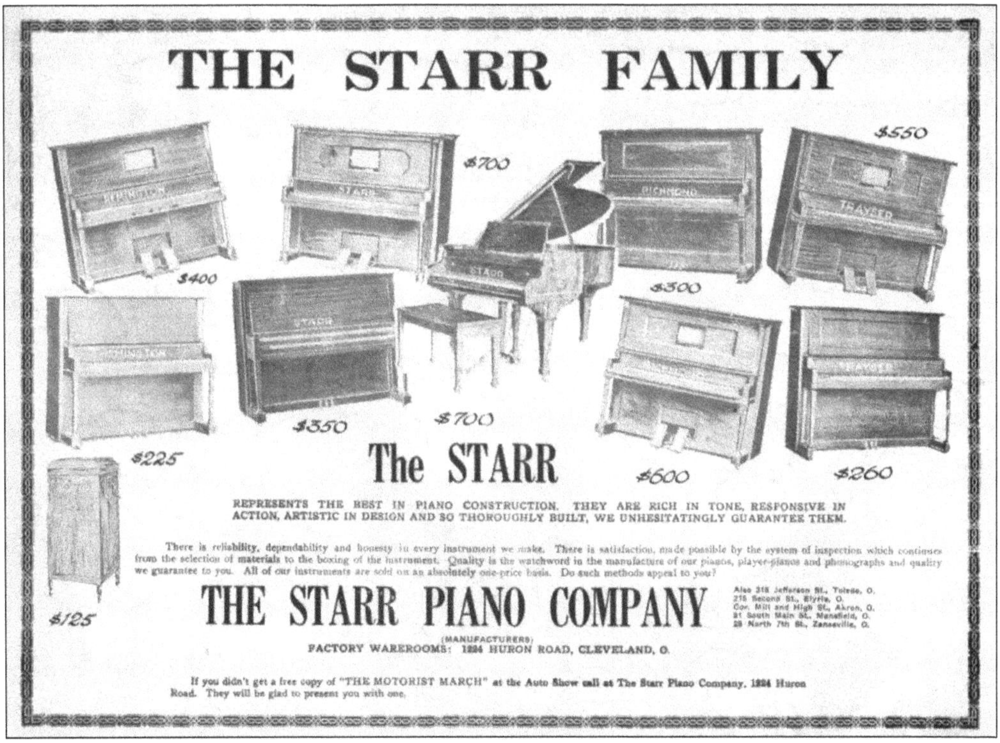

THE STARR FAMILY

$550 $700 $400 $300 $350 $700 $225 $600 $260 $125

The STARR

REPRESENTS THE BEST IN PIANO CONSTRUCTION. THEY ARE RICH IN TONE, RESPONSIVE IN ACTION, ARTISTIC IN DESIGN AND SO THOROUGHLY BUILT, WE UNHESITATINGLY GUARANTEE THEM.

There is reliability, dependability and honesty in every instrument we make. There is satisfaction, made possible by the system of inspection which continues from the selection of materials to the boxing of the instrument. Quality is the watchword in the manufacture of our pianos, player-pianos and phonographs and quality we guarantee to you. All of our instruments are sold on an absolutely one-price basis. Do such methods appeal to you?

THE STARR PIANO COMPANY

(MANUFACTURERS)

FACTORY WAREROOMS: 1224 HURON ROAD, CLEVELAND, O.

Also 318 Jefferson St., Toledo, O.
215 Second St., Elyria, O.
Cor. Mill and High St., Akron, O.
21 South Main St., Mansfield, O.
28 North 7th St., Zanesville, O.

If you didn't get a free copy of "THE MOTORIST MARCH" at the Auto Show call at The Starr Piano Company, 1224 Huron Road. They will be glad to present you with one.

The Starr family advertisement is on the back of sheet music for "The Motorist March" by Louis Rich. It was given to guests at the 15th annual Cleveland Auto Show. Starr Piano made pianos using the labels Starr, Richmond, Remington, and Trayser. The ad reads, "The Starr represents the best in piano construction. They are rich in tone, responsive in action, artistic in design and so thoroughly built, we unhesitatingly guarantee them." (LGI.)

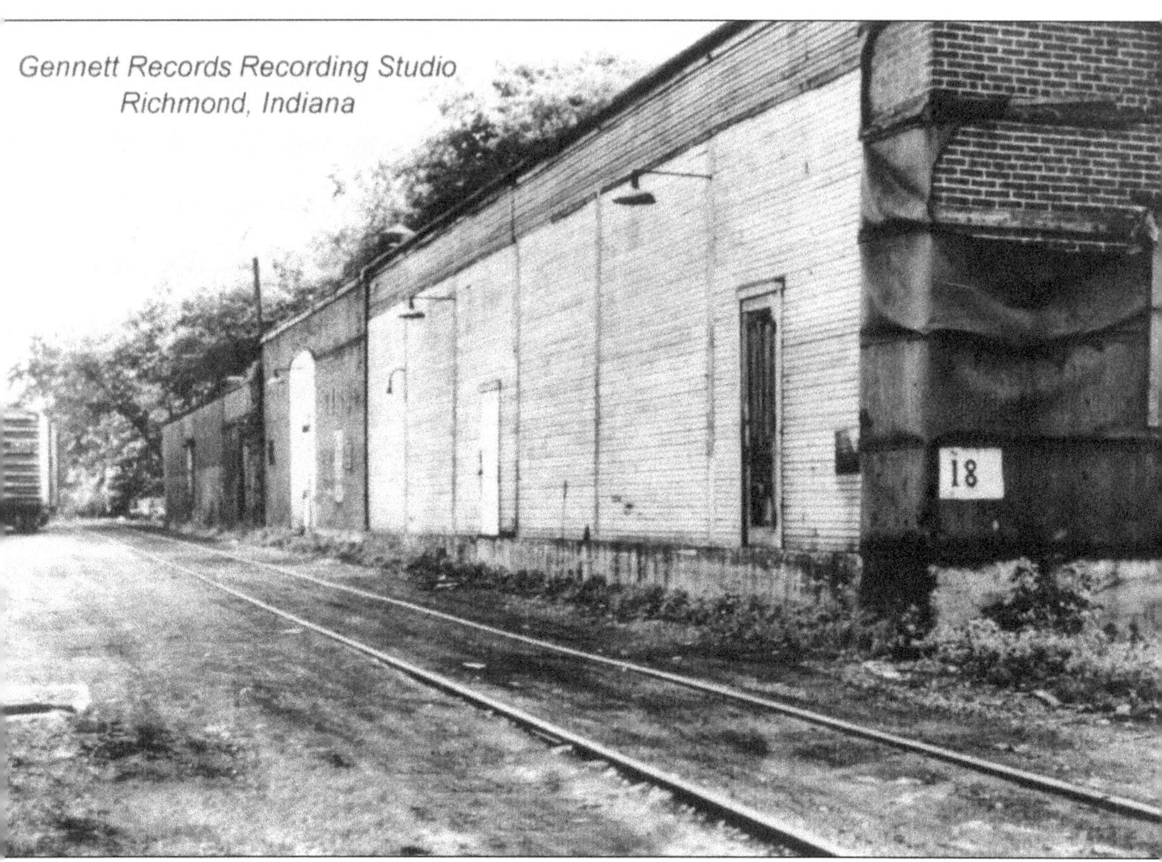

In 1921, Starr Piano employees cleared out a wood kiln situated between the Whitewater River and the railroad spur and converted the building into a recording studio. They hung drapes and rugs to deaden the sound in the live room, and Ezra Wickemeyer installed the recording apparatus in an adjoining room. The studio remained active for over a decade and recorded thousands of people, some for just that one time, but many others who went on to have illustrious careers. (LGI.)

Two

The Birth of a Record Company 1916–1922

Special
Record of Minutes of Board of Directors *Meeting* June 12 *19* 15 *Sheet No.*

Pursuant to call, notice and waiver, a special meeting of the Board of Directors of The Starr Piano Company, of Indiana, was held at the office of the Company at 11 A. M., on Saturday, June 12, 1915. Every member of the Board was present and signed the waiver of call and notice of this special meeting, which waiver appears here upon the record of these proceedings as follows:

THE STARR PIANO COMPANY, OF INDIANA.

WAIVER OF CALL AND OF NOTICE OF SPECIAL MEETING OF

THE BOARD OF DIRECTORS.

We, the undersigned, being all of the Directors of The Starr Piano Company, a corporation of Indiana, being all this day at 11 A. M., Saturday, June 12, 1915, present in person, as appears below, do hereby consent that a special meeting of the Board of Directors of this corporation be held at the office of the Company, in the City of Richmond, Indiana, at aforesaid time, for the purpose of ratifying and concurring in the adoption by the stockholders of The Starr Piano Company, of Indiana, at their special meeting of this date, of the following amendment and enlargement of the charter objects and powers of said corporation, towit:

"The object of its foundation is the manufacture, purchase, sale, lease and use of all and every kind of instruments, machines, devices, processes and materials necessary and suitable in and about the production, preservation, use and control of sound-vibrations for musical, commercial and other economic purposes, including all accessories and parts, and to buy and sell and generally deal in merchandise of kinds similar or incident to aforesaid objects and purposes."

Also for the purpose of considering and acting upon the motion to be introduced by the secretary, Mr. Fred Gennett, as follows:

"Resolved that the officers of the Company be and are hereby instructed to set aside, on July 1st, from the reserve funds of the Company, the sum of approximately $30,000., to be held as a reserve against losses by fire of property not otherwise insured, and as a reserve against loss to the Company by liability to employes for accidents; that appropriate payments equal to the standard payments for like risks, as charged by insurance Companies, shall be paid into, and all losses and cost of operating shall be paid from said fund. Full power to invest and control said fund, shall lie in the officers of the Company, and all gains or losses resulting from investments made, shall be credited and charged to said fund. Said guarantee fund shall not appear upon the current books of the corporation as an asset, and shall not be pledged as the basis for obtaining credit. The treasurer is instructed to report fully to the directors at their semi-annual meeting upon the condition of said fund."

On Saturday, June 12, 1915, Starr Piano's board of directors convened a special meeting. The directors unanimously agreed to amend and expand the company's charter beyond the manufacture of pianos to include all facets in the "production, preservation, use and control of sound vibrations for musical, commercial and other economic purposes." Starr Piano entered the record business as a logical expansion of its thriving piano company. This wise business decision profoundly affected the history of the recording industry and American music and culture. (Wayne County Historical Museum.)

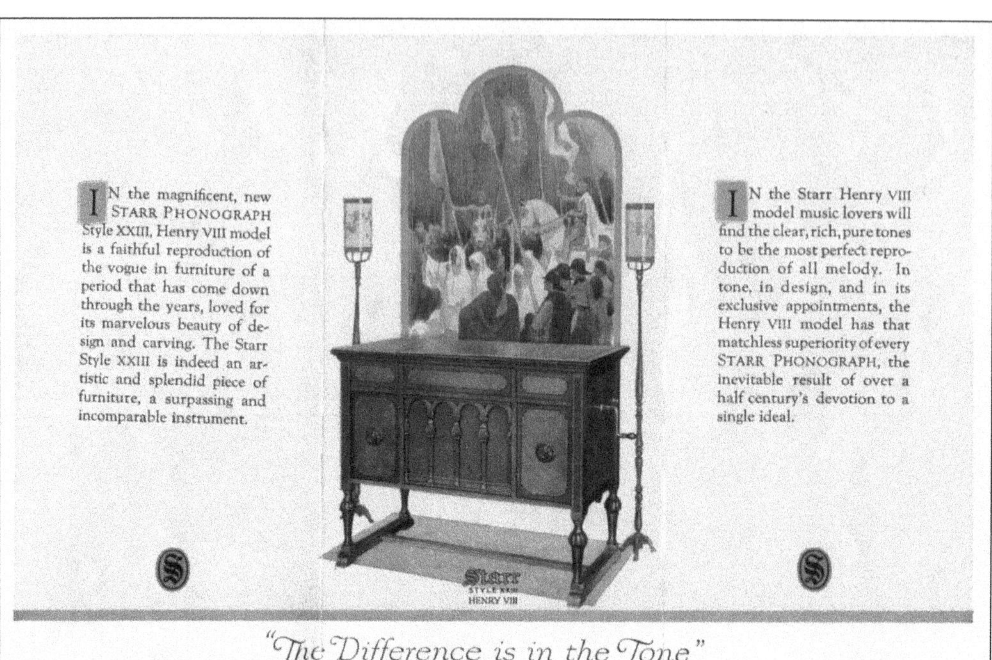

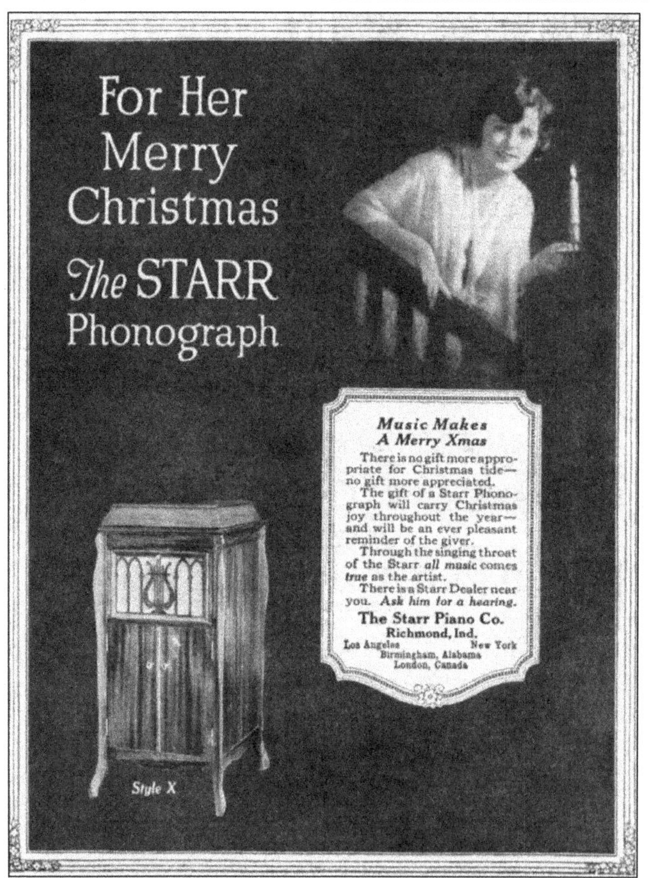

With a large stockpile of lumber, experienced craftsmen, and a distribution network from its piano business, Starr started to manufacture some of the finest phonographs. Starr's Henry VIII model boasted "marvelous beauty of design and carving" and "clear, rich, pure tones to be the most perfect reproduction of all melody." (LGI.)

To promote its new lines of phonographs, Starr aggressively advertised in many of the popular magazines and newspapers of the day, including the *Saturday Evening Post* and *Life*. Within four years of its entry into the phonograph industry, Starr sold approximately 3,000 units a month. (LGI.)

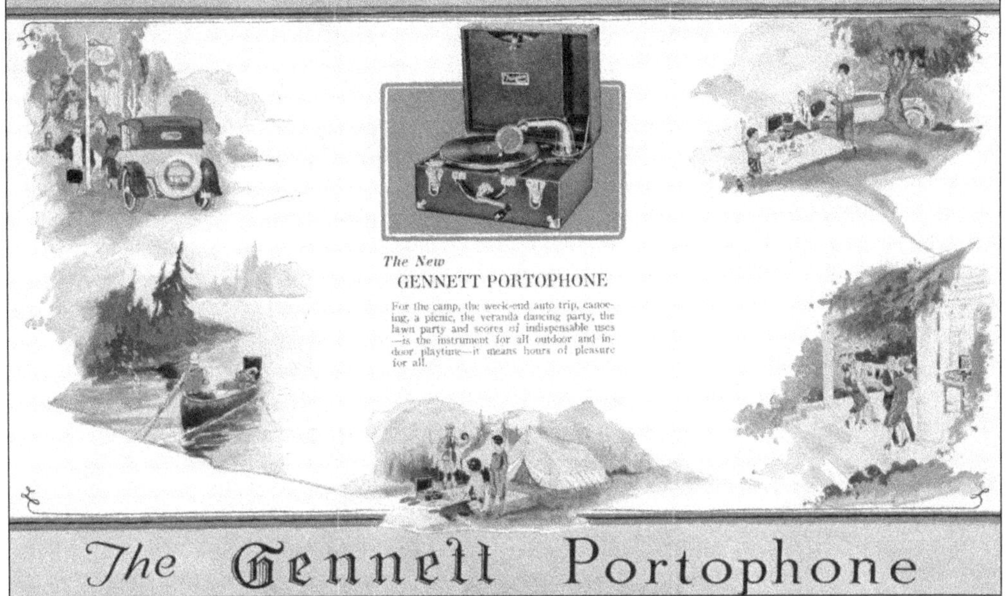

As the phonograph industry grew, the creation of cost-effective and portable units catalyzed its rapid rise. Starr Piano released a portophone under both the Starr and Gennett monikers. These leather- or cloth-covered units featured a stable winding crank, a smooth and long-running motor, and a holder for up to 11 records. (LGI.)

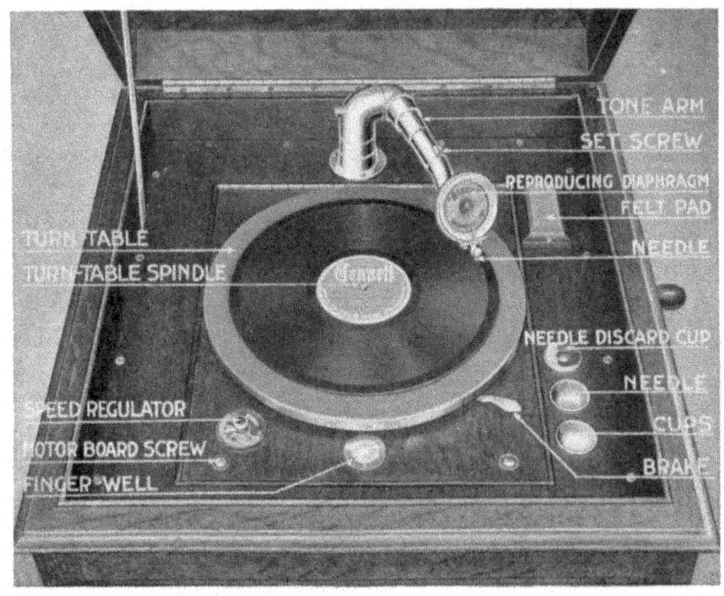

Top of Instrument Showing Various Parts
Sound Box is set to play "Hill and Dale" Records

Each Starr phonograph included a detailed instruction book to insure the proper setup and use. This diagram illustrates the many parts and features on the playing surface. It also shows that these models could play both the less popular vertical or "hill and dale" records and the industry standard "lateral" discs released by Victor and Columbia. (LGI.)

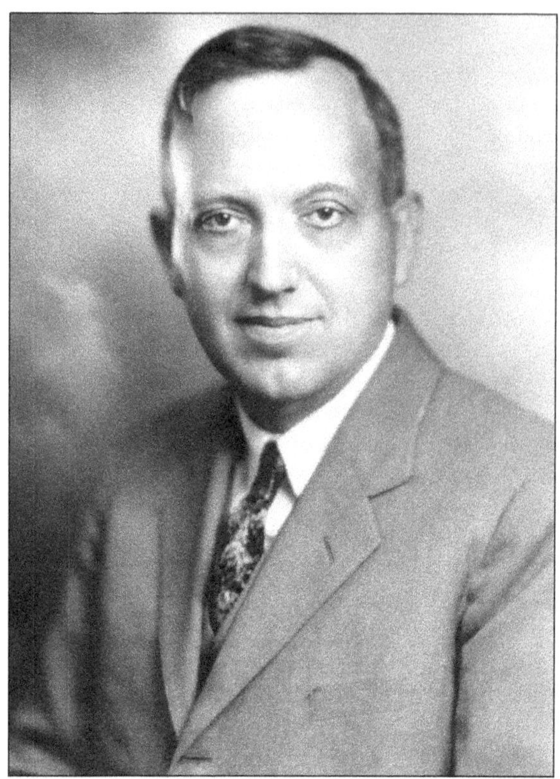

Upon the death of his father in 1922, Harry Gennett Sr. became the president of Starr Piano, though for all intents and purposes, Henry Gennett had retired in the mid-1910s. As Starr Piano expanded into sound recordings, Harry oversaw the piano manufacturing business and put his younger brother, Fred, in charge of the record division. (LGI.)

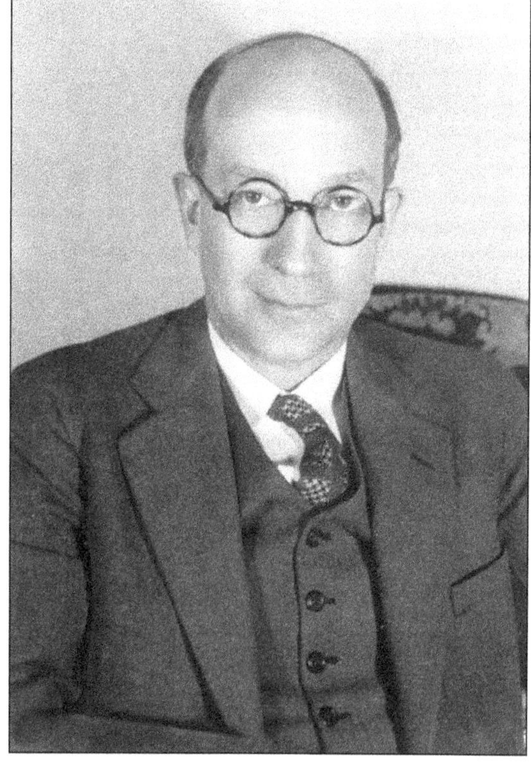

In addition to serving as Starr Piano's secretary, Fred Gennett oversaw the recording division from its inception in 1916 through its demise in the 1930s. While Fred was more standoffish than the prototypical music men of this age, perhaps it was this very characteristic that allowed the record company to move into new genres. (Mike Gennett.)

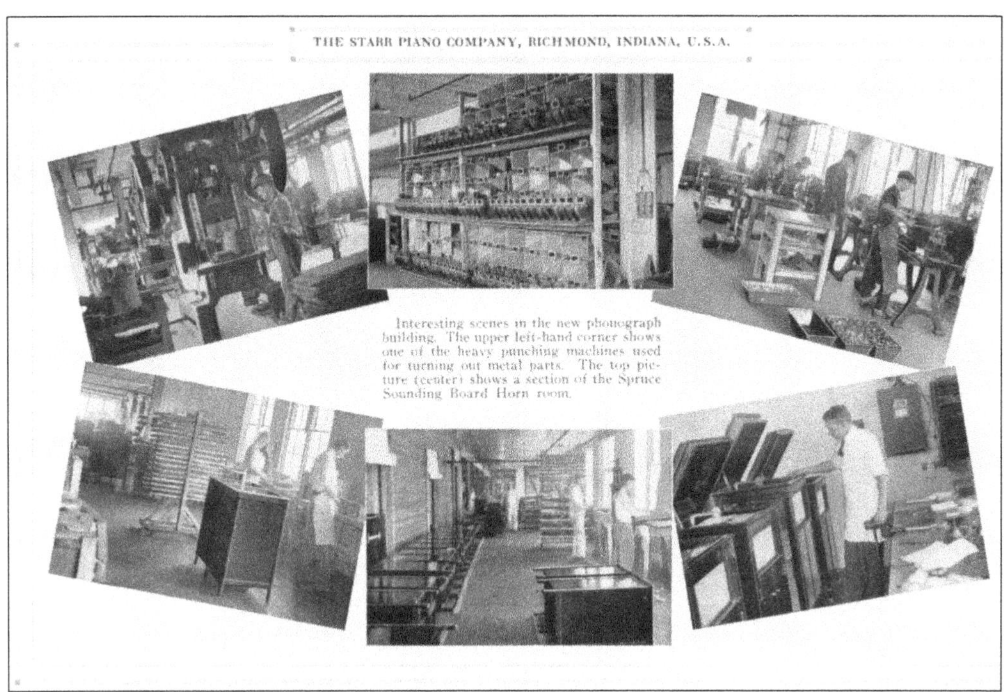

THE STARR PIANO COMPANY, RICHMOND, INDIANA, U.S.A.

Interesting scenes in the new phonograph building. The upper left-hand corner shows one of the heavy punching machines used for turning out metal parts. The top picture (center) shows a section of the Spruce Sounding Board Horn room.

Starr Piano produced a viewbook in 1917 that illustrates the piano, player piano, phonograph, and record departments. It notes "interesting scenes in the new phonograph building" as workers crafted the various machinery and cabinetry in each new phonograph. After a brief association with an outside pressing plant, the Gennetts brought all levels of the record manufacturing business in-house. After all, the complete control of the manufacturing process had made its piano company successful. (LGI.)

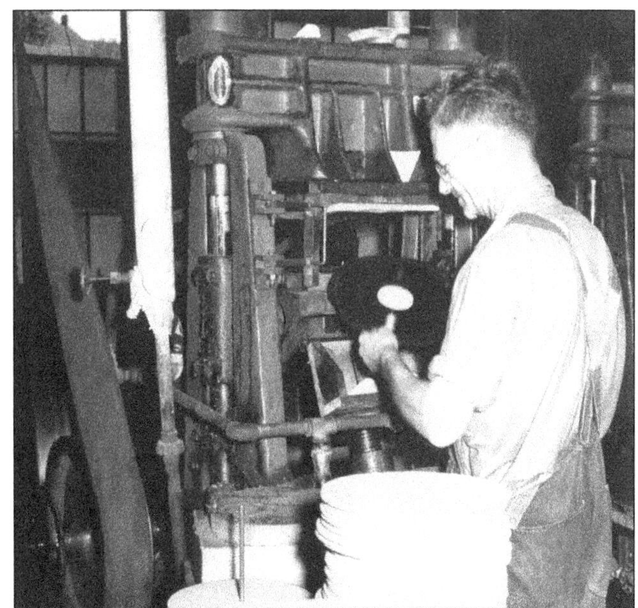

In addition to manufacturing phonographs, Starr Piano soon opened a record pressing plant. It pressed Starr, Gennett, and other company-owned labels, including Champion, Superior, and Supertone. Starr Piano soon offered its services to other labels and developed a custom recording and pressing package for local and regional artists. At its peak, Starr Piano pressed over three million 78-rpm discs a year. This component of the business remained active years after the Gennetts exited the music business when Decca and Mercury took over the pressing plant. (Wayne County Historical Museum.)

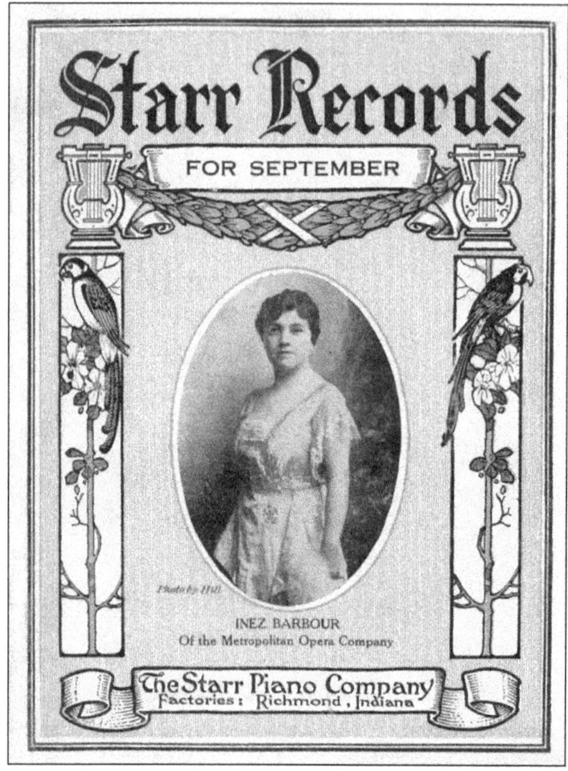

The early records released by Starr Piano matched the mainstream fare of the larger Victor Talking Machine Company and Columbia Records. Inez Barbour was a successful singer with the Metropolitan Opera Company who married New York Philharmonic conductor Henry Hadley. Hadley also recorded for Gennett during its brief partnership with the Ginn Company's Music Appreciation Series. (Brenda Starr Duckworth.)

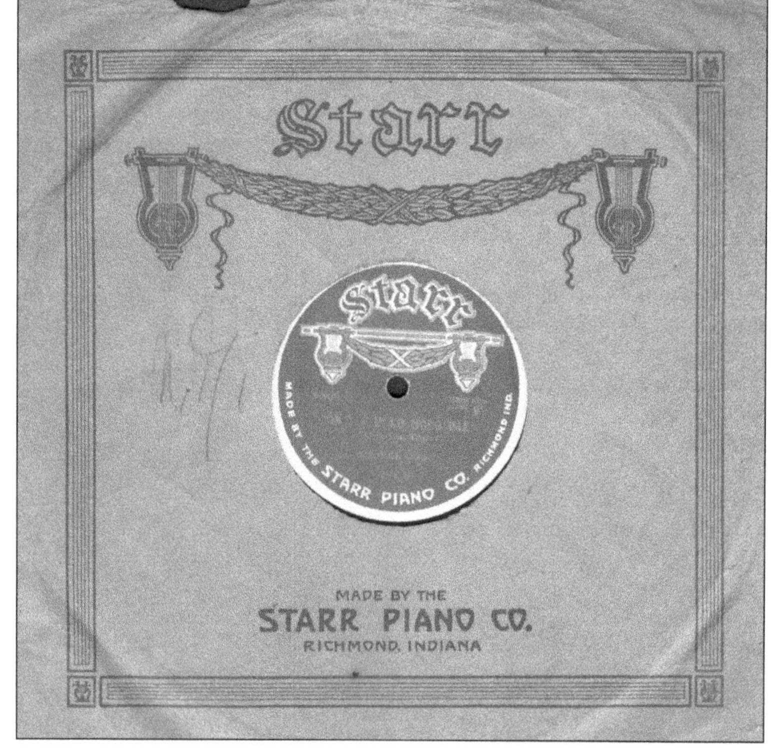

Initially, Starr Piano dubbed its new label Starr Records, as the company primarily sold its phonographs and records through its piano stores in the United States and Canada. Starr Piano recorded standard pop and mainstream music from its newly opened studio at 9–11 East Thirty-Seventh Street in New York City. These vertical records made little impact in the music marketplace. (LGI.)

Vernon Dalhart started his recording career singing pop and light opera in 1916 and for Starr/Gennett in 1917. He added hillbilly songs to his repertoire in the 1920s and released one of the best-selling discs, "The Wreck of the Old '97" b/w (backed with) "The Prisoner's Song," in 1924. He recorded over 100 sides for Gennett and its various affiliates through 1926 and was one of the most prolific artists in the 1920s. Dalhart is one of four Gennett recording artists inducted into the Country Music Hall of Fame. (George Grantham Bain Collection, Library of Congress.)

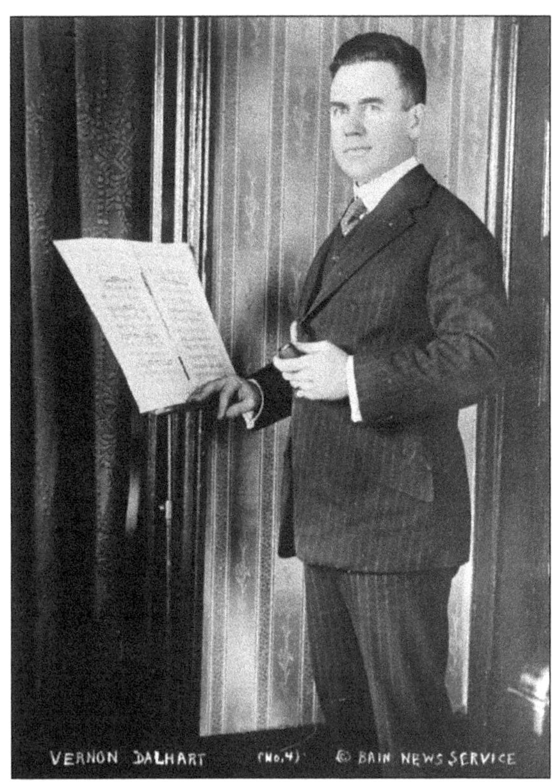

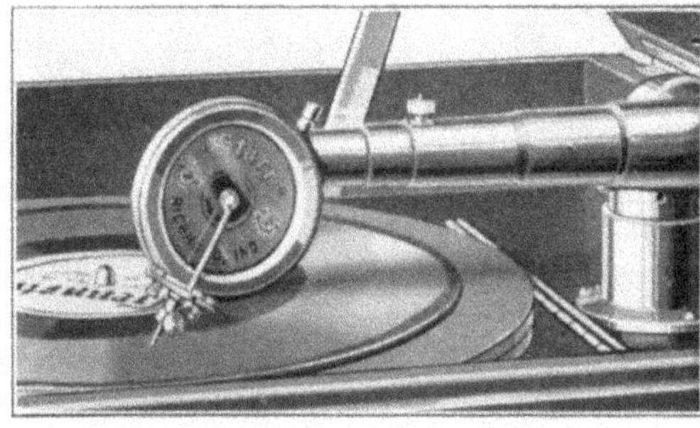

Figure B. Position for Gennett "Lateral" or any "Lateral" Record.

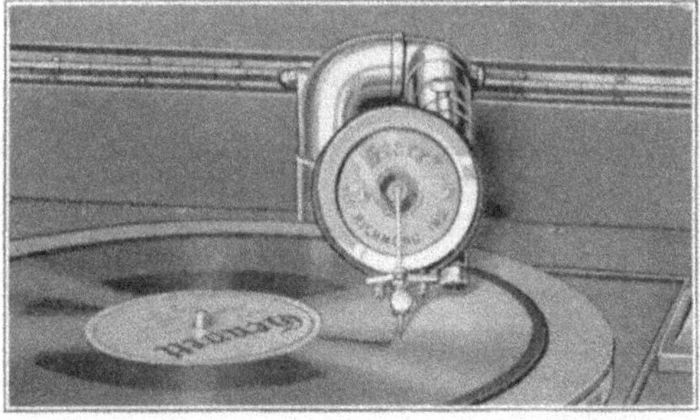

Figure C. Position for Gennett "Hill and Dale" or any "Hill and Dale" Record

In an attempt to both compete with Victor and Columbia's lateral duopoly and provide an option for the public, Starr manufactured a dual tone arm that played both styles of records. However, Starr's attempt to entice owners of lateral phonographs to purchase vertical discs was too little and too late, as Victor and Columbia's lateral cut records dominated the marketplace. (LGI.)

GILLILAN, STRICKLAND, Humorist

Have you ever heard of the genius who extracted sunshine from cucumbers? Well, he isn't in it with Gillilan This popular humorist, poet, lecturer and all around entertainer is a device for the extraction of humor from everyday life. He is a sure cure for discouraged minds. Strickland Gillilan doesn't invent his humor, but notices it in the rest of us and calls our attention to it. In other words, he teaches us to laugh at ourselves—after which we are better company, even for ourselves. His Gennett offerings are full of jolly good humor that appeals to everybody. You can not help but delight in listening to the quaint and distinctly individual renditions of this inimitable humorist. The "Art Tone" record, listed and described on the front pages of this issue, is made up of some of Gillilan's best known bits of humorous verse, including "Finnigin to Flannigan."

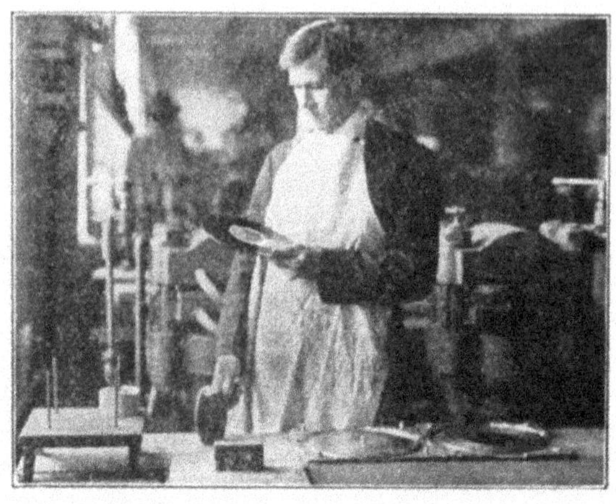

Gillilan Filling a Pressing Engagement

Absent Mindedness	(A)(N)(D)	*Nothing to Unload—Too Good to Miss*	**7581**	.75
Jumping at Conclusions	(A)(N)(D)	*Me an' Pap an' Mother—Traffic Cop Murphy*	**10000**	1.00
When Our Gal Spoke a Piece	(A)(N)(D)	*Swellhead*	**7571**	.75
When Papa Holds My Hand—Crossed Fingers	(A)(N)(D)	*Family Group—Fidgets*	**10018**	1.00

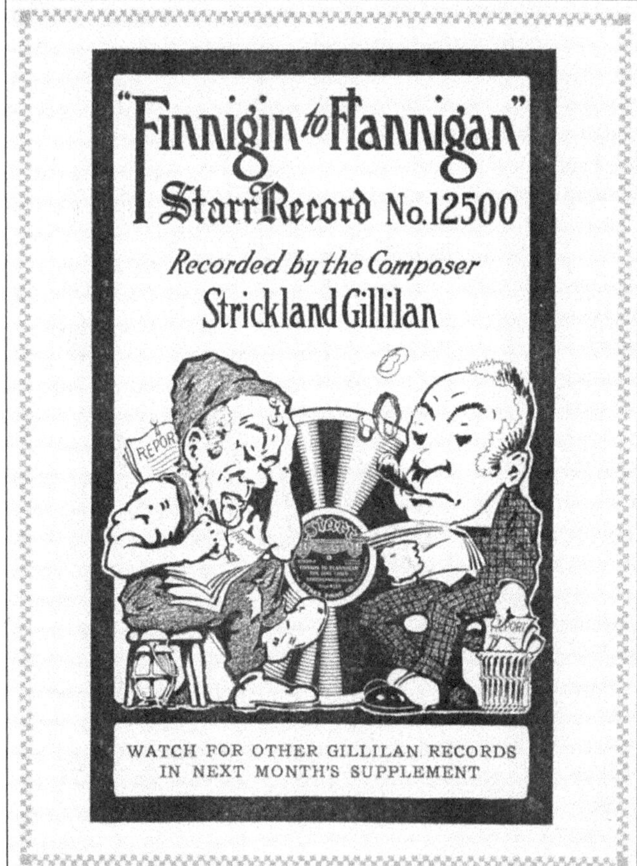

Strickland Gillian was one of the first artists to record for Starr Records in 1916. Gillian was a popular poet, journalist, and humorist, whose poem "The Reading Mother" became a Mother's Day mainstay. The following passage frequently appears in greeting cards today, "You may have tangible wealth untold; Caskets of jewels and coffers of gold. Richer than I you can never—I had a Mother who read to me." (Brenda Starr Duckworth.)

Strickland Gillilan's poem "Finnigin to Flannigan" uses Irish dialect parody and portrays a conversation between the railroad boss, Finnigin, and his employee, Flannigan, as the train is about to crash. The poem features the well-known phrase, "On again, off again, gone again—Finnigin." (Brenda Starr Duckworth.)

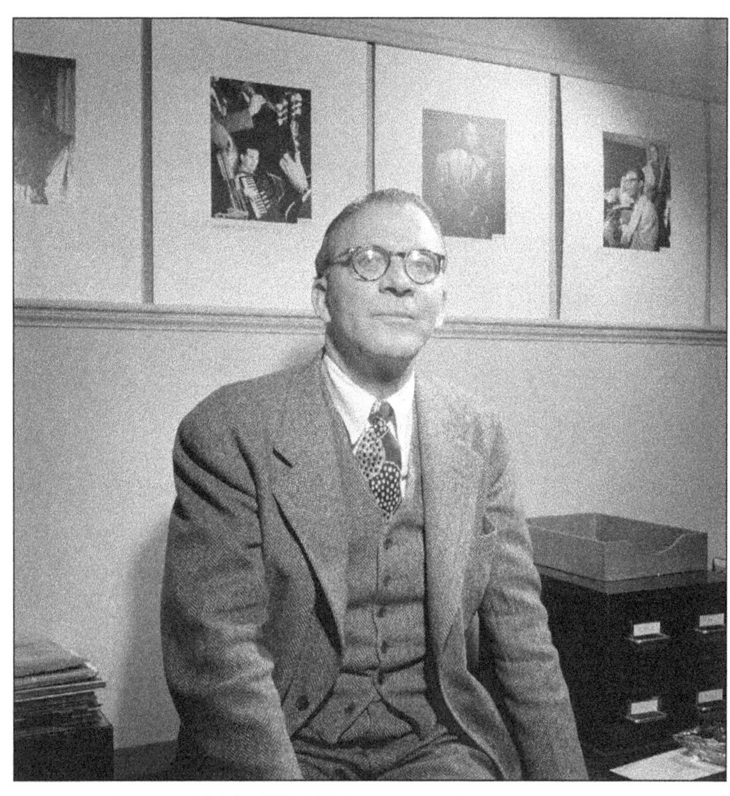

Jean Goldkette led one of the most talented bands in the 1920s, and it featured Tommy and Jimmy Dorsey, Joe Venuti, Bix Beiderbecke, Frankie Trumbauer, and Eddie Lang. In 1918, Goldkette accompanied saxophonist Duane Sawyer on piano. The two recordings appeared on Gennett no. 8512. (William P. Gottlieb Collection, Library of Congress.)

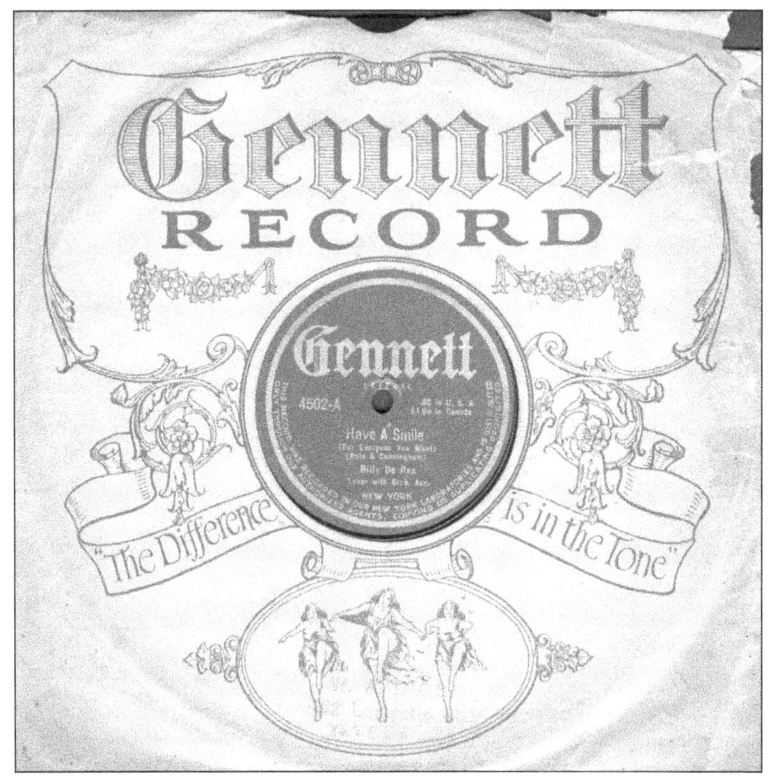

In 1919, Fred Gennett determined Victor and Columbia's lateral patent duopoly was no longer valid. He saw an opportunity to challenge this duopoly when Columbia Records' patent expired. Gennett released its new releases on lateral cut discs. Victor quickly sued for patent infringement, but Fred Gennett's belief and ability to argue his case in court led to a major upheaval in the young recording industry. (LGI.)

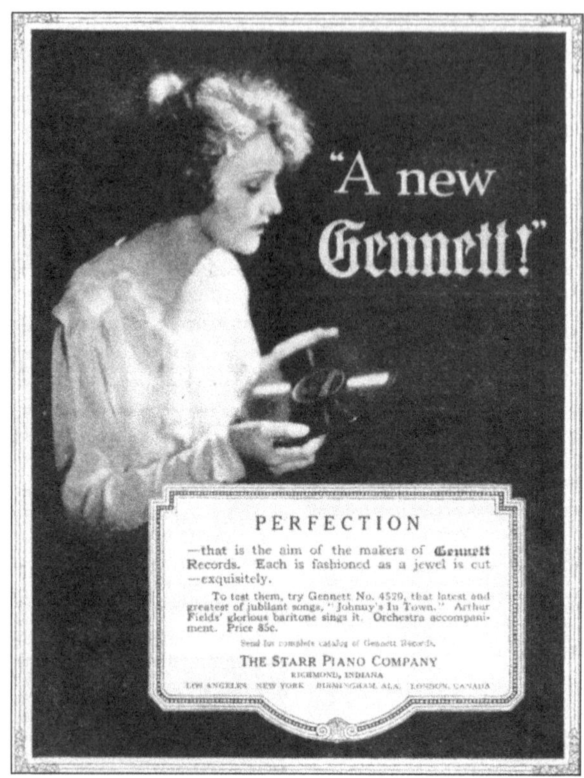

Arthur Fields was an American baritone from the vaudeville circuit and among the earliest recording stars. He recorded over 1,000 sides for almost every label, including Edison, Victor, and Gennett. He sang on well over 100 sides for Gennett, including with Bailey's Lucky Seven, Ladd's Black Aces, Harry Raderman's Orchestra, and on the Moxie Soda theme song. (LGI.)

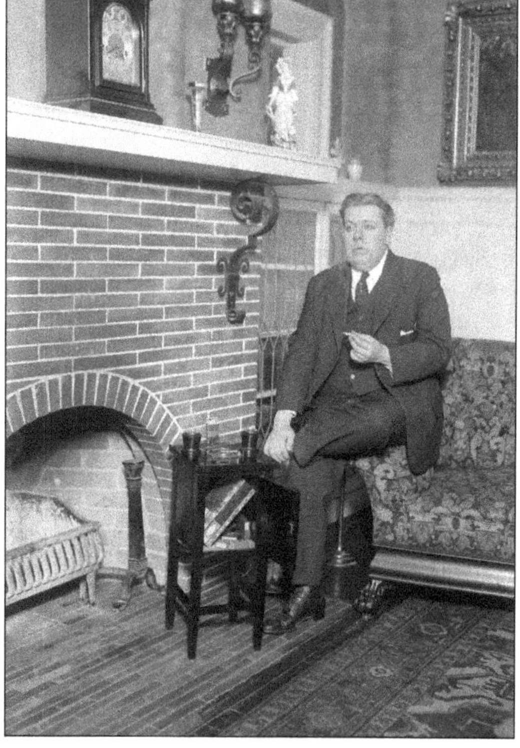

Henry Burr was one of the most popular recording artists in the first 20 years of the 20th century. He was a member of many singing ensembles, including the Peerless Quartet and the Sterling Trio. Burr appeared on approximately 50 recordings on various Gennett labels between 1917 and 1926. (George Grantham Bain Collection, Library of Congress.)

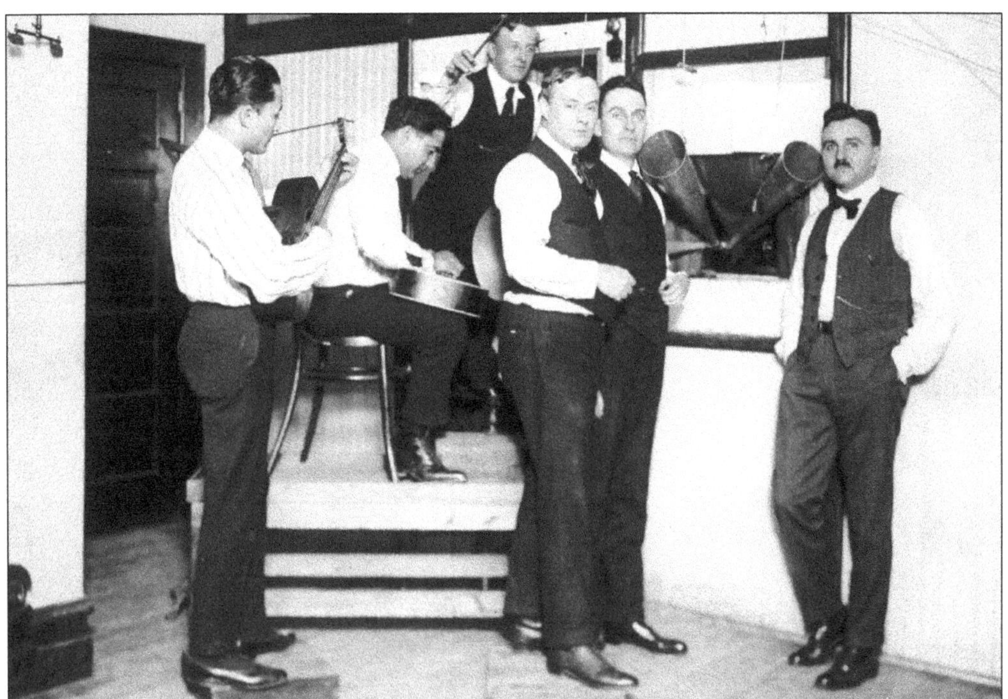

Hawaiian music became very popular in the 1920s, and guitarist Frank Ferera was one its signature artists. He recorded for many labels, including Gennett, in several different ensembles. In this photograph, Ferera (seated) is pictured with fellow guitarist Anthony Franchini (left) and the Crescent Trio—Lewis James, Charles Harrison, and Elliott Shaw. This assemblage of musicians recorded together in 1921 at Gennett's New York City studio. (Library of Congress.)

Helen Ware was a stage and film actress at the turn of the 20th century. She recorded over 20 sides for Gennett between 1917 and 1923. Gennett released the majority of her recordings on its Art Tone Series, which emulated Victor's Red Seal line and generally cost more per disc than those on the plain Gennett label. (LGI.)

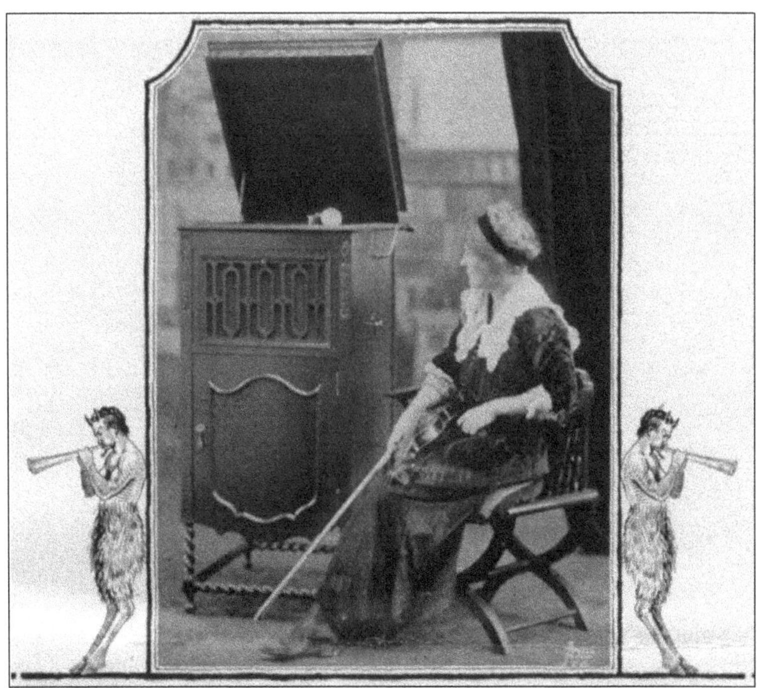

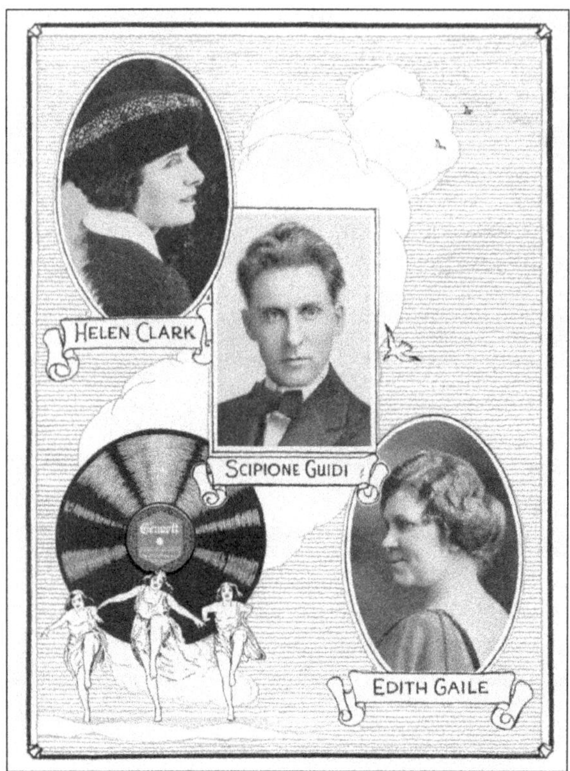

Other artists in the Art Tone and Green Label Series included Helen Clark, Scipione Guidi, and Edith Gaile. Clark was a popular actress and recording artist on many labels, including Victor and Gennett. Guidi was a longtime violist with the New York Philharmonic in the 1920s. He recorded over two dozen sides for Gennett between 1921 and 1929. Gaile recorded only four sides for Gennett in the early 1920s and was a prominent soprano on the theater circuit. (LGI.)

The Criterion Quartet was a popular vocal ensemble that actively recorded between 1916 and 1930. The group consisted of Walter Downie, Robert Rainey, William Washburn, and founder Reinald Werrenrath. The quartet made over 100 sides in Gennett's New York City studio, including "The Bright and Fiery Cross" and "Mystic City" for a Ku Klux Klan record label. (LGI.)

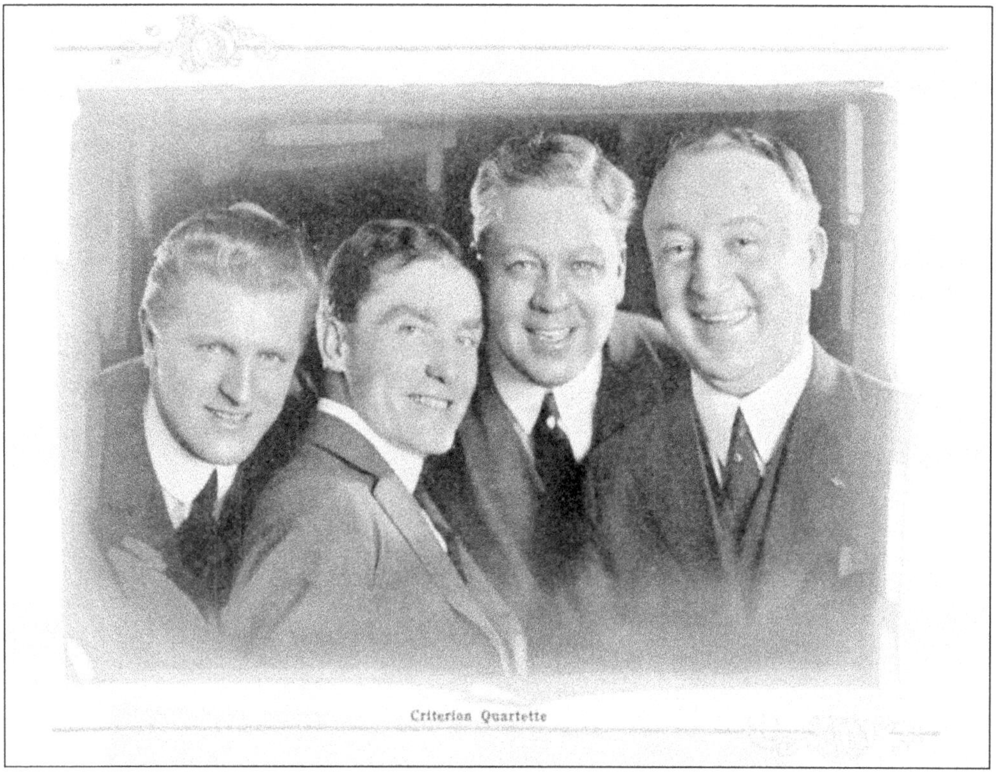

Criterion Quartette

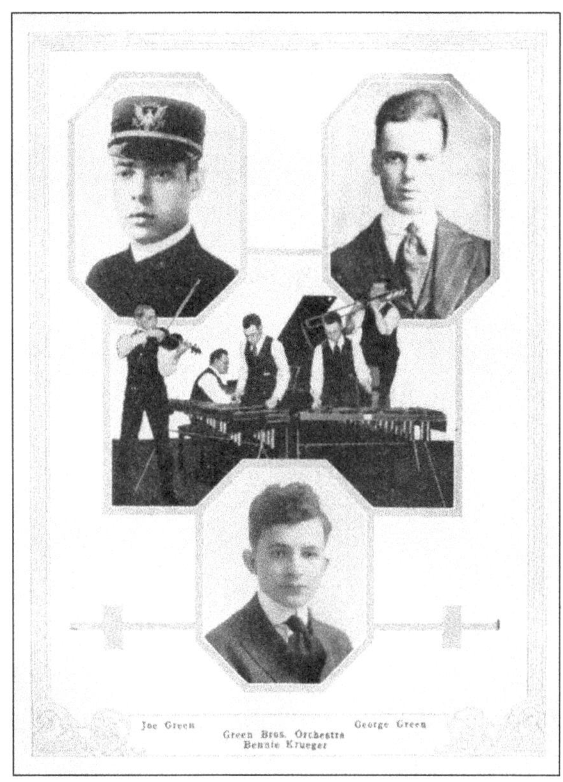

This May 1920 Gennett Records catalog page advertises recordings by the Green Brothers Xylophone Orchestra and Bennie Krueger. The Green Brothers, Joe and George, recorded for Gennett between 1919 and 1923. Jazz saxophonist Bennie Krueger recorded for Gennett with his own orchestra and Bailey's Lucky Seven throughout the 1920s. In the 1930s, Krueger served as the musical director for both Rudy Vallee and Bob Crosby. (LGI.)

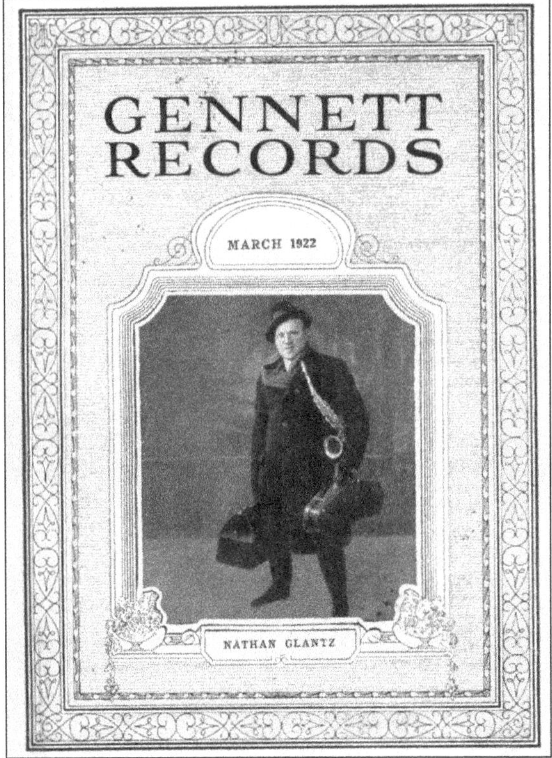

Nathan Glantz started his career as an alto and tenor saxophonist. He performed with Fred Van Eps and Frank Banta and is best known for being the first person on record to make his saxophone "laugh." Although Glantz organized, led, or played on nearly 1,000 sides for Gennett under several dozen monikers, he did not play on many of the recordings actually released by Gennett and its subsidiaries. (LGI.)

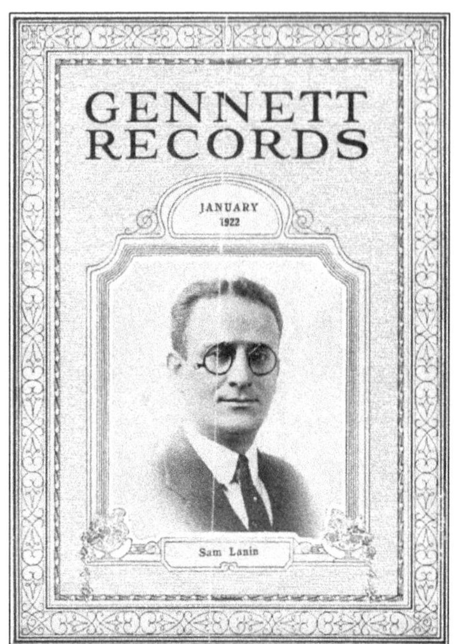

In the 1920s, Sam Lanin was one of the most productive bandleaders and organized sessions for practically every record label. For Gennett, Lanin recorded with his Roseland Ballroom Orchestra and coordinated some of the label's most popular artists, such as Ladd's Black Aces and Bailey's Lucky Seven. Additionally, Lanin possessed an impeccable ear for talent, as many jazz greats appeared on his sessions, including Bix Beiderbecke, Jimmy McPartland, Tommy Dorsey, Jimmy Dorsey, Red Nichols, and Miff Mole. (LGI.)

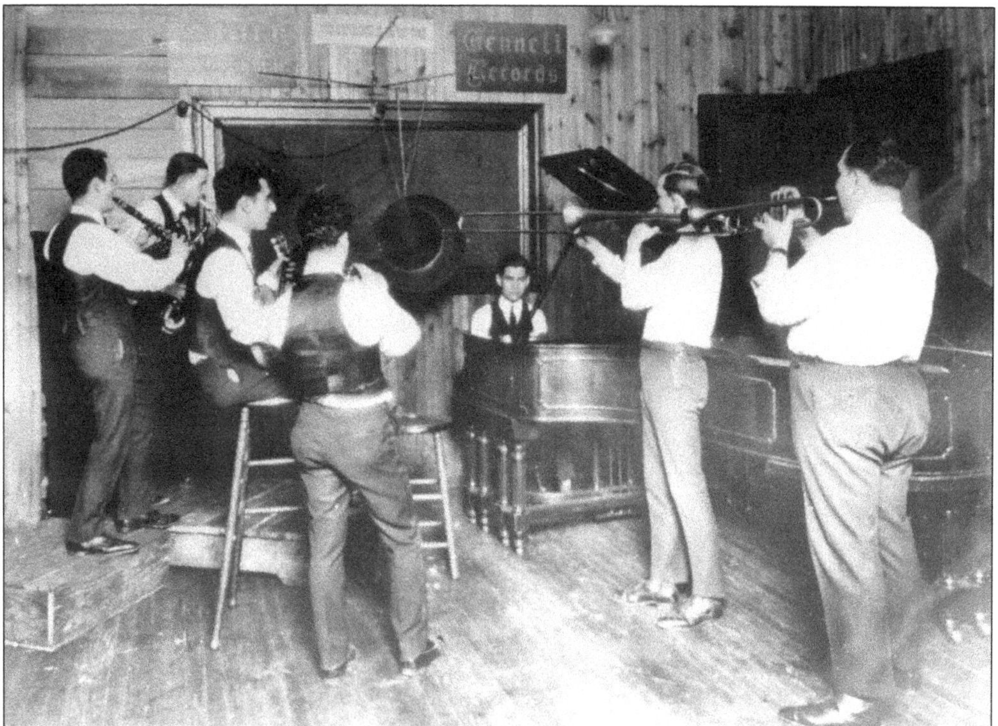

Bailey's Lucky Seven, a studio band of revolving musicians organized by Sam Lanin, was one of Gennett's most popular recording artists. They recorded well over 100 sides between 1921 and 1926. One of their most popular recordings, "Nobody Lied" b/w "Homesick," features Cliff "Ukulele Ike" Edwards scat singing and mimicking the sound of a muted trumpet. Edwards is the voice of Jiminy Cricket in Disney's *Pinocchio*. From left to right are Sam Lanin, unidentified, Nick Lucas, Phil Napoleon, Joe Lanin, Miff Mole, and Jules Levy Jr. (Starr-Gennett Foundation.)

Miff Mole was a dynamic and in demand jazz trombonist in the 1920s. He recorded on the majority of Bailey's Lucky Seven sides and with Ladd's Black Aces, McMurray California Thumpers, Husk O'Hare's Super Orchestra of Chicago, and Johnny Clesi's Areolians for Gennett. Additionally, Mole organized and led sessions with the Sioux City Six featuring Bix Beiderbecke. (William P. Gottlieb Collection, Library of Congress.)

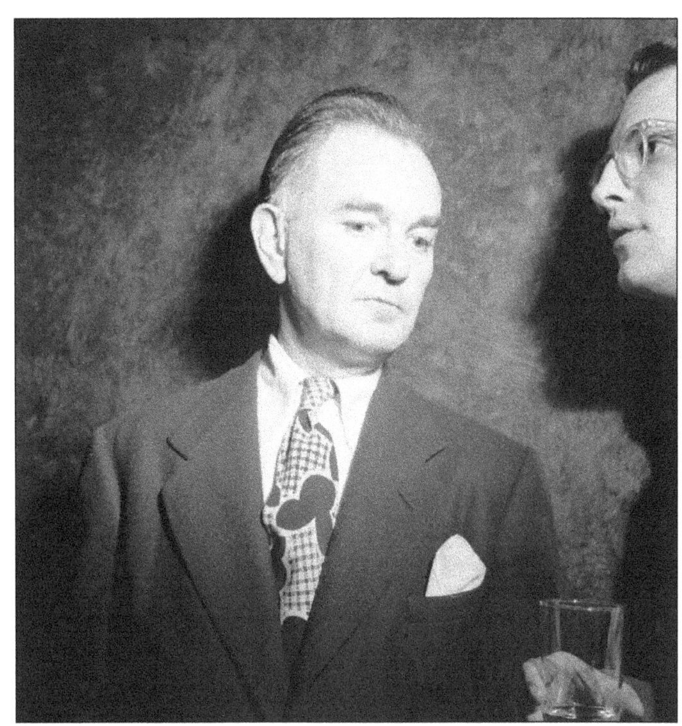

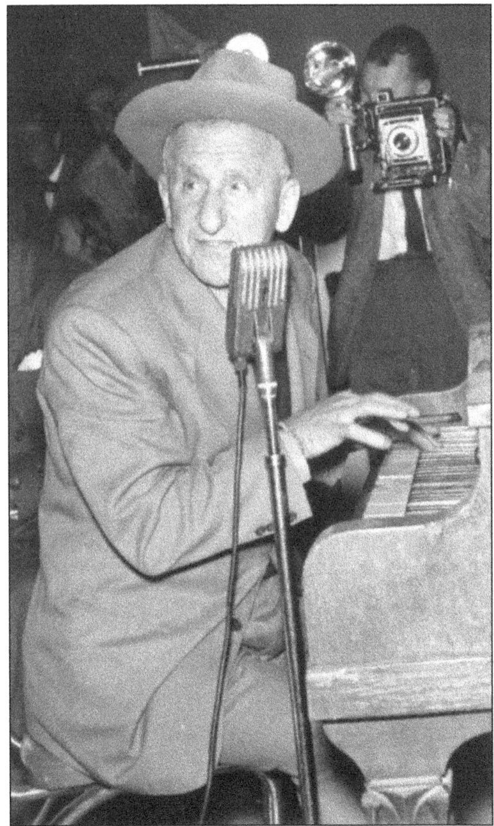

While best known as an actor and comedian, Jimmy Durante was also a popular jazz pianist and bandleader in the 1920s. For Gennett, Durante recorded with Ladd's Black Aces, Bailey's Lucky Seven, Original New Orleans Jazz Band, and Jimmy Durante's Jazz Band. He had a major hit with his song "Inka Dinka Doo." Durante later hosted a television variety show in the 1950s and starred in many other shows and motion pictures. (CBD.)

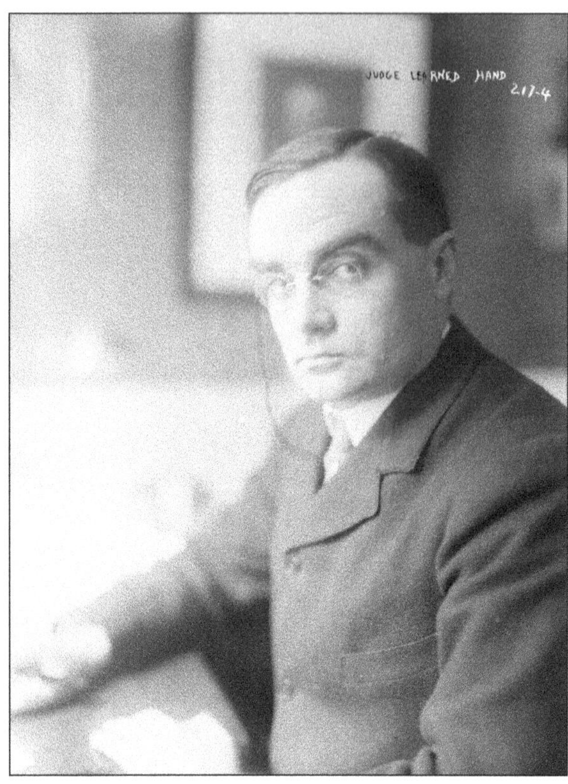

Judge Learned Hand was one of several judges to preside over and adjudicate the *Victor Talking Machine Company v. Starr Piano* patent infringement lawsuit between 1919 and 1923. Victor argued Starr Piano violated its patented technology when Starr released lateral records without Victor's permission. Judge Learned Hand agreed with Starr Piano's argument that the Victor patent was invalid and entered the process into the public domain. This decision acted as a catalyst for the rapid growth of smaller record labels and the recording of blues, jazz, and country music in the 1920s. (Library of Congress.)

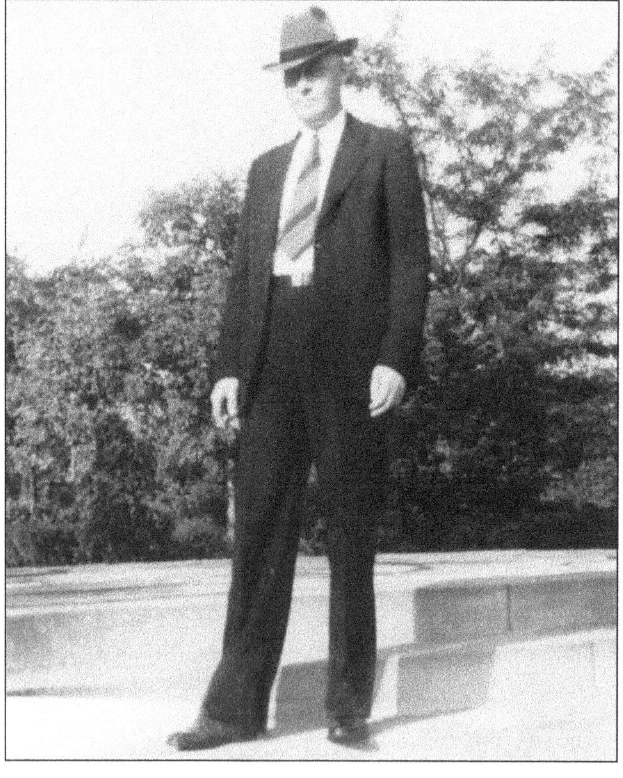

Ezra Wickemeyer worked at Starr Piano from 1914 through 1927. Starting in 1921, Wickemeyer served as Gennett's chief recording engineer in the one-story former lumber storage building towards the end of Starr's Richmond industrial complex. Wickemeyer supervised the recording of over 1,000 sides with artists that ranged from local pundits to world-renowned jazz artists. He was always attuned to capturing a well-balanced mix and performance. (LGI.)

Better known as "Singing Sam, the Barbasol Man," Harry Frankel recorded "How Are You Going To Wet Your Whistle" in 1919 at Gennett's New York City studio. Frankel was also one of the first artists to record in the newly opened studio in Richmond and recorded his popular "It Ain't Gonna Rain No More" there in 1924. Frankel passed away in 1948 in his Richmond, Indiana, home. (Wayne County Historical Museum.)

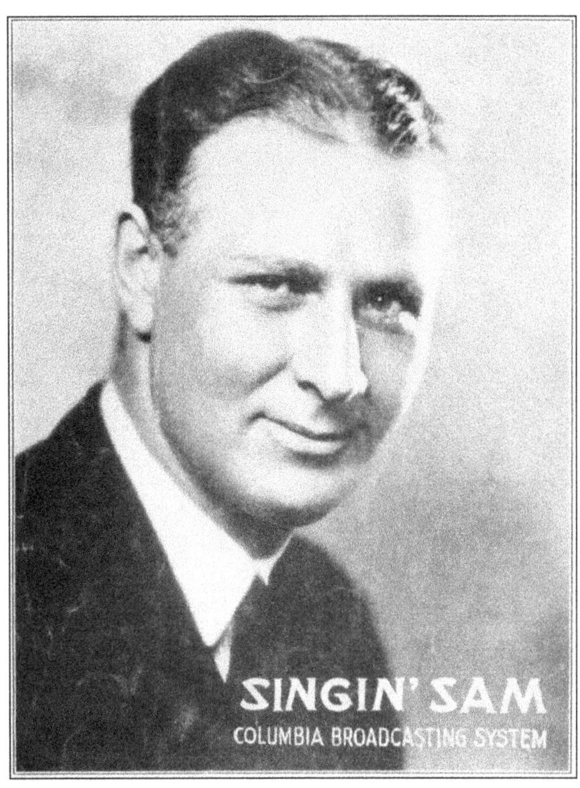

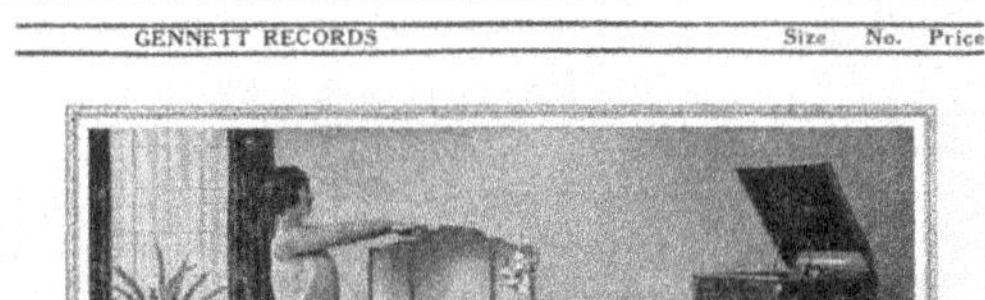

GENNETT RECORDS — Size — No. — Price

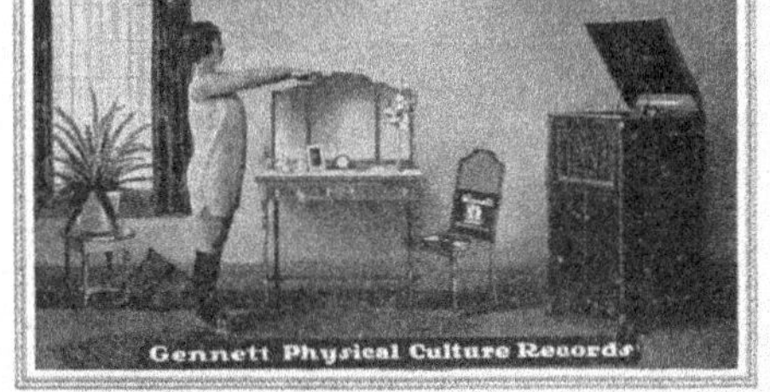

The Gennett Physical Culture Records were prepared by Clarence A. Nichols, the well known New York City Physical Director who was formerly physical director at the 57th Street Y. M. C. A. and who now holds the same position in the Gary Health Studios, New York. Their purpose is to give every person the opportunity to keep in good physical condition. An active, outdoor life is unfortunately denied many of us. We do not get enough bodily exercise. Our muscles become soft, our system becomes sluggish, we are not our best. The Gennett Physical Culture Records though simple, are effective and will meet the constantly growing demand for home exercises. A few minutes spent in going through these exercises will keep you in shape, bring health and make you "feel fine." Old time spirit will be renewed, muscles will harden, your vim, vigor and pep will return. Every person owes this to himself.

The Gennett Physical Culture Record set consists of twelve exercises on three double-sided records, two exercises to a side. They are beautifully set to music and the instructions are given in a clear voice and easily followed. You will find them complete, practical, most enjoyable and invaluable.

You'll be delighted with these exercises. Have your dealer show the set to you. He'll be glad to demonstrate to your complete satisfaction.

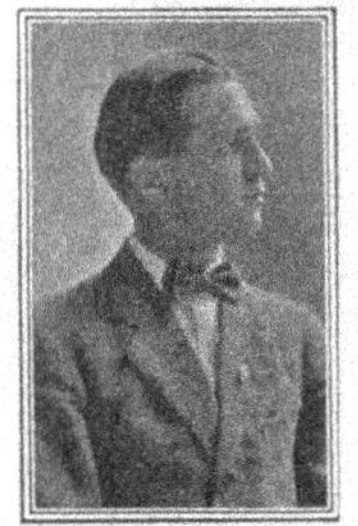

Clarence A. Nichols

NICHOLS, C. A.—Physical Culture Supervisor

	Size	No.	Price
Gennett Physical Culture—Exercise No. 1 and No. 2 and *Gennett Physical Culture—Exercise No. 3 and No. 4*	10	5031	Set $2.75
Gennett Physical Culture—Exercise No. 5 and No. 6 and *Gennett Physical Culture—Exercise No. 7 and No. 8*	10	5032	
Gennett Physical Culture—Exercise No. 9 and No. 10 and *Gennett Physical Culture—Exercise No. 11 and No. 12*	10	5033	

91

In addition to recording musical acts, Gennett also found success in various novelty and lifestyle products. A series of Physical Culture records with exercise guru Charles A. Nichols were amongst its most successful. On each disc, Nichols describes the exercise and then shouts the count and encouragement as a small orchestra accompanies him. (LGI.)

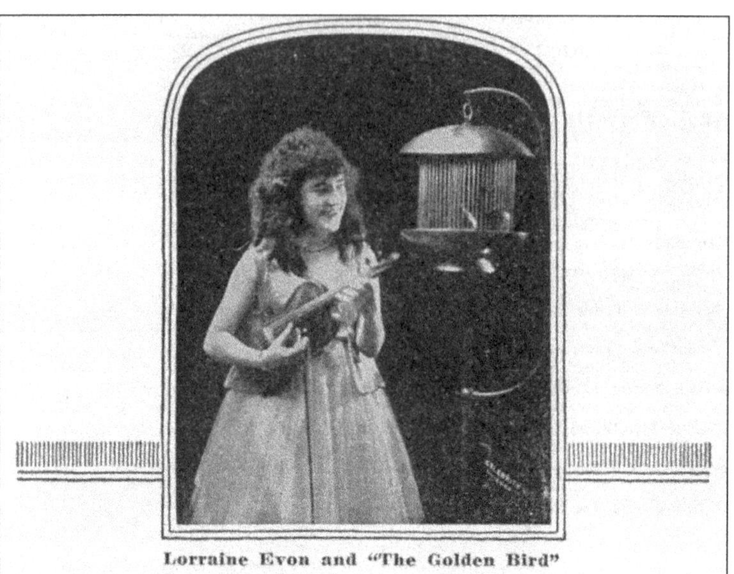

Lorraine Evon and "The Golden Bird"

A Gennett Record of exceptional interest among the great variety of Gennett Recordings is the canary solo by Lorraine Evon's "Golden Bird" a record of such charm as to be worthy of a place in every music lover's library. The sweet, enrapturing, golden notes of the canary have given us a record of inspiration, of distinction and of genuine musical worth. Although the real theme of the music is carried in the accompaniment the notes of the bird blending with violin and piano offer a melody of such harmony and fascination that it will never be forgotten and forever cherished (See page 48.)

47

Gennett aggressively marketed the various singing canary records featuring violinist Lorraine Evon and pianist Norman Brown. Gennett showcased Evon, Brown, and Norman Provol's canary in various markets, like Milwaukee, and "every Gennett dealer was forced to restock on Golden Bird numbers," according to the *Talking Machine Trade*. While these two musicians played such standards as "Souvenir" or "Glow Worm," Norman Provol's trained canary sang along with them. (LGI.)

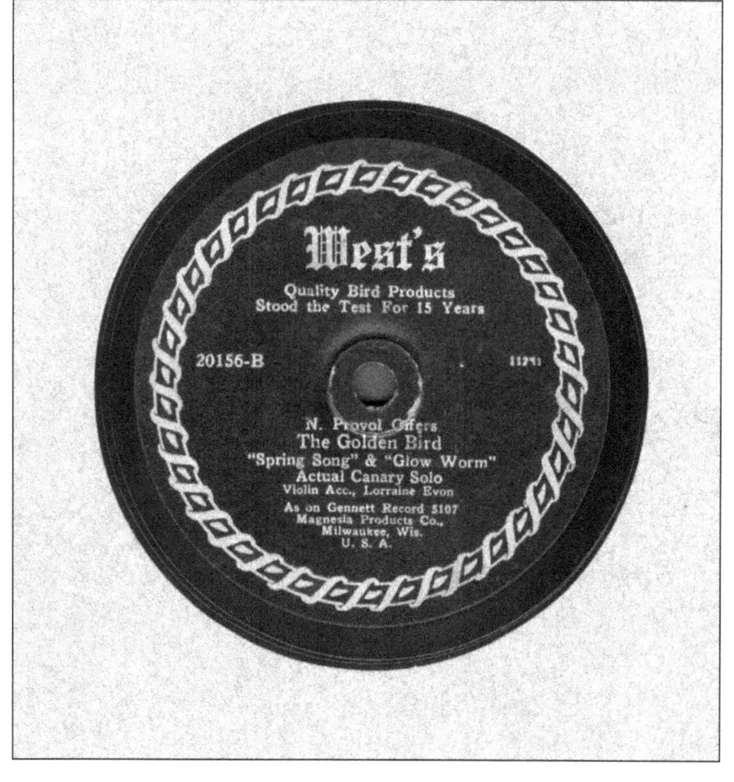

Starr Piano released the singing canary records on both Gennett and a custom label for West's, a company that offered "quality bird products" and "stood the test for over 15 years" in Milwaukee, Wisconsin. Surprisingly, both the Gennett and West's issues sold very well, as copies turn up all the time on auction sites and in antique stores. (LGI.)

Homer Rodeheaver, music director for Rev. Billy Sunday from 1909 to 1927, was the most prolific sacred singer on acoustic records other than Henry Burr. Rodeheaver recorded for Victor, Columbia, Edison, Emerson, Vocalion, Brunswick, BD&M, and Gennett, in addition to his own Rainbow label. Rodeheaver and Virginia Asher were the first artists to make issued records in Gennett's Richmond studio. Their partnership began in 1910, and they introduced both "In the Garden" and "The Old Rugged Cross," hymns that remain popular today. (LGI.)

GENNETT RECORDS—SACRED

SACRED GENNETT RECORDS

Gennett Records by Homer Rodeheaver and Virginia Asher

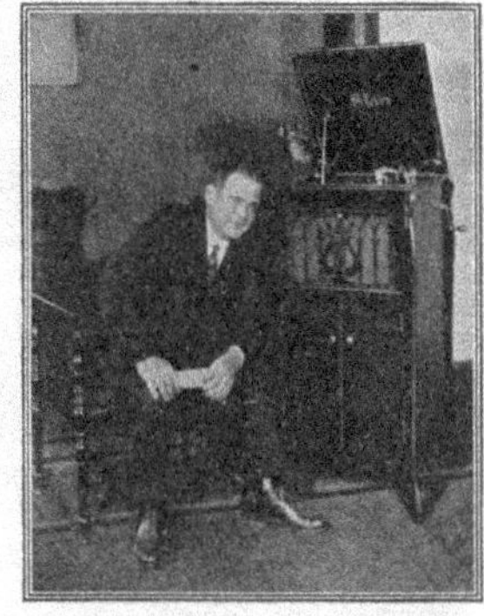

Homer Rodeheaver

Homer Rodeheaver, Billy Sunday's famous choir leader, is the world's greatest as well as the most popular evangelistical singer. His followers number into the thousands. He and Mrs. Virginia Asher, who is associated with him in his musical work record exclusively for Gennett Records. They present their recordings in that characteristic style which has gained for them followers who number into the thousands.

Rodeheaver began his career in a Southern logging camp. He attended high school at Delaware, Ohio, after which he was admitted to the preparatory department of the Ohio Wesleyan University. Here he became popular as a leader of college songs and yells, and also as a trombone player. It was his cleverness as leader of the College minstrels that first brought him into prominence, and when a call came to the college from a neaby town for a leader for the music of a revival, then being conducted by Evangelist Walton, he was sent to fill the place for the evening meetings, returning to school each day for his regular work.

After chorus work at differeut places he cast his lot with Rev. W. A. Sunday, arising from semi-obscurity to a position second to no other living song evangelist.

Don't overlook a single one of the Rodeheaver, Asher, or any of the other sacred Gennett Records which follow.

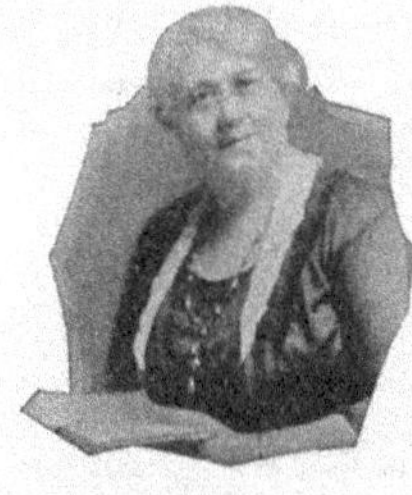

Mrs. Virginia Asher

102

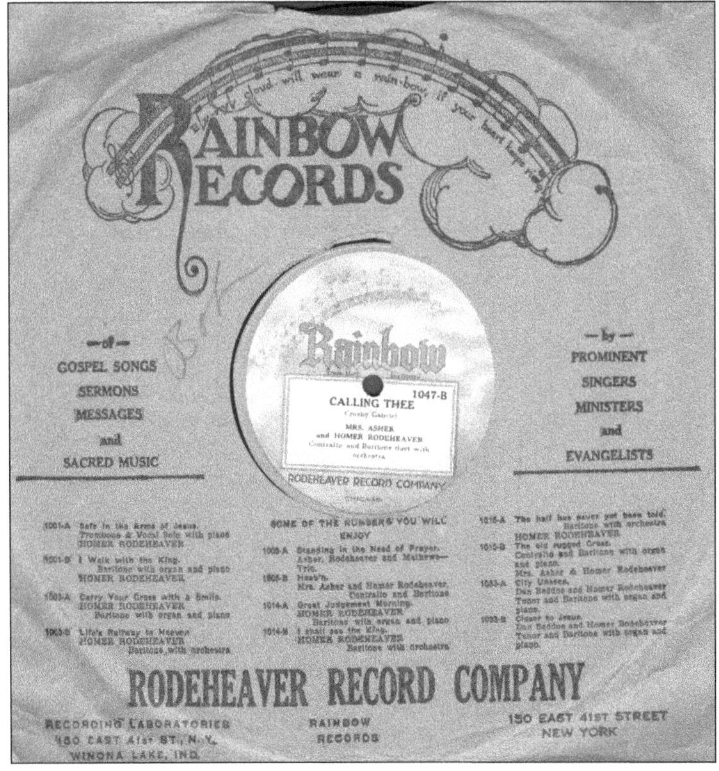

In 1920, Homer Rodeheaver established the Rodeheaver Record Company and its primary label, Rainbow, in Winona Lake, Indiana. He later moved the company to New York and, ultimately, Chicago. Starr Piano pressed Rainbow from 1921 to 1928 and released many of the same titles on Gennett. Both companies maintained a Personal Series and cooperated to some extent on its production. Certain Rodeheaver/Gennett titles still appeared on Sears' Silvertone label as late as 1930. (LGI.)

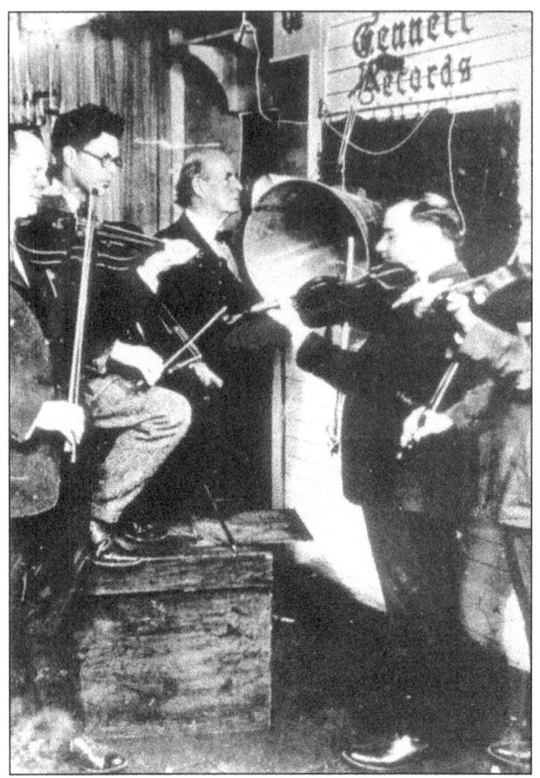

Three-time presidential candidate and Woodrow Wilson's secretary of state William Jennings Bryan arrived at Gennett's Richmond studio in July 1923 to record several sides. "The Great Commoner" re-created his 1896 Democratic Party Convention "Cross of Gold" speech. In this photograph, Bryan recites Psalm 23 with the string quartet from the Hotel Gibson Orchestra, which Gennett also released in its Christmas Greetings Series. (LGI.)

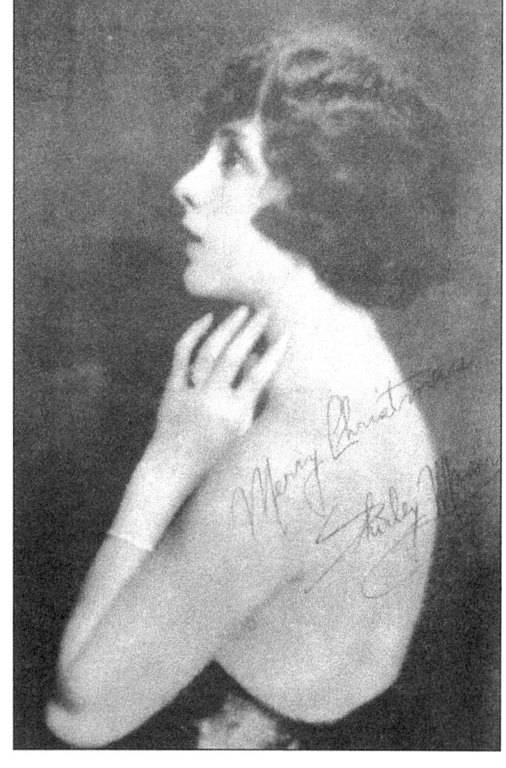

Shirley Mason starred in over 100 films in the 1910s and 1920s, including *Vanity Fair*, *Treasure Island*, and *Little Miss Smiles*. In 1923, she made a Christmas Greetings record entitled "Christmas in Hollywood" with Taylor Trio's "O Christmas Tree" on the reverse side of Gennett 5237. (LGI.)

Wilbur D. Nesbit was a celebrated author, poet, and humorist. He recorded two Christmas Greetings sides entitled "Always Christmas" (Gennett 5228) and "God Bless Us All" (Gennett 5229). His most popular poem was "Your Flag and My Flag," and he authored several books for the Volland Publishing Company. Volland also released one of his recordings on its custom label pressed by Starr Piano. (Library of Congress.)

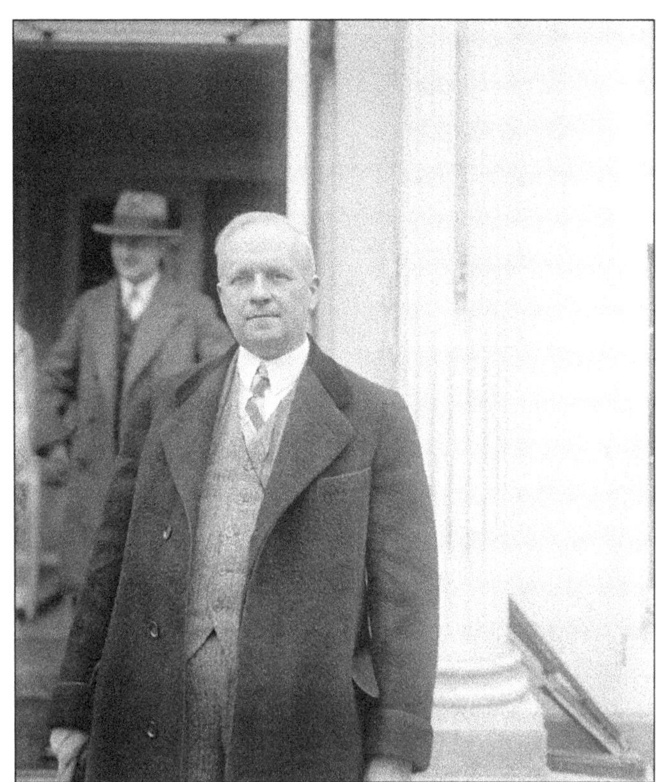

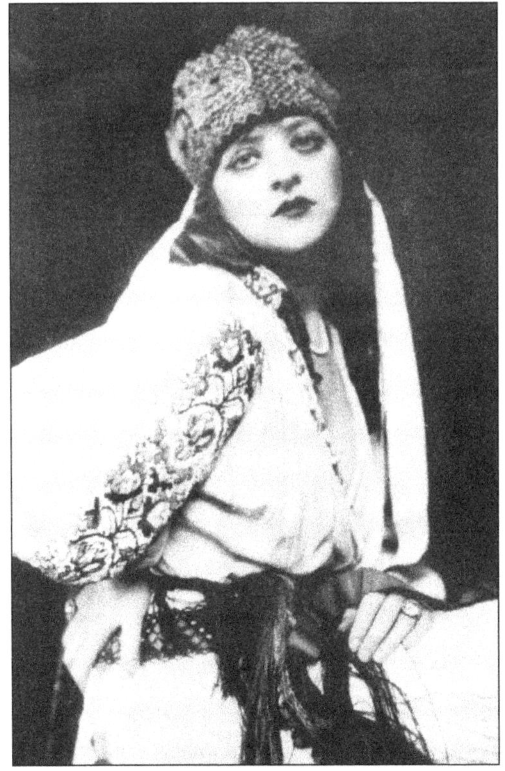

Bebe Daniels was a popular actress and singer, who starred in such classic films as *42nd Street*, *The Maltese Falcon*, and *Rio Rita*. Her popularity in film led to a recording contract with RCA Victor, but in 1923, she recorded a Christmas Greetings side on Gennett 5236 with the Criterion Quartet's "The First Noel" on the reverse. (LGI.)

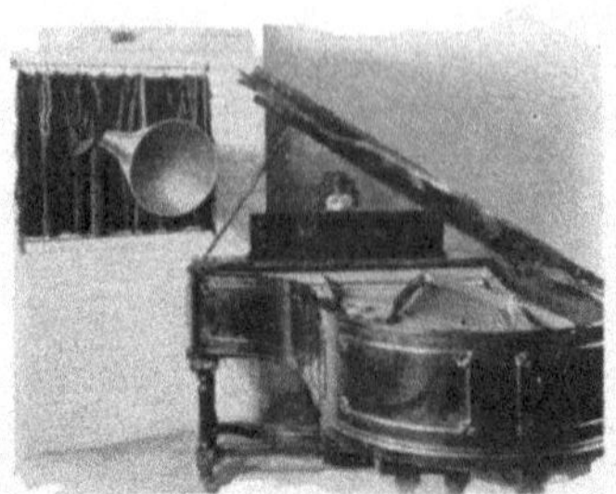

Recording is Instructive as well as Interesting
Write us for Further Details

THE Personal Recording Laboratory of The Gennett Record Division of The Starr Piano Company is fully equipped. Professional attention is given to every recording.

Address your application for a quotation for the original copper engraving together with the description of what work you desire done to the Personal Recording Department, Division of The Starr Piano Company, Richmond, Indiana. Appointments may also be made through any Starr Store.

By special arrangement appointments may also be made for work to be done in our New York City Laboratory.

Personal Recording Department
Gennett Record Division,
THE STARR PIANO COMPANY
Richmond, Indiana

GENNETT PERSONAL RECORDINGS

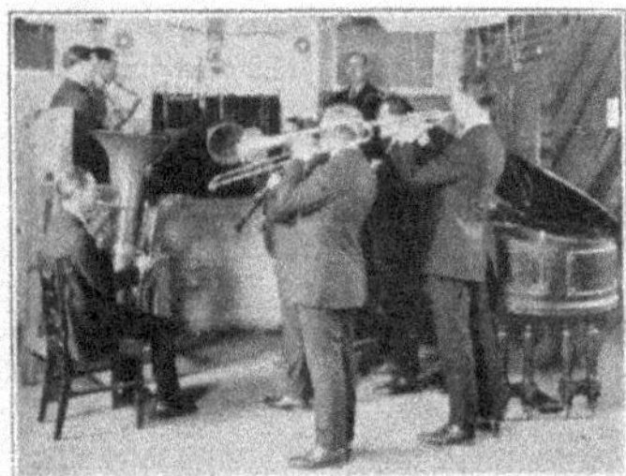

An Orchestra Recording at the Starr Laboratories

GENNETT RECORDS
Division of
THE STARR PIANO COMPANY
RICHMOND, INDIANA

NICHOLSON PRESS, RICHMOND, IND.

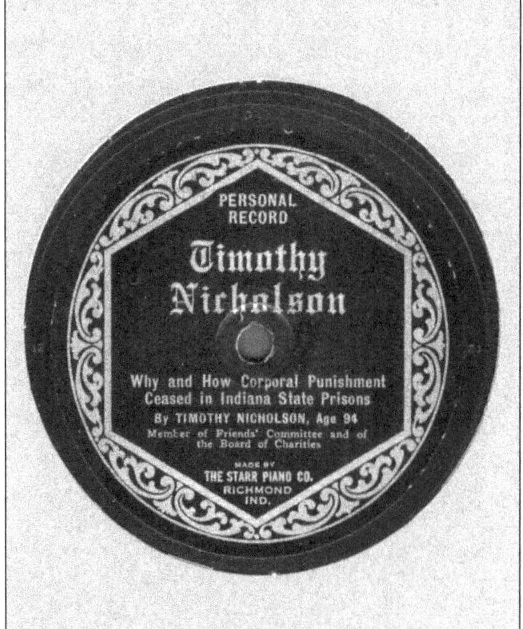

Gennett also offered the rental of its studios and record-pressing services to the general public. This advertising flyer encourages salesmen to "ginger-up talks to your dealers" with a personal recording. Gennett Records also encouraged musicians to perform a song by their mothers or daughters, as "it would be a possession to be forever cherished." (LGI.)

Timothy Nicholson (1828–1924) was a public servant and activist in Richmond. He served as a trustee at Earlham College for over 50 years, in Richmond's public schools, and for the Morrisson Library. On December 7, 1922, the 94-year-old Nicholson recorded his thoughts on "Why and How Corporal Punishment Ceased in Indiana State Prisons" and a "Statement Concerning Friend's (Quaker's) Richmond Declaration of Faith and the Organization of the Five Years Meeting." (LGI.)

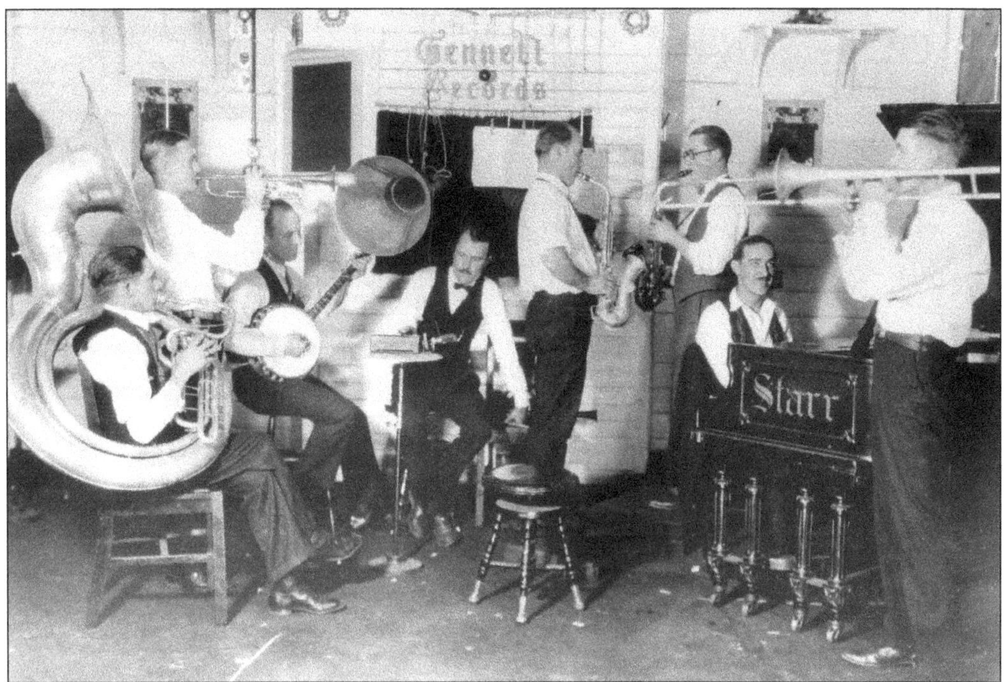

The Miami Lucky Seven was a territory jazz band that performed regularly at the Casino Gardens in Indianapolis, Indiana. The Casino Gardens, located at Eighteenth Street and Lafayette Road, was a popular dance venue during the Jazz Age/Prohibition era and was later renamed the Municipal Gardens in 1927. The Miami Lucky Seven first made some personal sides before Gennett put the group's records on its label. From left to right are Lester McCoun, Art McCammon, Bernard Whelan, Edwin McClure, Fred Housekeeper, Jack Risk, and Bert Repine. (CBD.)

MAX TERHUNE

● It's one of the mysteries how one man can carry along such a menagerie of animals, birds and insects as Max Terhune, the Hoosier Mimic. He seems to speak the language of almost every animal and bird of the forest, and can imitate a railroad train or a mosquito with equal accuracy. Max is known to a great many people throughout the country from his stage appearances with Weaver Brothers and Elviry. In the lower picture he is talking with his pal "Scully." He hails from Anderson, Indiana.

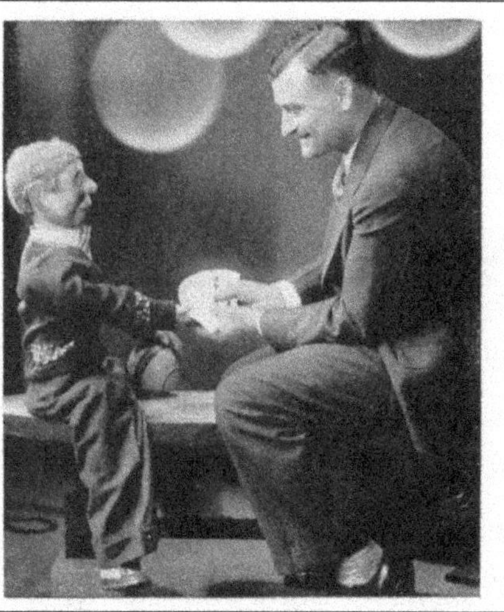

Max Terhune, the Hoosier Mimic, was a top-notch ventriloquist, magician, and imitator of sounds and voices. He recorded a personal side of barnyard noises at Gennett in 1922 and later with Ezra Buzzington's Rustic Revelers in 1929. He is best known as a regular on the WLS *National Barn Dance* and as "Lullaby Joslin" in the *Three Mesquiteers* cowboy films of the late 1930s. Terhune stars with Robert Livingston, Gene Autry, and John Wayne in these Western B movies. (Berea College Special Collections and Archive.)

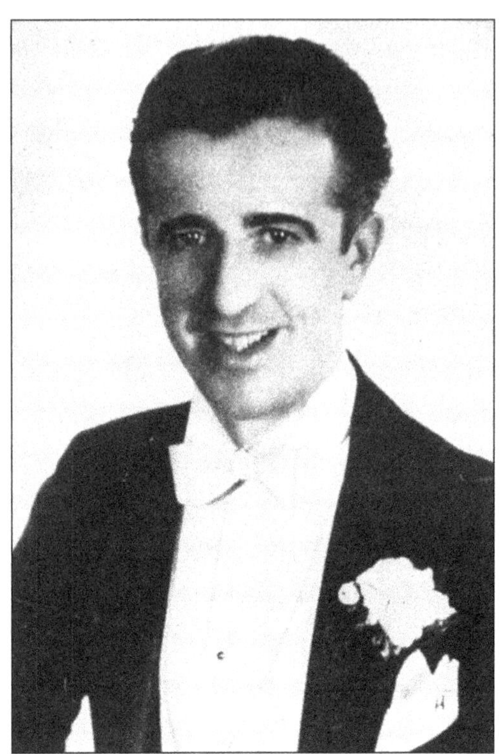

The recording relationship developed between Husk O'Hare and Gennett Records served as a pivotal moment in the label's history. Fred Wiggins, Starr Piano's Chicago store manager, persuaded Gennett to record both the white and black hot New Orleans–style jazz bands that were popular in the city. O'Hare organized his "Super Orchestra" and recorded in both New York City and Richmond in 1922. O'Hare then facilitated a recording session with a band that was quite popular at Chicago's Friar's Inn, the New Orleans Rhythm Kings. (CBD.)

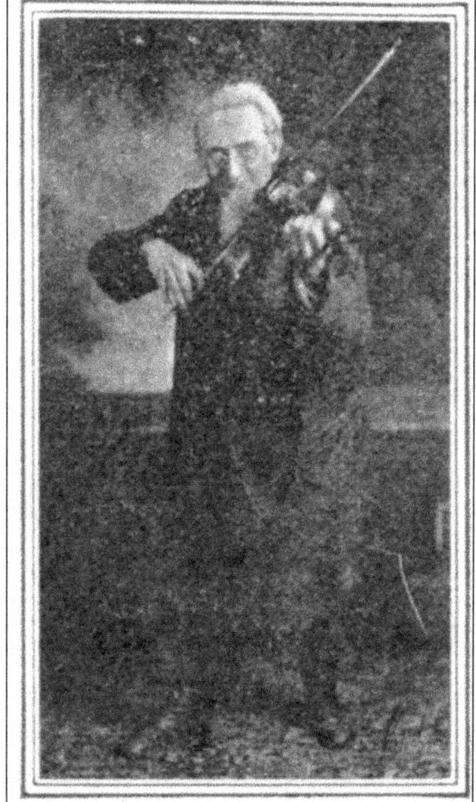

Wm. B. Houchens

Gennett was one of the first labels to record and market old-time/hillbilly music. Its first hillbilly artist, fiddler William B. Houchens, recorded some traditional old-time tunes on September 18, 1922, almost a year before the genre's breakthrough artist, Fiddlin' John Carson. While the Houchens sides sold dismally and missed their chance to become a historic milestone, Gennett quickly developed into one of the preeminent hillbilly/country music labels in the 1920s. (LGI.)

Three

Jazz Me Blues
1923–1929

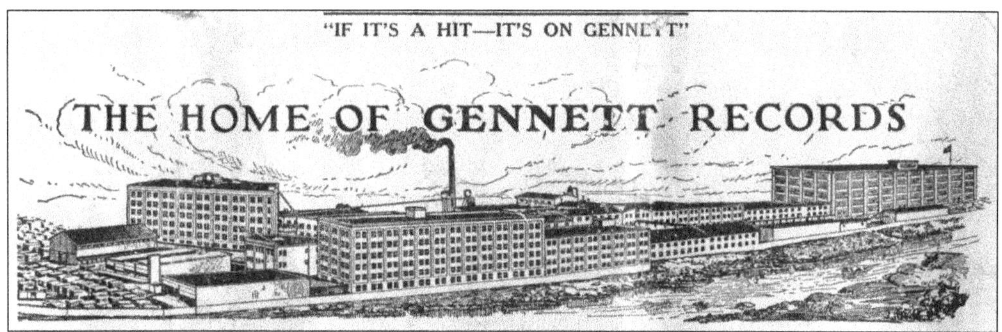

With the studio established in Richmond, Gennett took advantage of its location as the only permanent studio in the middle of the United States and recorded musicians from nearby Chicago, Indianapolis, Cincinnati, and Kentucky. Gennett discovered a vibrant and underrecorded group of groundbreaking jazz, blues, country, sacred, and ethnic musicians who changed the face of American music and culture. Starr Piano declares in its 1928 Electrobeam catalog, "If It's a Hit–It's on Gennett." (Berea College Special Collections and Archive.)

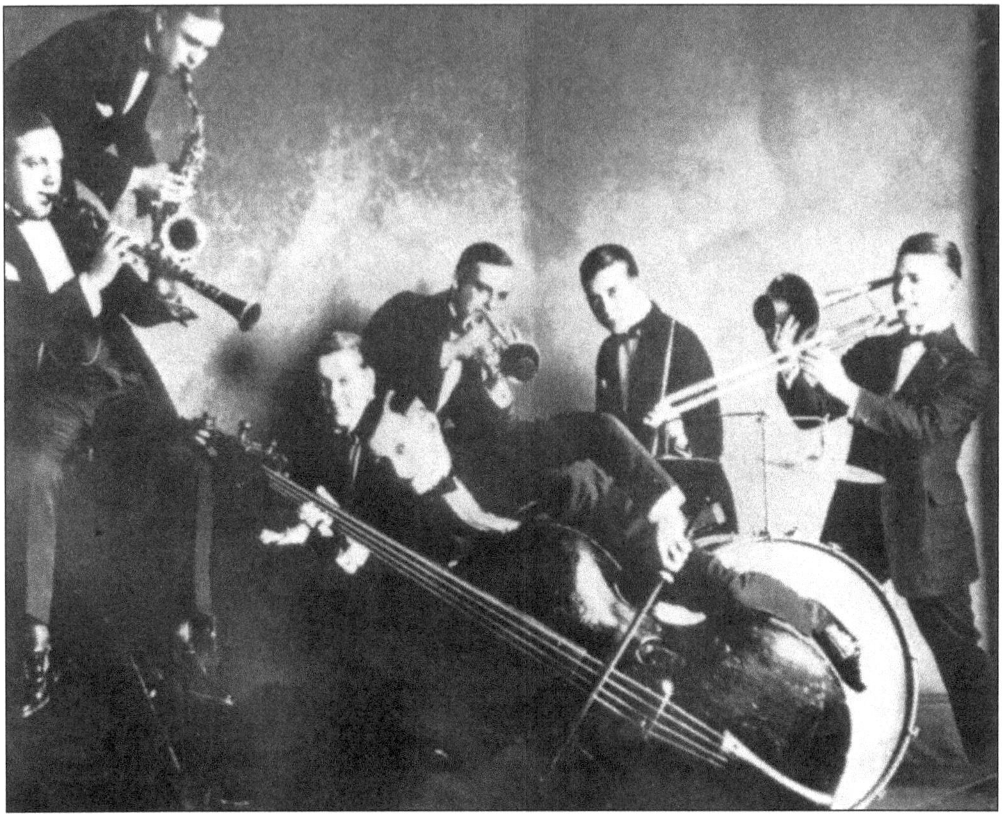

The New Orleans Rhythm Kings first recorded for Gennett as Friar's Society Orchestra in August 1922. These New Orleans natives waxed over 20 sides of hot jazz, including as accompanist to pianist Jelly Roll Morton. Some of the group's most popular recordings include "Tin Roof Blues," "Shimmeshawabble," and "Mr. Jelly Lord." From left to right are Leon Roppolo, Jack Pettis, Elmer Schoebel, Arnold Loyacano, Paul Mares, Frank Snyder, and George Brunies. (LGI.)

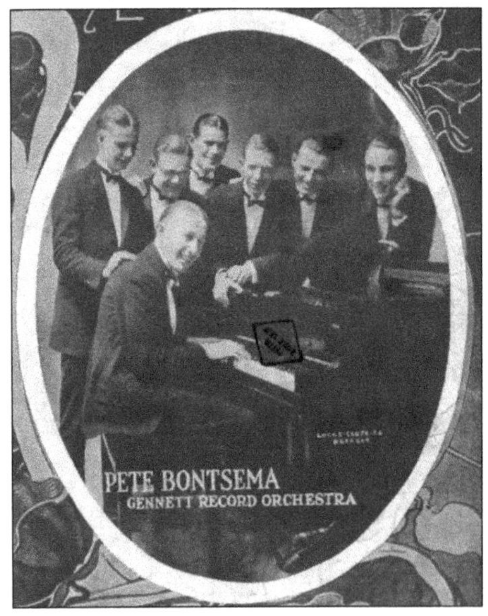

Pianist Pete Bontsema and His Hotel Tuller Orchestra of Detroit recorded 10 sides in Richmond on September 18, 1923. Despite this limited relationship, Bontsema marketed his orchestra as a Gennett recording artist, as is evidenced in this promotional photograph. Bontsema soon joined Chicago's WLS radio in the 1930s as a member of its popular "Al and Pete" act. (Morrisson-Reeves Library.)

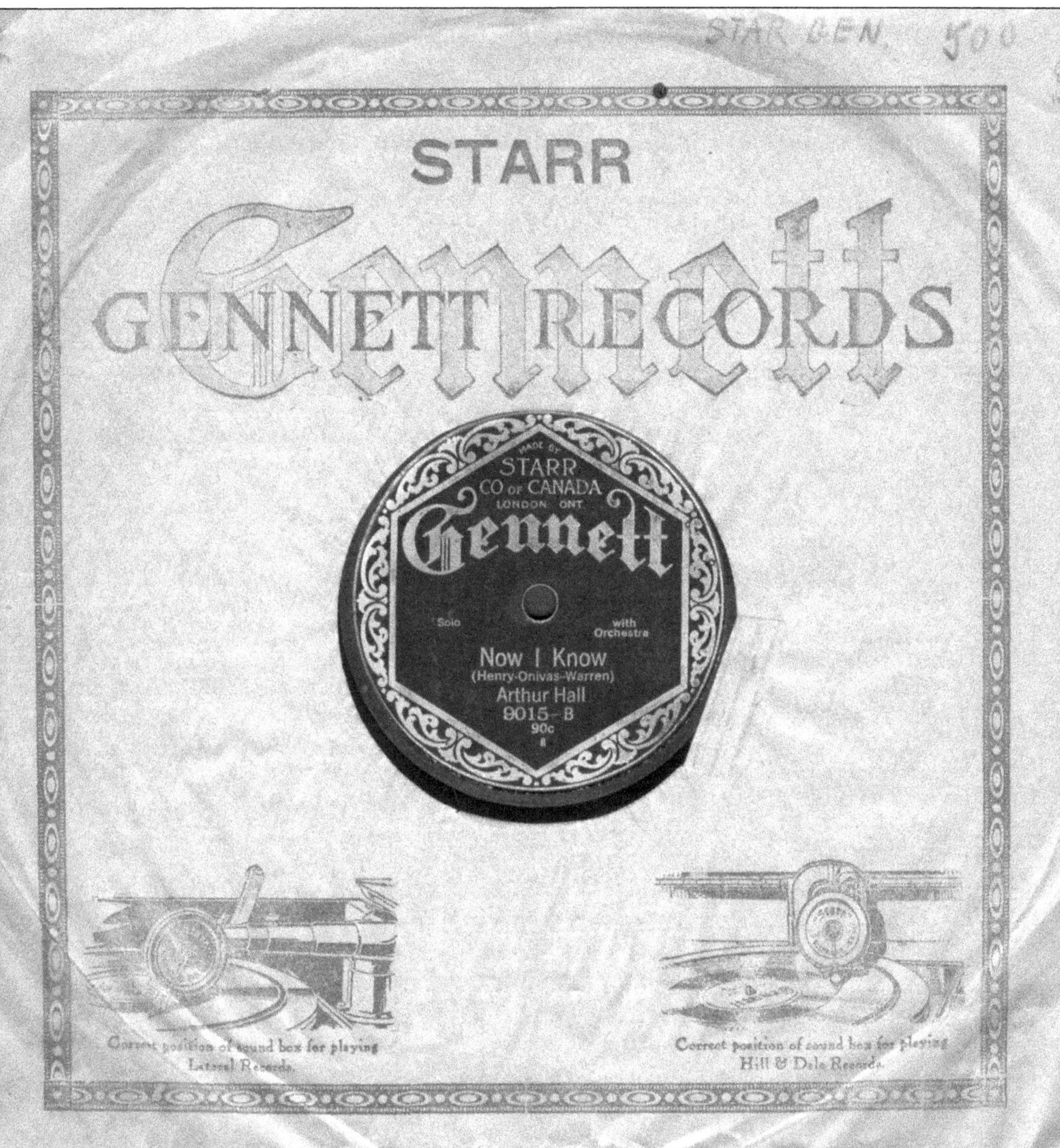

In April 1917, W.D. Stevenson and J.A. Croden founded the Canadian Phonograph Supply Company. Impressed with Starr Piano's "modern equipment and product quality," the Canadian company became the distributor of Starr's records and phonographs. A year later, a prohibitive tariff forced Stevenson and Croden to negotiate a move of Starr Piano's manufacturing operations to Canada. Herbert Berlinger joined the company and pressed the American Starr-Gennett masters for Starr Canada. In 1922, a peak year, Toronto alone had over 100 Starr dealerships. A disastrous fire at the London, Ontario, warehouse on April 28, 1922, resulted in a massive sell-off of damaged goods. In 1923, Starr Company of Canada became a public company and Croden left. By 1925, the Starr Piano Company in Richmond liquidated its stock and assets and discontinued the Starr label. Stevenson briefly served as vice president of Starr Piano in Richmond. (LGI.)

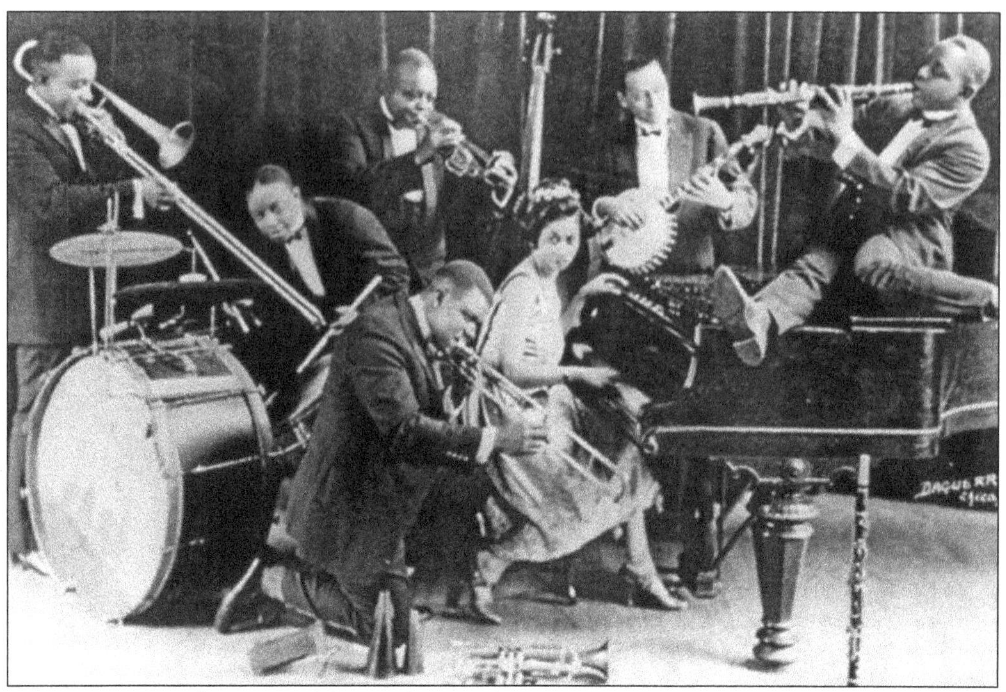

King Oliver's Creole Jazz Band featured some of New Orleans's greatest hot jazz musicians. Starr Piano's Fred Wiggins noticed them during their successful run at Chicago's Lincoln Gardens and arranged for a two-day recording session in April 1923. This session and a subsequent one on October 3, 1923, yielded such mainstay jazz sides as "Chimes Blues," "Canal Street Blues," and "Dipper Mouth Blues." From left to right are Honore Dutrey, Baby Dodds, King Oliver (back), Louis Armstrong (front), Lil Hardin Armstrong, Bill Johnson, and Johnny Dodds. (CBD.)

Recording Information of Wax No. 11632 / 11632A / 11632B / 11632C

Date Recorded 10-5-23 By E.C.A. Wickemeyer At Richmond, Ind.

Subject "WHEN YOU LEAVE ME ALONE TO PINE"

By King Oliver & his Creole Jazz Band Accompanied by

Composed by Music by Armstrong - Hardin

Words by Armstrong - Hardin Published by Melrose

Copyright 19 Royalties

Recording Expense

Wax Shipped Trunk No. Via

Suggest Using in Supplement

Remarks

King Oliver's Gennett sides are jazz's first masterpieces, so one has to wonder why Gennett rejected one of the band's sides. This recording card shows evidence that King Oliver's Creole Jazz Band recorded four takes of "When You Leave Me Alone to Pine," written by Louis Armstrong and his future wife, Lil Hardin. To date, none of the recordings have seen the light of day. (CBD.)

In 1922, Louis Armstrong answered King Oliver's call to join the band in Chicago, and they made their recording debut in 1923. Armstrong recorded again for Gennett in 1924 as a member of the Red Onion Jazz Babies and soon became the most popular recording artist of the 20th century. He produced some of the greatest jazz sides with his Hot Five and Hot Seven bands and recorded some of the biggest pop singles over the next four decades with such mainstays as "Hello, Dolly" and "What a Wonderful World." (CBD.)

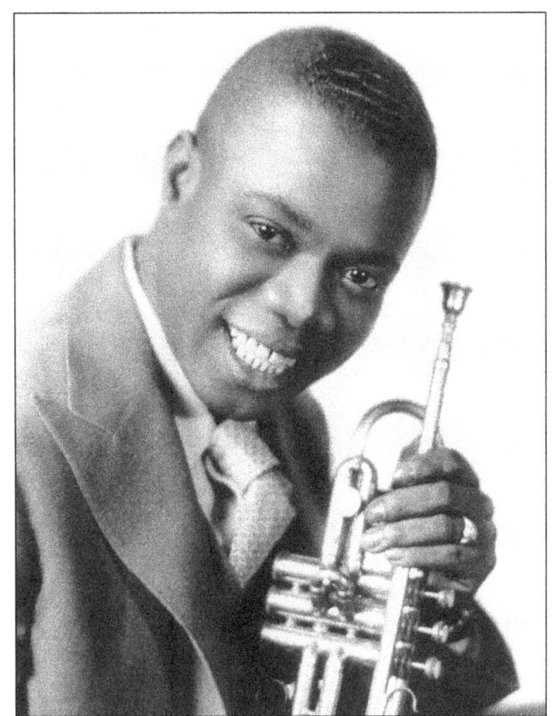

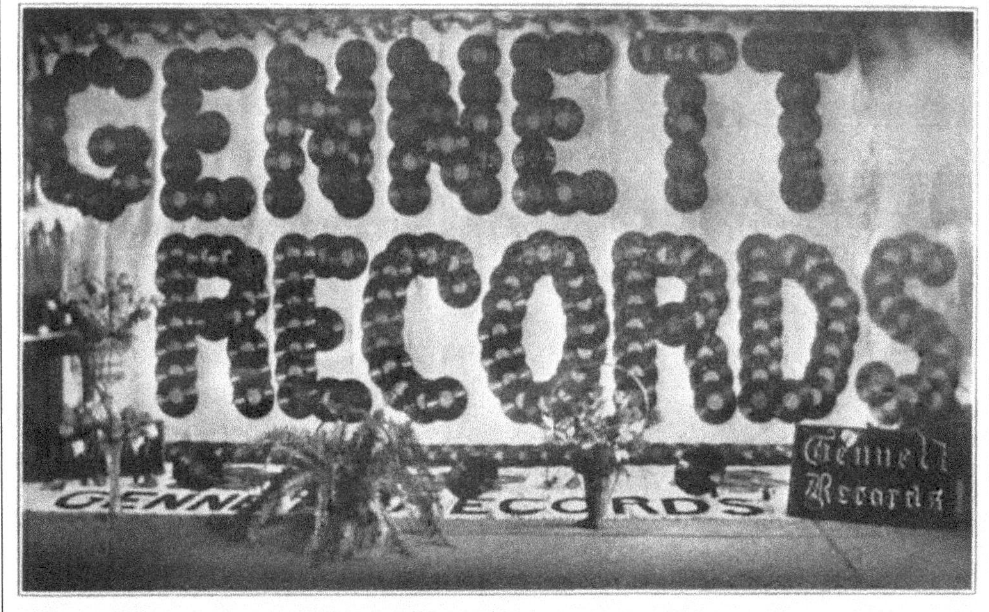

Murphy Music Co. Display, First Prize Winner

In October 1924, Fred Wiggins, the head of Gennett Records, announced the winner of its window display contest—the Murphy Music Company of Mulberry. The Murphy Music Company used over two hundred twenty-eight 78-rpm discs to spell out "Gennett Records" with various floral accents that produced an "artistic effect." In addition to the award, the Murphy Music Company notes in a November 15, 1924, *Talking Machine World* article that sales also increased during the display contest. (CBD.)

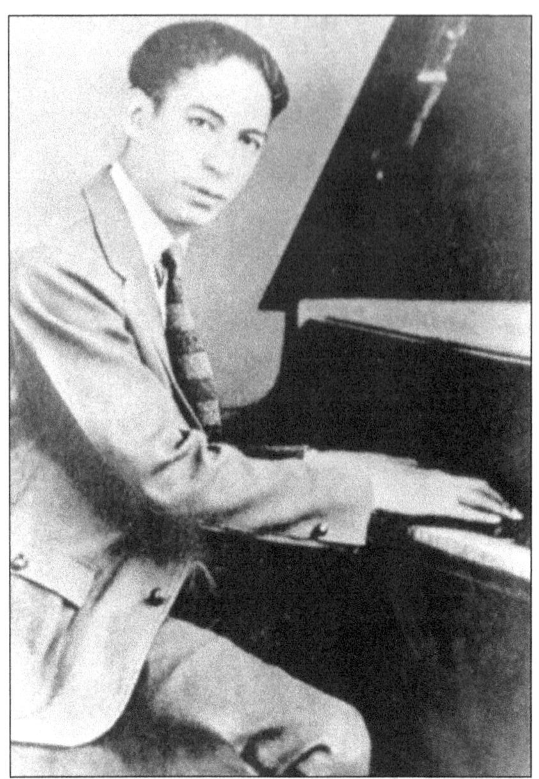

New Orleans pianist Ferdinand "Jelly Roll" Morton composed and recorded some of the first hot jazz sides for Paramount and Gennett in 1923. He initially recorded with the New Orleans Rhythm Kings at Gennett, which was among the first integrated recordings in jazz. Gennett properly credited the musicians on the label. His Gennett sides included many future jazz standards, including "Milenburg Joys," "Wolverine Blues," and "King Porter Stomp." (CBD.)

HEAR THESE LATEST POPULAR SONGS AND SNAPPY DANCE HITS ON GENNETT RECORDS BY EXCLUSIVE GENNETT COLORED ARTISTS

VOCAL HITS

If You Want To Keep Your Daddy Home (Grainger-Ricketts-Paisley)
Laughin' Cryin' Blues (Grainger-Ricketts)
Viola McCoy. Piano Acc. Porter Grainger — 5108 .75

Midnight Blues (A Wee Hour Chant) (Thompson-Williams)
Triflin' Blues (Daddy Don't You Trifle On Me) (Grainger-Ricketts) Viola McCoy—Piano Acc. Porter Grainger — 5128 .75

Gulf Coast Blues (Williams)
Tired O' Waitin' Blues (Grainger-Ricketts)
Viola McCoy and Bob Ricketts' Band — 5151 .75

Crazy Over Daddy (Dowell)
Cootie Crawl (Booker)
Sammie Lewis—Piano Acc. Mandy Randolph — 5147 .75

Chirpin' The Blues (Hunter)
Just Thinkin' (A Blues) (Grainger-Ricketts)
Viola McCoy
Piano Acc. Porter Grainger — 5162 .75

Maybe Someday (Spikes Bros.)
All Night Blues (Jones)
Callie Vassar
Piano Acc. Richard Jones — 5172 .75

Long Lost Mama (Woods)
Wish I Had You (And I'm Gonna Get You Blues) (Grainger-Ricketts)
Viola McCoy
Piano Acc. Porter Grainger — 5175 .75

That Thing Called Love (Bradford)
Liza Johnson Got Better Bread Than Sally Lee (Bailey)
Julia Jones, Contralto
Piano Acc. Perry Bradford — 5177 .75

Viola McCoy

In 1923, Gennett expanded into the race music field and produced a special "Colored Artist" catalog. The catalog features Gennett's releases by King Oliver's Creole Jazz Band, Viola McCoy with Porter Grainger, Sammie Lewis, Callie Vassar, Josie Miles with Fletcher Henderson, Julia Jones with Perry Bradford, and hot jazz sides recorded by all-white ensembles the New Orleans Rhythm Kings and Ladd's Black Aces, which in some catalogs features a picture of an all-black ensemble. (LGI.)

Wendell Hall recorded one of Gennett's biggest-selling releases, "It Ain't Gonna Rain No Mo" b/w "Red Headed Music Maker," in 1923. These songs, written by Hall, featured his old-time minstrel-style vocals and masterful ukulele. Gennett describes this record as the "most genial clever melodies with words full of human interest" in its catalog. Hall soon began a career on radio and worked with such stars as Milton Berle and Grandpa Jones. (LGI.)

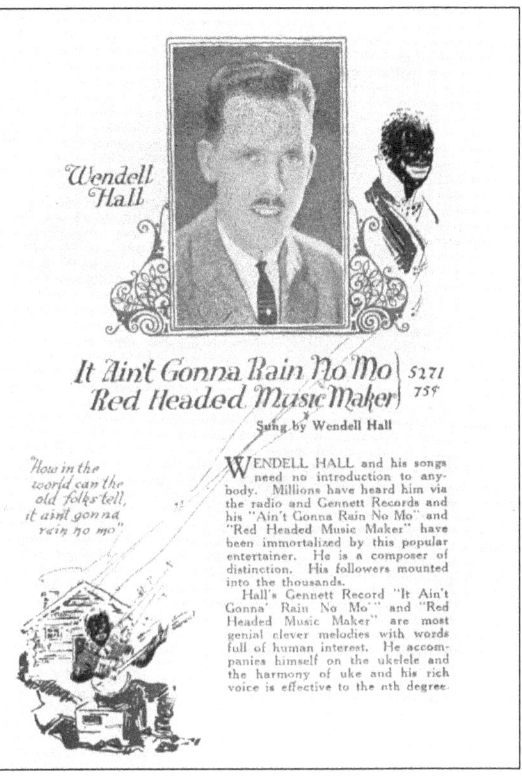

Wendell Hall

It Ain't Gonna Rain No Mo / Red Headed Music Maker — 5271 75¢

Sung by Wendell Hall

"How in the world can the old folks tell, it ain't gonna rain no mo"

WENDELL HALL and his songs need no introduction to anybody. Millions have heard him via the radio and Gennett Records and his "Ain't Gonna Rain No Mo" and "Red Headed Music Maker" have been immortalized by this popular entertainer. He is a composer of distinction. His followers mounted into the thousands.

Hall's Gennett Record "It Ain't Gonna' Rain No Mo'" and "Red Headed Music Maker" are most genial clever melodies with words full of human interest. He accompanies himself on the ukelele and the harmony of uke and his rich voice is effective to the nth degree.

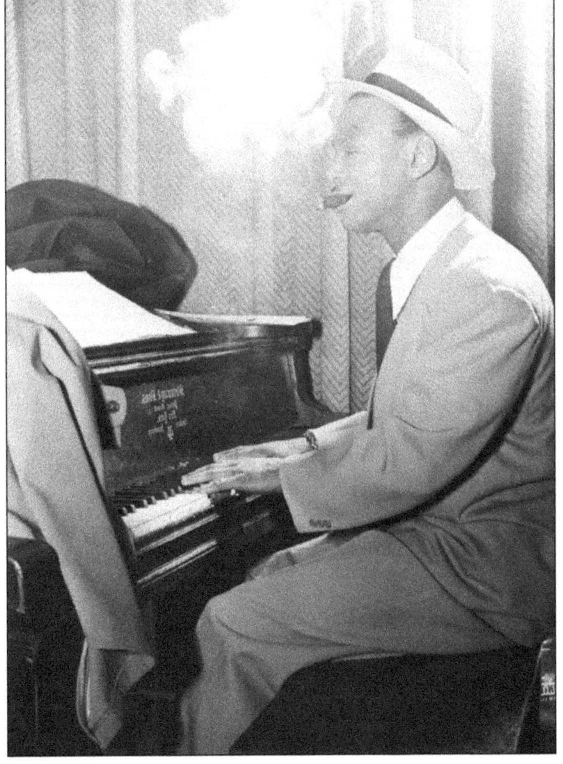

Most music fans and historians consider Earl "Fatha" Hines as the father of modern jazz piano. In 1923, Hines recorded seven sides in the Richmond studio as a member of Lois Deppe's Serenaders. Gennett released six of the seven sides on a personal pressing, and the seventh was unissued. After a stint with Louis Armstrong's Hot Five, Hines led a big band that featured future bebop pioneers Charlie Parker and Dizzy Gillespie. (William P. Gottlieb Collection, Library of Congress.)

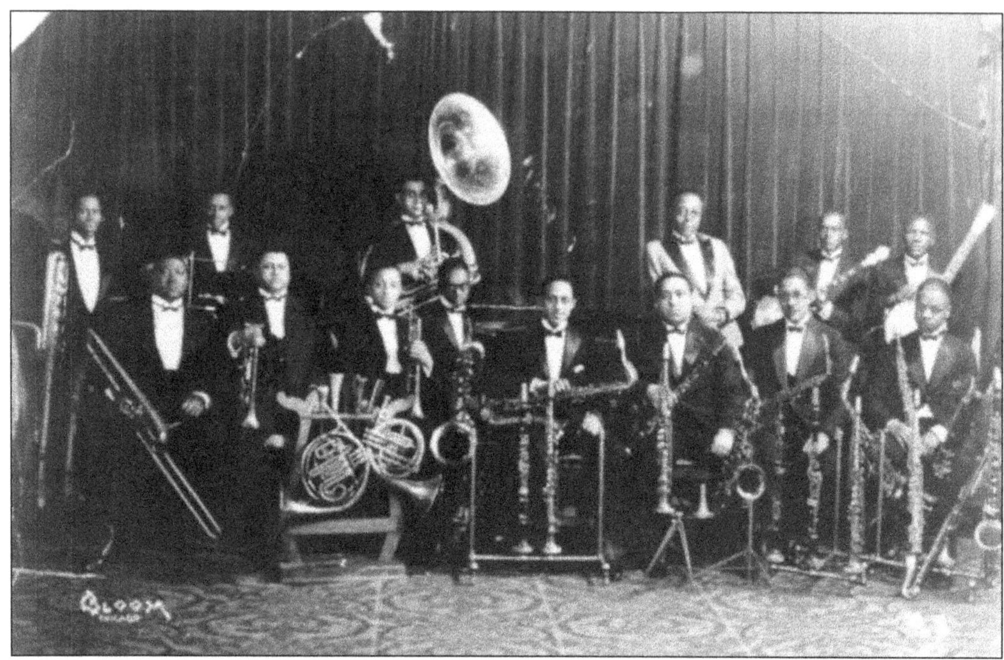

Charles "Doc" Cook led his Dreamland Orchestra to Gennett's Richmond studio for a January 21, 1924, recording date. The Dreamland Orchestra was rich in early jazz talent and featured Freddie Keppard (cornet) and Jimmy Noone (clarinet). Doc Cook soon became an arranger at New York City's Radio City Music Hall and RKO theaters in the 1930s and 1940s. (CBD.)

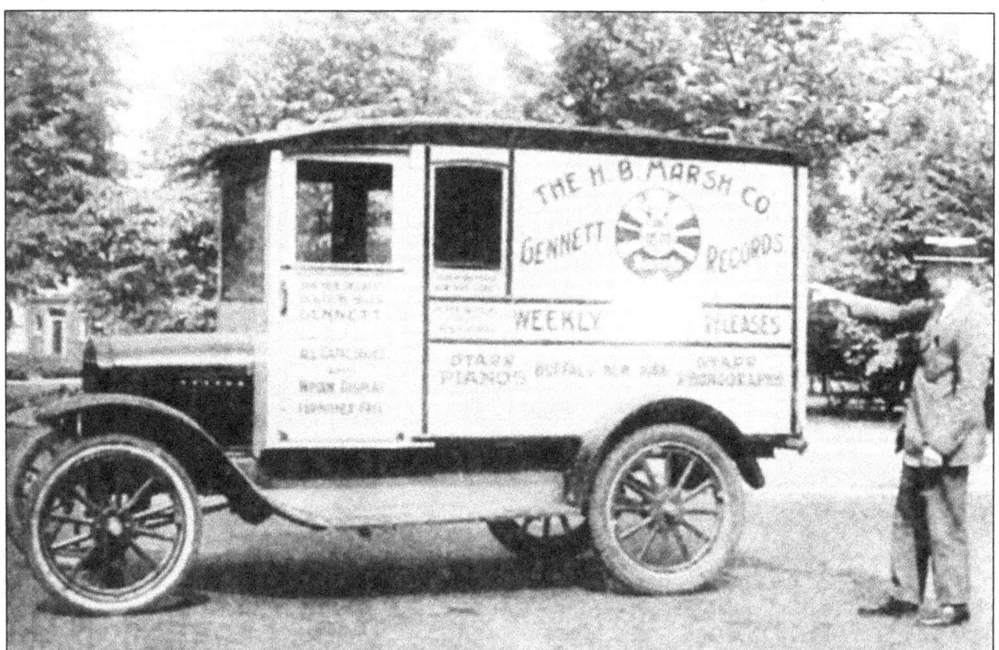

The H.B. Marsh Company in Buffalo, New York, was one of the most aggressive and successful regional wholesalers for Starr Pianos/Gennett Records. Marsh customized a fleet of delivery trucks with Starr and Gennett advertising and made them available to its retailers in this territory. H.B. Marsh is pictured next to one of his trucks. (CBD.)

In the July 5, 1924, *Talking Machine World* trade paper, Starr Piano announces the promotion of Fred D. Wiggins from Chicago branch manager to the head of the record division. Wiggins's elevation no doubt was tied to his recommendations to record the Chicago-based jazz artists New Orleans Rhythm Kings, King Oliver's Creole Jazz Band, and Jelly Roll Morton. Wiggins's 10-year career as a record man does not receive the same historic accolades as many of his contemporaries and warrants serious reexamination and celebration. (CBD.)

F. D. Wiggins Takes Charge of Gennett Record Sales

RICHMOND IND., July 5.—The Starr Piano Co. of this city, manufacturer of Starr phonographs and Gennett records, announced this week that Fred D. Wiggins, who had been manager of the company's branch in Chicago, had been transferred to the factory, where he would have complete charge of Gennett record sales. Mr. Wiggins has been associated with the Starr Piano Co. for the past twenty-five years, having occupied important posts in the organization. He is ideally qualified for his new work, and under his direction it is expected that an extensive plan of expansion and co-operation will be conducted successfully this Fall.

C. R. Hunt, formerly associated with the Starr Piano Co.'s branch at Kansas City, Mo., has succeeded Mr. Wiggins as manager of the Chicago branch. He has also been identified with the organization for a number of years and is a thoroughly competent sales executive.

Whistler's Jug Band was one of the first African American jug bands to record. The group hailed from nearby Lexington, Kentucky, and entered the Richmond studio on September 25, 1924, to record nine sides. Gennett released only four of them. Buford "Whistler" Threlkeld was the guitarist and leader, and the Gennett recordings also feature banjoist Willie Black. (CBD.)

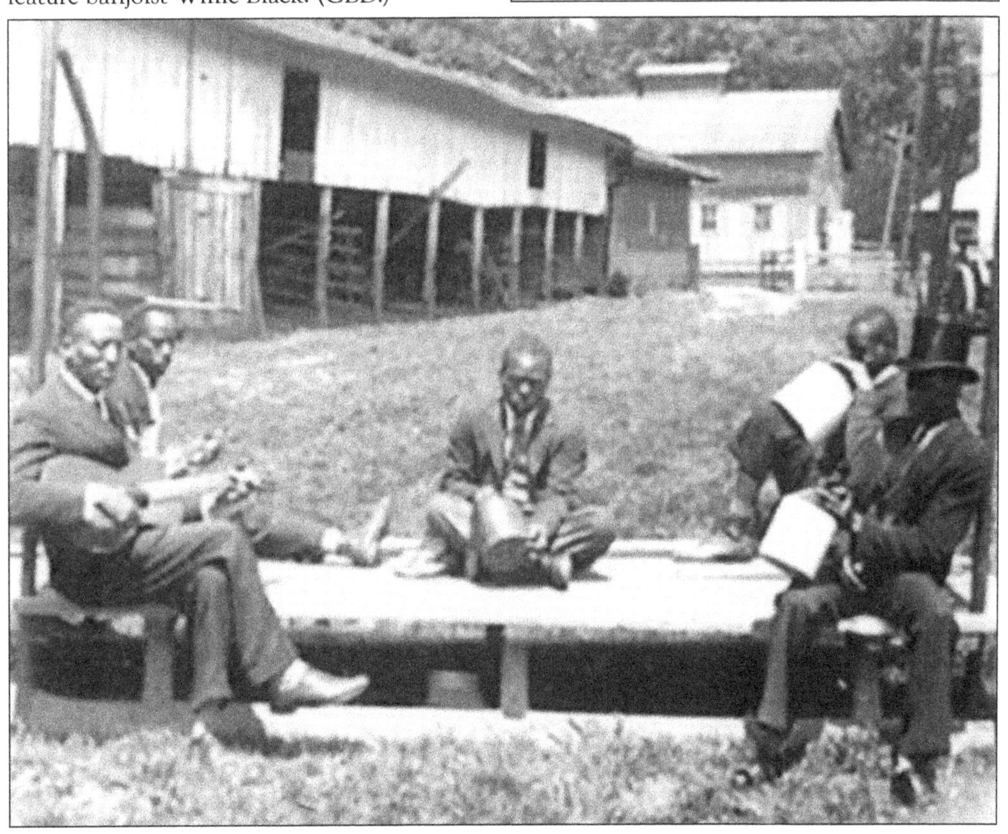

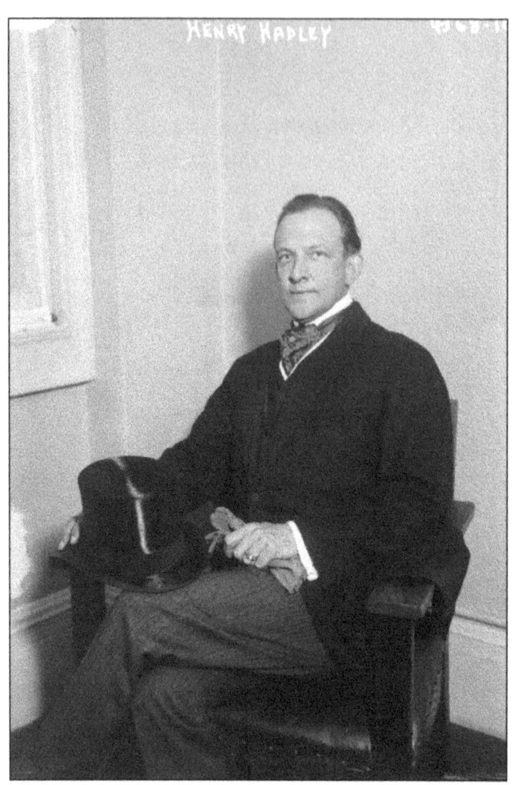

In the 1920s, Henry Hadley served as a conductor of the famed New York Philharmonic. The Ginn Music Company and its Music Appreciation Series contracted with Hadley to record classical music for elementary schools with members of the philharmonic. Gennett also released many of these sides on its own label. Ginn soon departed Gennett for Columbia due to its dissatisfaction with the acoustic recording quality. (Bain News Service Collection, Library of Congress.)

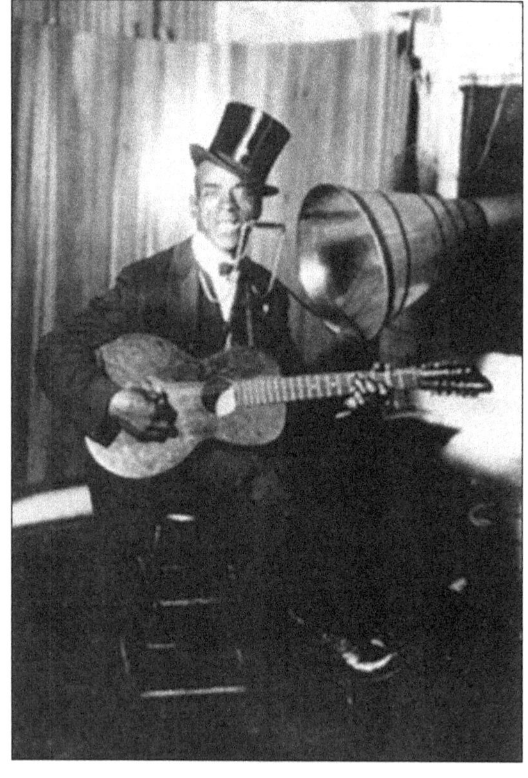

Johnny "Daddy Stovepipe" Watson was one of the first blues artists recorded when the Maxwell Street "one-man band" visited Gennett's Richmond studio on May 10, 1924. Daddy Stovepipe recorded three sides, and Gennett released two of them, "Sundown Blues" and "Stovepipe Blues." Gennett issued these recordings two years before Blind Lemon Jefferson's breakthrough blues sides on Paramount Records. (CBD.)

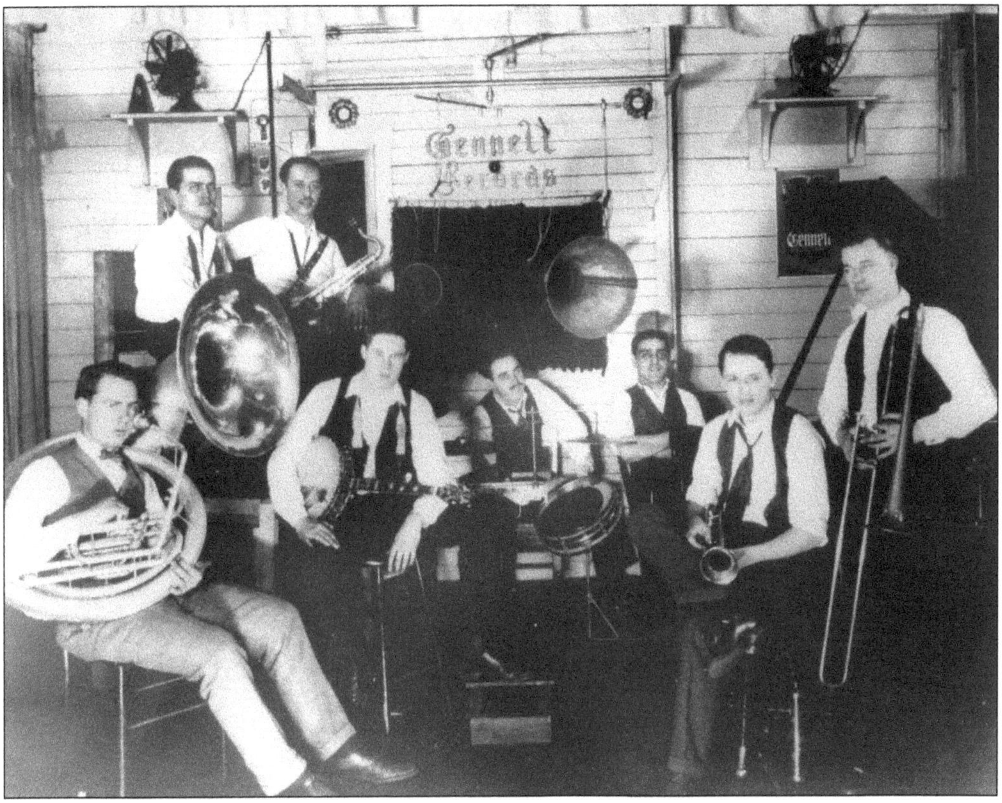

The Wolverine Orchestra was one of the most popular and successful territory bands in the 1920s, largely due to its dynamic cornetist, Leon "Bix" Beiderbecke. The Wolverine Orchestra first recorded for Gennett in February and May 1924. Some of the landmark recordings waxed in Richmond included "Copenhagen," "Fidgety Feet," and "Jazz Me Blues." From left to right are Min Leibrook, Jimmy Hartwell, George Johnson, Bob Gillette, Vic Moore, Dick Voynow, Beiderbecke, and Al Gandee. (LGI.)

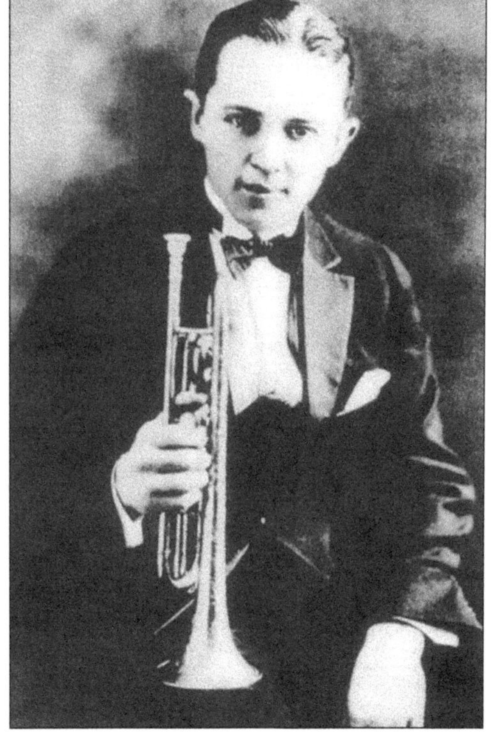

Cornetist Bix Beiderbecke began his recording career at Gennett as a member of the Wolverine Orchestra and later with the Sioux City Six and Bix and His Rhythm Jugglers. He later joined orchestras led by Jean Goldkette and Paul Whiteman. Historians and music fans cite Beiderbecke and Louis Armstrong as the most important and influential cornetists in jazz music. Beiderbecke died at the age of 28 and is buried in his hometown of Davenport, Iowa. (LGI.)

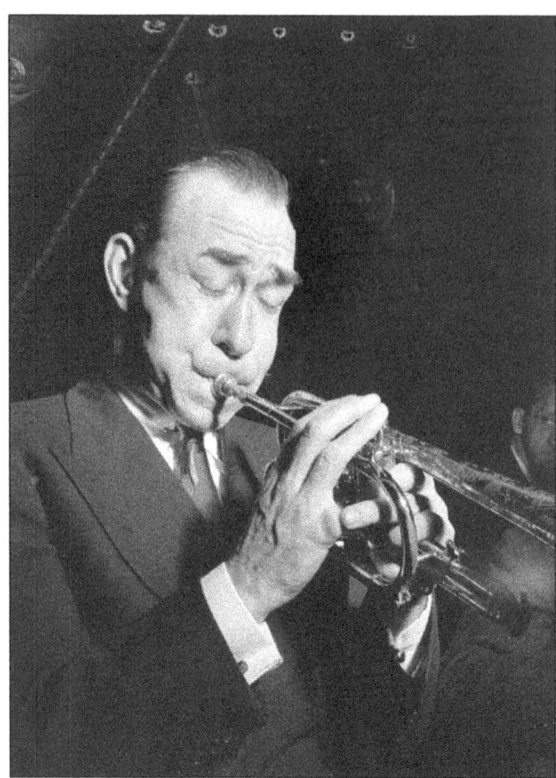

Muggsy Spanier was another of the top and influential cornetists to record debut sides with Gennett. On February 25, 1924, Spanier, with the Bucktown Five, recorded seven sides in Richmond. Later, he played and recorded with Ray Miller, Ted Lewis, and his own ensemble, the Ragtimers. (William P. Gottlieb Collection, Library of Congress.)

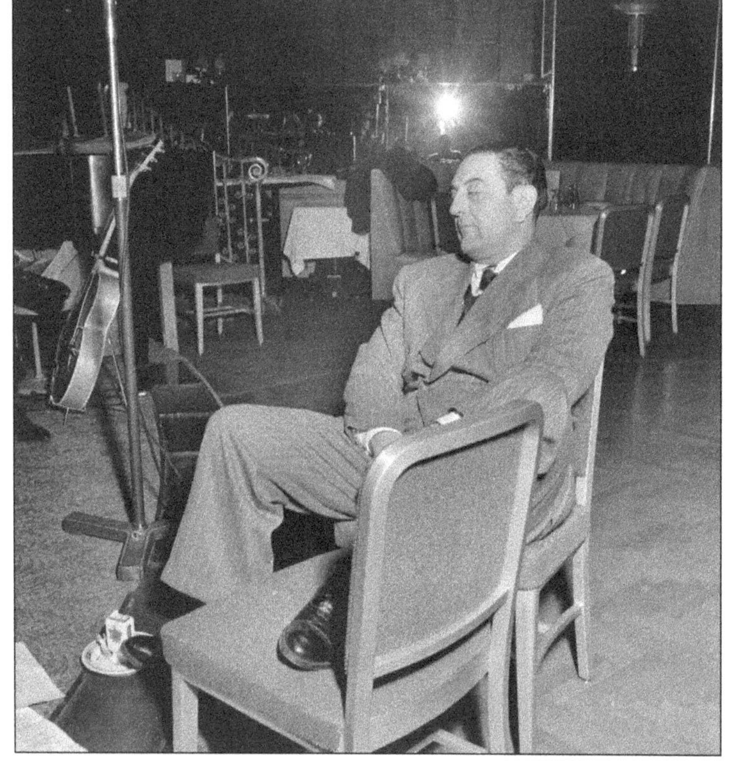

Guy Lombardo and His Royal Canadians made their recording debut in Richmond on March 10, 1924, and Gennett issued four of their five sides. Lombardo and his ensemble quickly became popular on both radio and record. Lombardo's recording and performance of "Auld Lang Syne" became synonymous with the New Year's Eve Times Square ball drop in New York City. (William P. Gottlieb Collection, Library of Congress.)

Thomas "Fats" Waller performed on several jazz and spiritual recordings with Gennett artists in April 1926, including Caroline Johnson and the duo of Alta Browne and Bertha Powell. Waller went on to record over 1,000 sides and appeared on radio and in several motion pictures. Additionally, Waller was a prolific songwriter and composed such standards as "Ain't Misbehavin'" and "Honeysuckle Rose." (Library of Congress.)

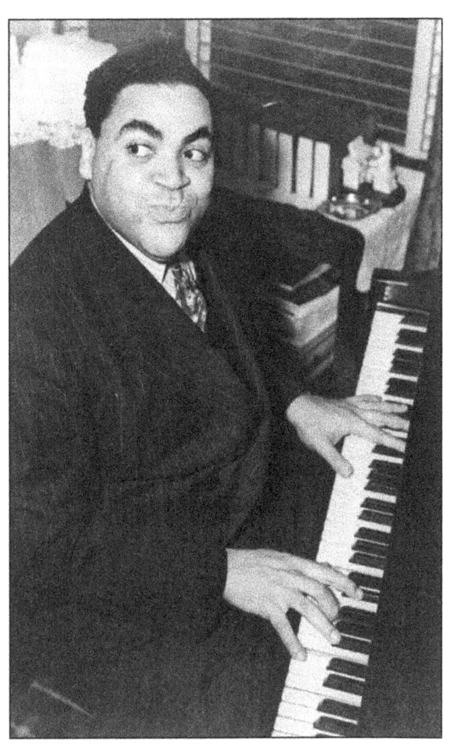

In 1924, legendary jazz pianist Edward "Duke" Ellington first recorded for Gennett as a member of Wilbur Sweatman and His Acme Syncopators. Ellington then recorded with Alberta Jones and his own ensemble, Duke Ellington's Washingtonians, at Gennett's 9–11 East Thirty-Seventh Street studio in New York City in 1926. There is no doubt that Ellington ranks as one of jazz's most beloved, talented, and prolific composers and recording artists of the 20th century. From left to right are Sonny Greer, Charlie Irvis, Bubber Miley, Elmer Snowden, Otto Harwick, and Ellington. (CBD.)

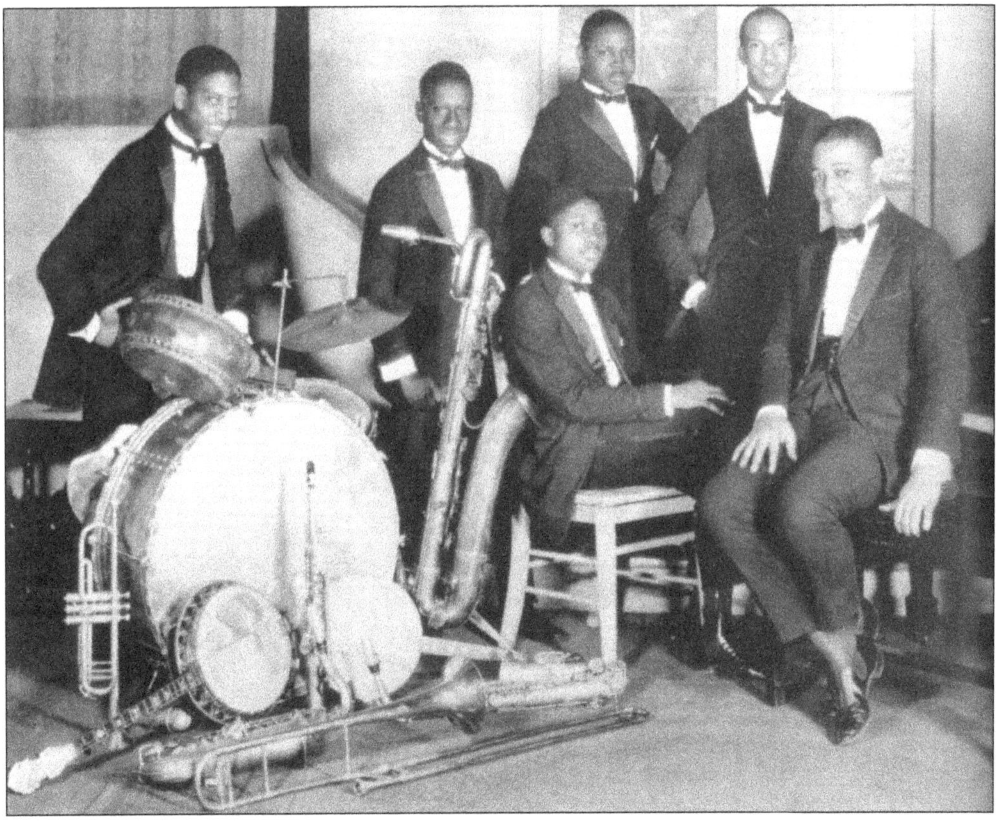

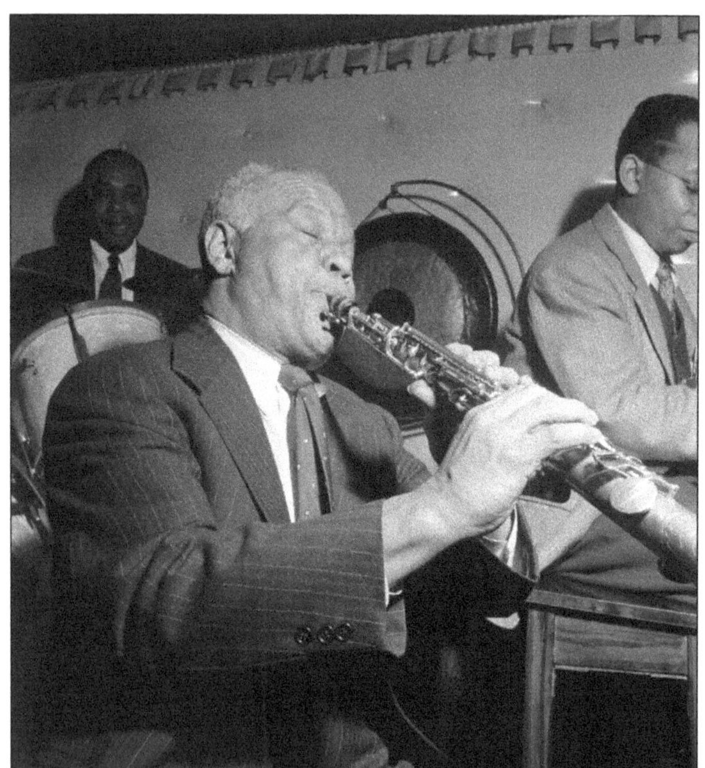

On December 23, 1924, the pioneering jazz clarinetist Sidney Bechet joined Louis Armstrong (cornet), Lil Hardin Armstrong (piano), Charlie Irvis (trombone), Buddy Christian (banjo), and vocalists Alberta Hunter, Eva Taylor, and Clarence Todd in Gennett's New York City studio as a member of the Red Onion Jazz Babies. All three sides—"Cake Walking Babies (from Home)," "Nobody Knows the Way I Feel Dis Morning," and "Early Every Morn"—showcase world-class musicians at the peak of their artistry. (William P. Gottlieb Collection, Library of Congress.)

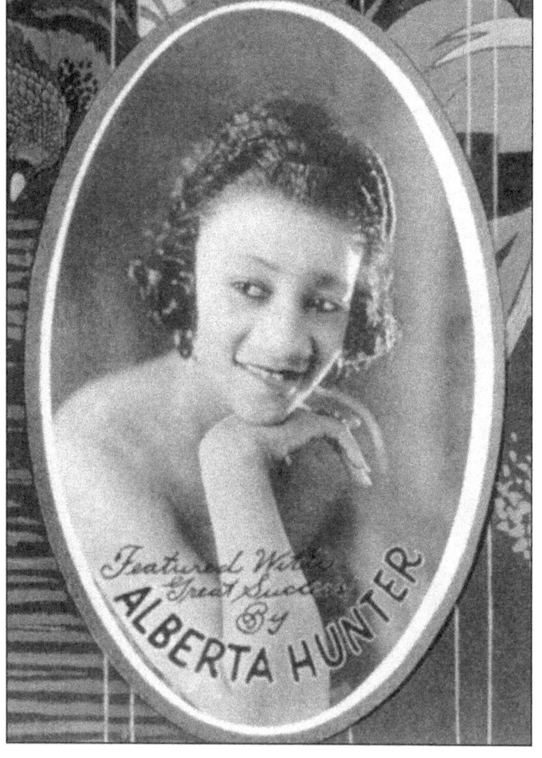

Alberta Hunter recorded four sides in Gennett's New York City studio with the Red Onion Jazz Babies under the pseudonym Josephine Beatty. Hunter was one of the most popular blues singers in the 1920s and recorded for Black Swan, Paramount, Okeh, Victor, and Columbia. She also penned "Downhearted Blues" and enjoyed a career comeback in the 1970s and 1980s. (CBD.)

Bix Beiderbecke returned to the Richmond studio on January 26, 1925, with Bix and His Rhythm Jugglers. The band includes, from left to right, Don Murray (clarinet), Howdy Quicksell (banjo), Tom Gargano (drums), Paul Mertz (piano), Beiderbecke, and Tommy Dorsey (trombone). The group recorded four sides, but Gennett only released "Davenport Blues" and "Toddlin' Blues." Dorsey developed into one of the most popular bandleaders and gave Frank Sinatra his big break. (Starr-Gennett Foundation.)

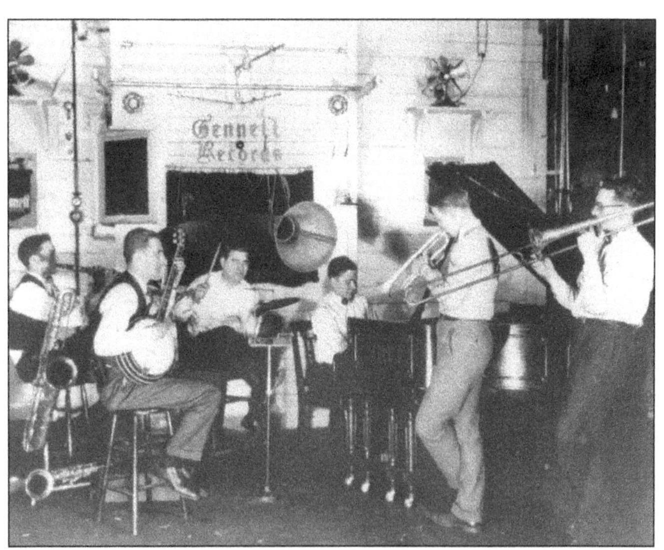

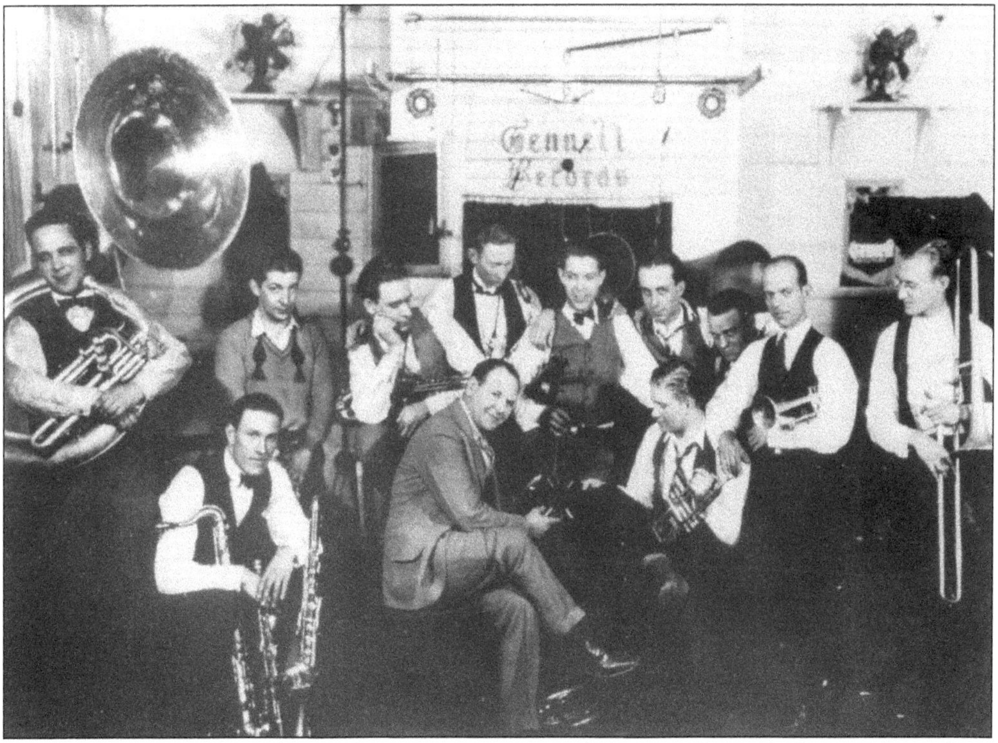

The Chubb-Steinberg Orchestra from Cincinnati recorded nine sides in Richmond throughout 1925, though Gennett only released three of them. The group featured some of the earliest recordings of the great jazz trumpet player Wild Bill Davison. From left to right are Ray Fetzer (sousaphone); Jack Weber (saxes); Carl Clauve (banjo); Homer Beecraft (sax); Otis L. Neirouter, also known as "Slim Evans" (alto sax); unidentified (possibly Chubb or Steinberg); Art Hicks (vocals); Bud Ebel (drums); Davison (cornet); Jack Saatkamp (piano); Bert Allen (cornet); and Frank Bamberger (trombone). (Starr-Gennett Foundation.)

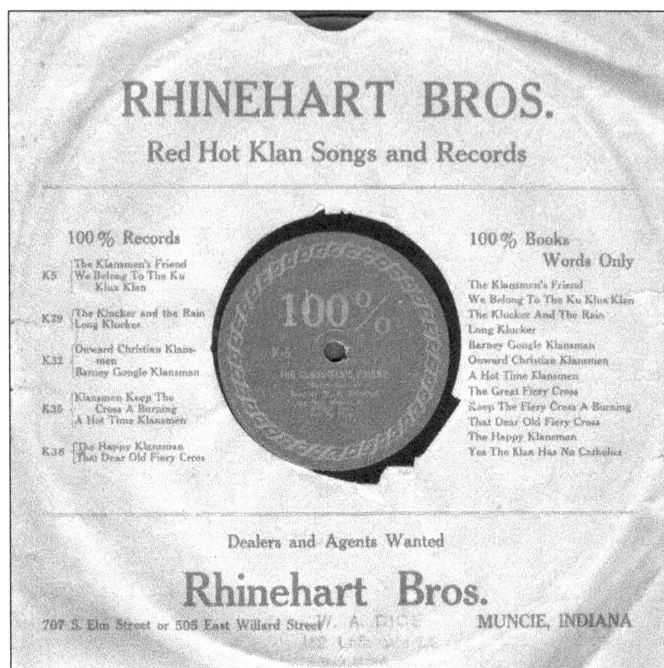

In the 1920s, Indiana witnessed a rapid regrowth of the Ku Klux Klan. The KKK used various forms of media, including sound recordings, to spread its propaganda and recruit new members. Several different Klaverns rented both the New York City and Richmond studios and pressed records at Starr Piano. While many Gennett employees were known KKK members, it was the various Klan organizations' ability to pay the studio rental and pressing fees that made them acceptable clients. (LGI.)

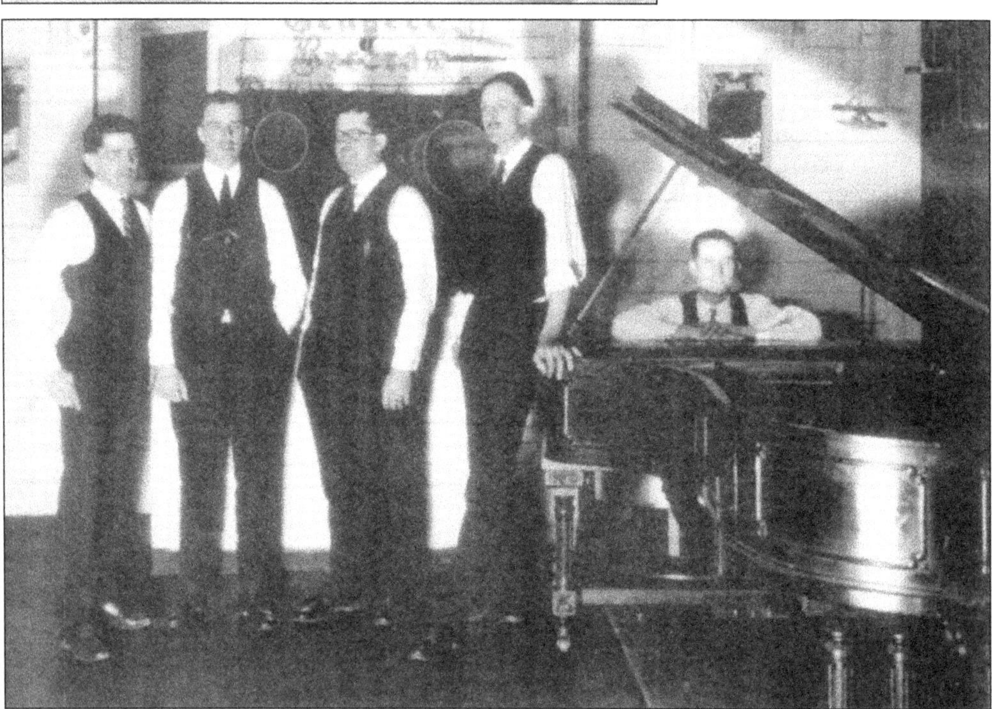

James D. Vaughan, "The Father of Southern Gospel," founded his Lawrenceburg, Tennessee–based music publishing company in 1900. Vaughan soon expanded into sound recordings and both recorded and pressed his releases with Starr Piano. The members of the Vaughan Quartet—from left to right, Hilman Barnard, G. Keifer Vaughan, Walter B. Seale, Roy Collins, and pianist Ted Shaw—recorded both together and separately on over 100 sides for Gennett and Vaughan Records. Vaughan also recorded and released KKK–themed sides at Starr. (CBD.)

Evangelist Exum Arthur Lewis (1880–1963) recorded over 30 sides in Richmond for his Chicago-based label and publishing company. The Chicago Aeolian Ladies Quartet, which included Lewis's sister Alice, often accompanied Lewis while he sang and played his specially crafted "Mandola-Mandolin." Lewis was a merchant and ragtime composer before his conversion at the old Moody Church around 1908. From the 1910s onward, he preached and performed across the continent and via radio broadcasts. (LGI.)

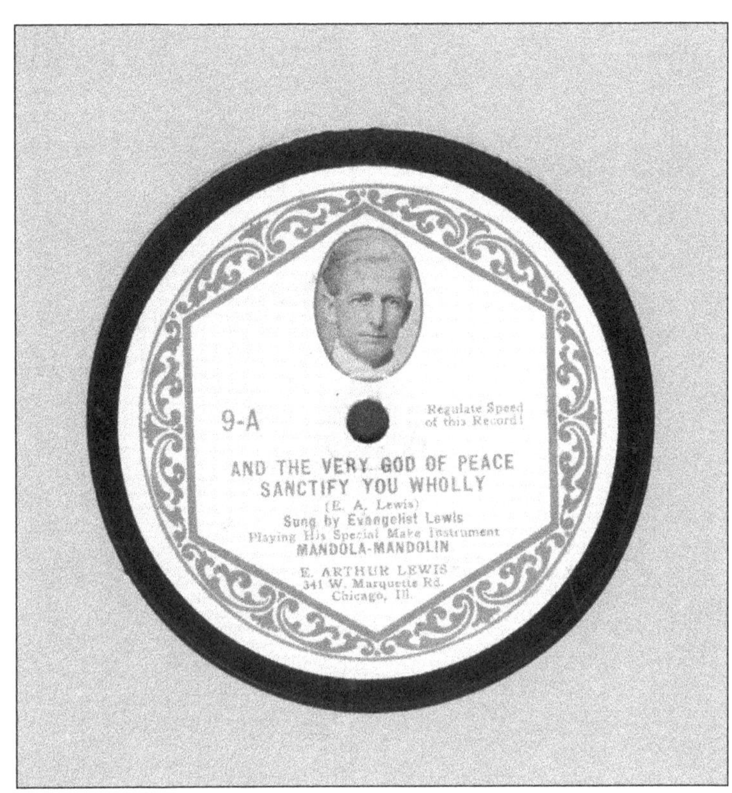

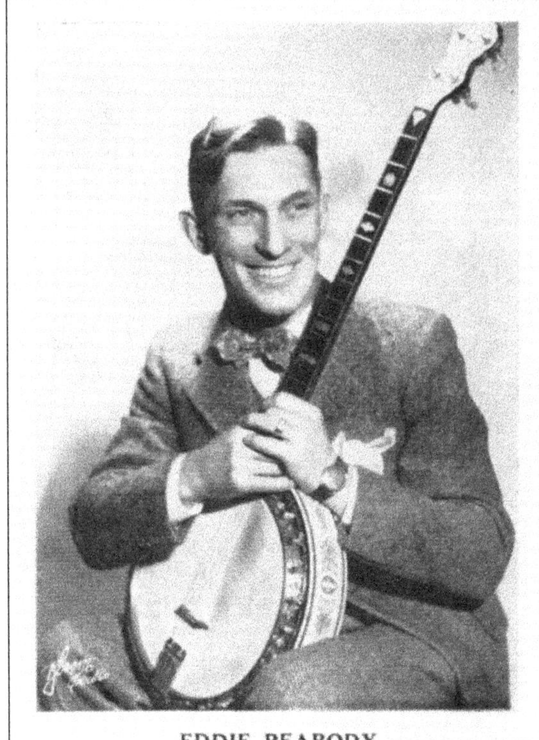

In March 1925, Eddie Peabody recorded four solo banjo numbers in Gennett's New York City studio. A veteran of the vaudeville circuit, Peabody soon became recognized as the "King of the Banjo" because of his virtuosic and innovative performances. Peabody is best known for the development of a chord melody style on the plectrum banjo and an electric banjo, called the banjoline. He also appeared on several radio shows and in movies, including *The Lemon Drop Kid*. (CBD.)

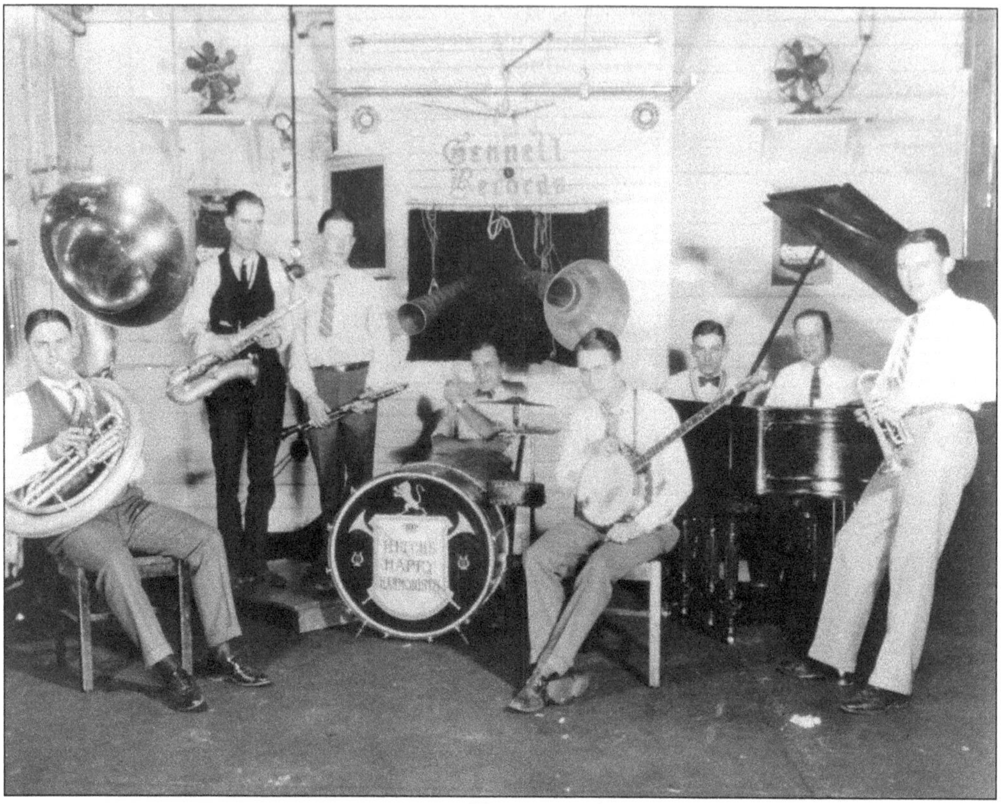

Then an Indiana University Law student, pianist Hoagy Carmichael first recorded as a member of Hitch's Happy Harmonists on May 19, 1925. The Happy Harmonists recorded two Carmichael-penned songs, "Boneyard Shuffle" and "Washboard Blues." Thus began one of the most successful recording and songwriting careers of the 20th century. From left to right are Haskell Simpson, Maurice May, Harry Wright, Buddy McDowell, Arnold Habbe, Carmichael, Curtis Hitch, and Fred Rollison. (LGI.)

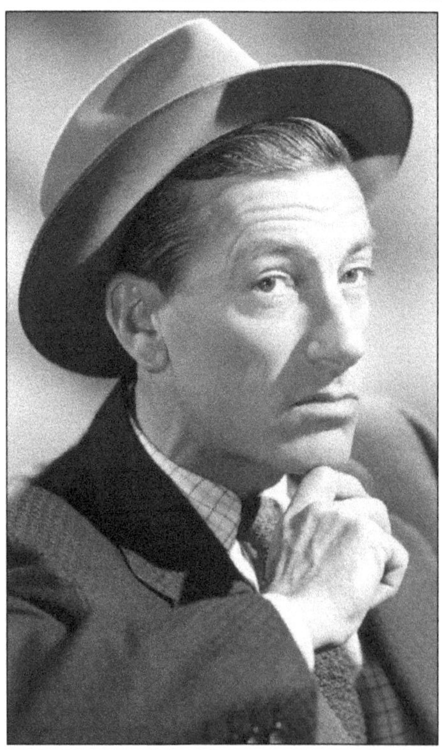

Hoagy Carmichael returned to the Richmond studio several times in 1927 and 1928 with his own bands and as a member of Emil Seidel's Orchestra. On Halloween day in 1927, Carmichael and His Pals recorded an instrumental version of his newly penned song, "Stardust." The record sold so poorly that when Carmichael took a second pass at it in 1928, Gennett rejected it. Carmichael and lyricist Mitchell Parrish soon rearranged "Stardust" into one of the most recorded songs in the 20th century and a standard in the American songbook. (Rick Kennedy.)

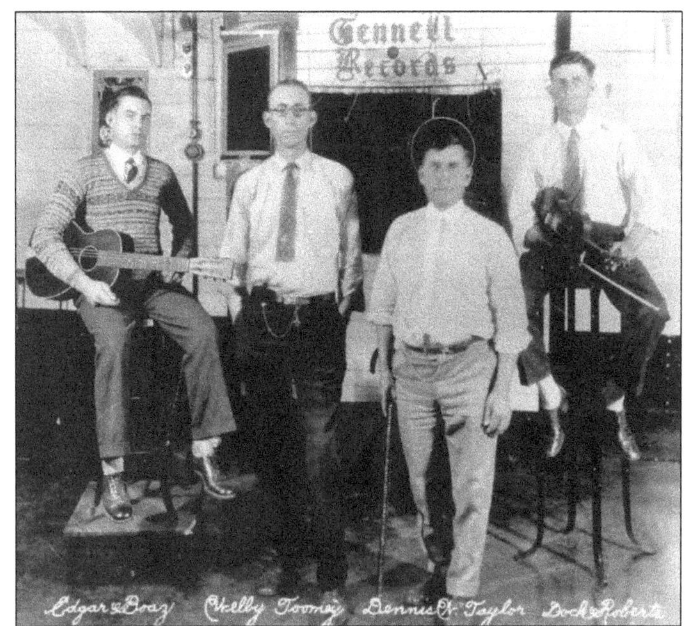

With the same vigor as its foray into jazz recording, Gennett Records entered the old-time/hillbilly music market in the mid-1920s. Gennett developed relationships with local talent scouts to source musical talent, primarily from Kentucky, to the Richmond studio. This picture captures two of Gennett's best hillbilly talent scouts, Dennis Taylor and Fiddlin' Doc Roberts. From left to right are Edgar Boaz, Welby Toomey, Taylor, and Roberts. (Berea College Special Collections and Archive.)

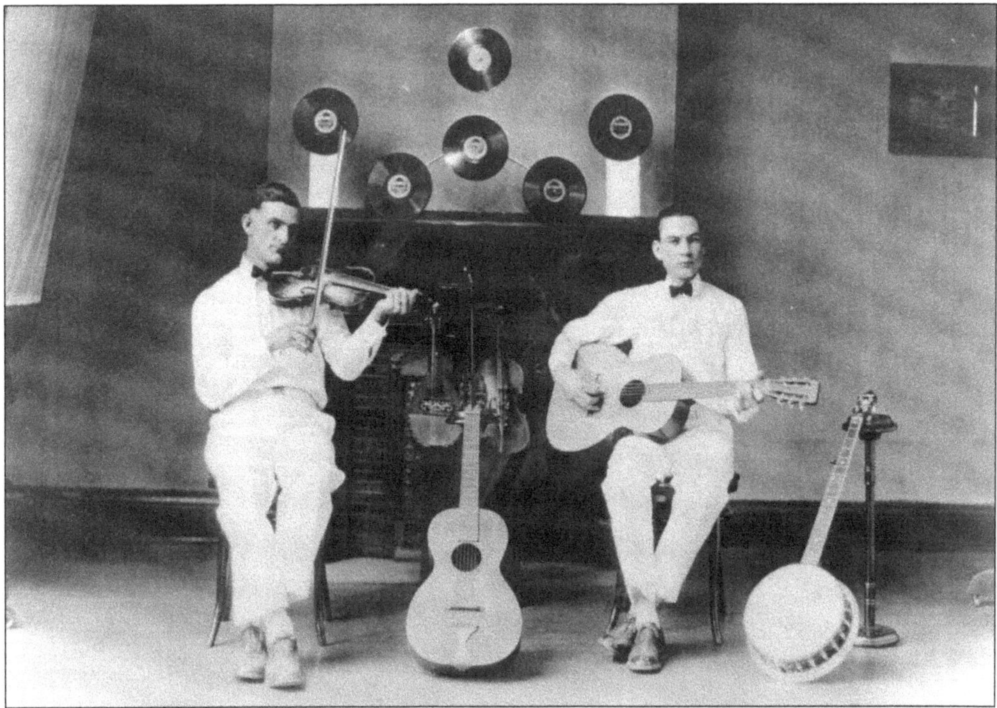

Fiddlin' Doc Roberts recorded on or organized approximately 100 sides for Gennett and its various affiliate labels, primarily Champion and Supertone. Roberts organized sessions with and for such noted Kentucky artists as Asa Martin, Ted Chestnut, Green Bailey, Dick Parman, Marion Underwood, and his son James Roberts. Additionally, Roberts appeared as a member of the racially integrated group known as Taylor's Kentucky Boys. In this photograph, Roberts (left) and Edgar Boaz pose in front of several of their Gennett releases. (Berea College Special Collections and Archive.)

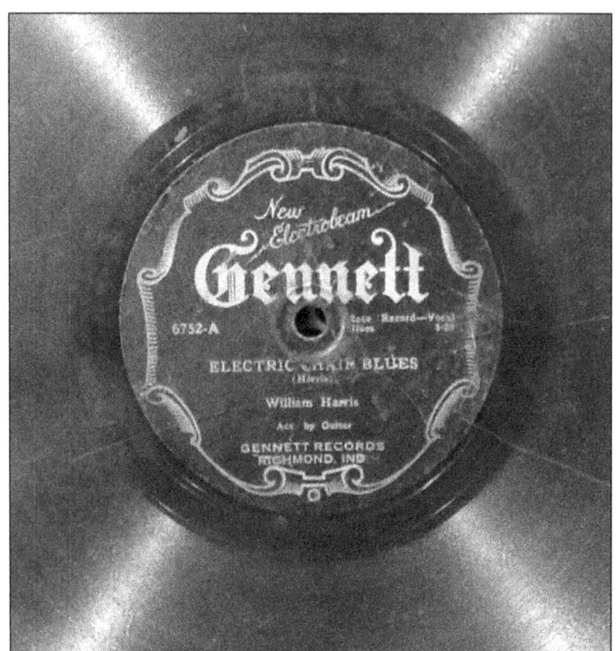

Blues guitarist and vocalist William Harris first recorded for Gennett during its 1927 Birmingham, Alabama, location recording sessions. Gennett later arranged for Harris to record 14 tracks between October 9 and 11, 1928, in Richmond. Harris waxed some of the finest blues sides, including "Kansas City Blues," "Bull Frog Blues," and "Electric Chair Blues." Gennett switched to an electric recording process in 1927 and added Electrobeam to its labels to signify the improved sound quality. (Richard Nevins.)

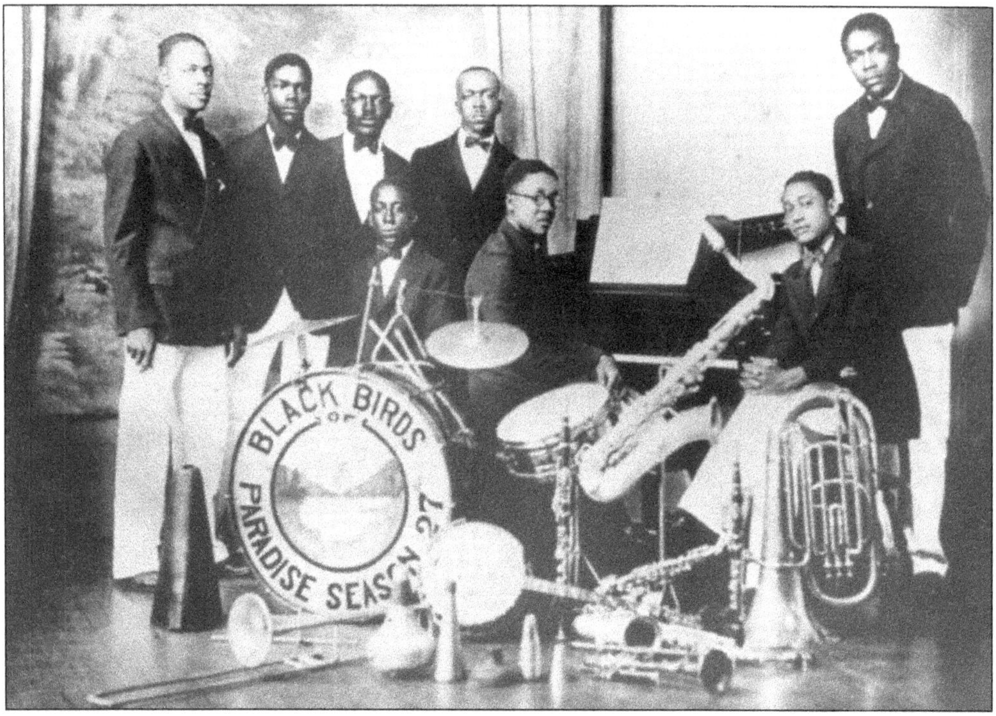

In 1927, Gennett arranged for some location recording trips, including a productive one over two months in Birmingham, Alabama. The Montgomery, Alabama–based jazz band, the Blackbirds of Paradise, recorded nine sides from which Gennett and Black Patti issued six. The band consisted of William "Buddy" Howard (vocals and trombone), Philmore "Shorty" Hall (cornet), James Bell (clarinet), Walter Boyd (sax), Melvin Small (piano), Ivory Johnson (bass), Tom Ivory (banjo), and Sam Bordees (drums). (Morrisson-Reeves Library.)

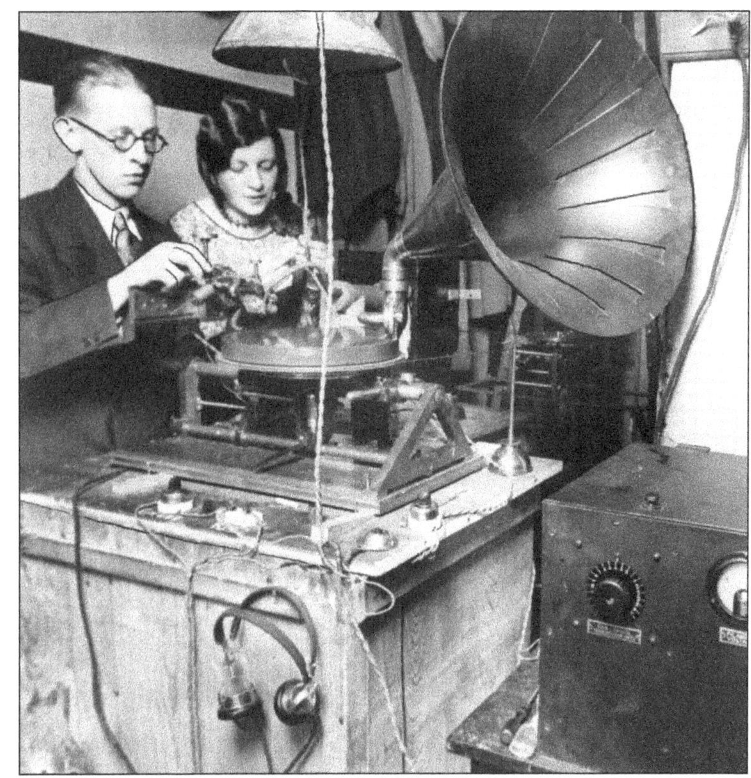

St. Paul, Minnesota, was another site for location recording for Gennett Records. The label set up temporary studio facilities in the Lowry Hotel. In this photograph, Gennett's chief sound engineer Harold Soule and Grace Slovetsky inspect the recording equipment after a session with Wally Erickson's Coliseum Orchestra. Soule replaced Ezra Wickemeyer, who left in 1927, and engineered some of Gennett's greatest jazz, blues, and country sides. (Minnesota Historical Society.)

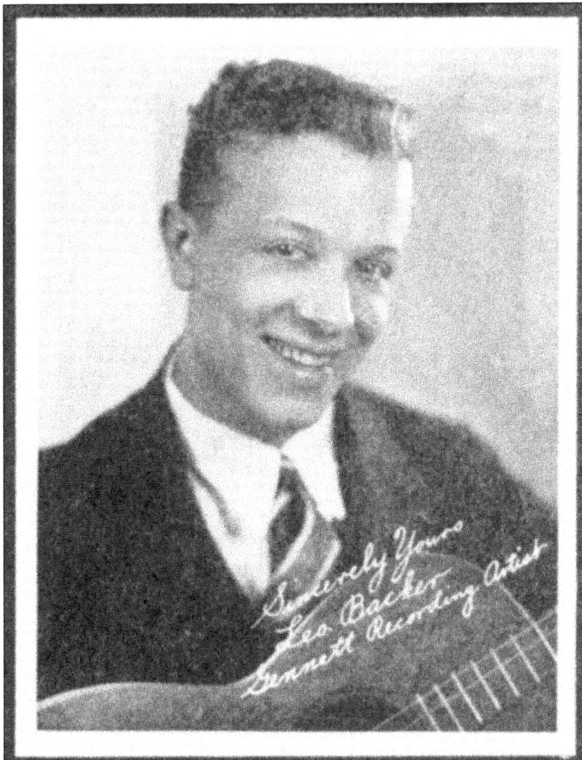

Guitarist and vocalist Les Backer was a prolific artist for Gennett. He recorded several dozen sides both as a featured artist and a sideman with Walter Anderson and His Golden Pheasant Hoodlums in sessions that occurred in Chicago, St. Paul, and Richmond. On many of his records, the label billed Backer as "The Gennett Aristocrat." Backer also marketed himself as a Gennett recording artist on his sheet music and at live appearances. (Morrisson-Reeves Library.)

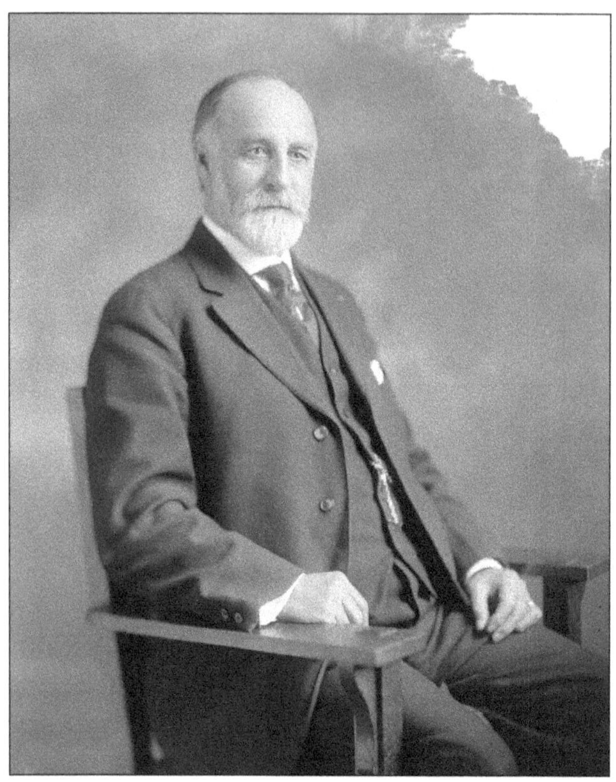

Jesse Walter Fewkes was an anthropologist who became the head of the Bureau of American Ethnology at the Smithsonian Institution. Fewkes was one of the first people to field record indigenous peoples in the 1890s. In 1926, he supervised a location recording of Hopi Indians at the El Tovar Hotel in East Mesa, Arizona. While these recordings have become a treasure trove for folklorist study, their original purpose was as a souvenir item for Grand Canyon tourists. (Library of Congress.)

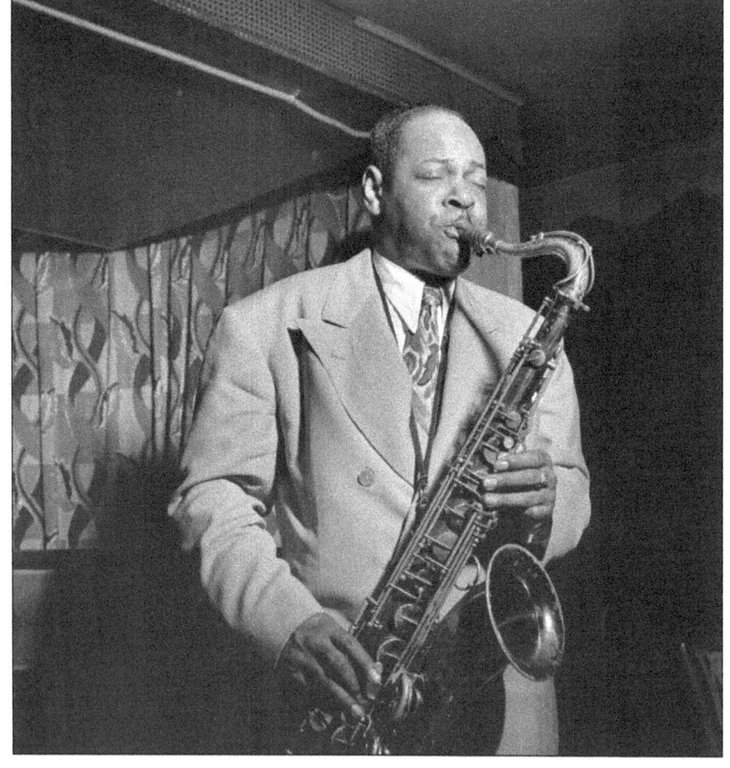

On March 26, 1926, tenor saxophonist Coleman Hawkins recorded two sides in Gennett's New York City studio as a member of Fletcher Henderson's Orchestra. Hawkins was one of the first great jazz tenor saxophonists and with his own orchestra recorded the definitive version of the jazz standard "Body and Soul" in 1939. Hawkins's career remained vital in the modern jazz era. He also recorded several sides for Joe Davis, who briefly revived the Gennett label in the 1940s. (William P. Gottlieb Collection, Library of Congress.)

Elmer Grosso and his orchestra were another of Gennett's most prolific recording artists. The violinist organized sessions that produced over 100 sides in Gennett's New York City studio between 1926 and 1930 under various monikers. Gennett used the pseudonym Champion Dance Kings on most of Grosso's Champion Records releases. (LGI.)

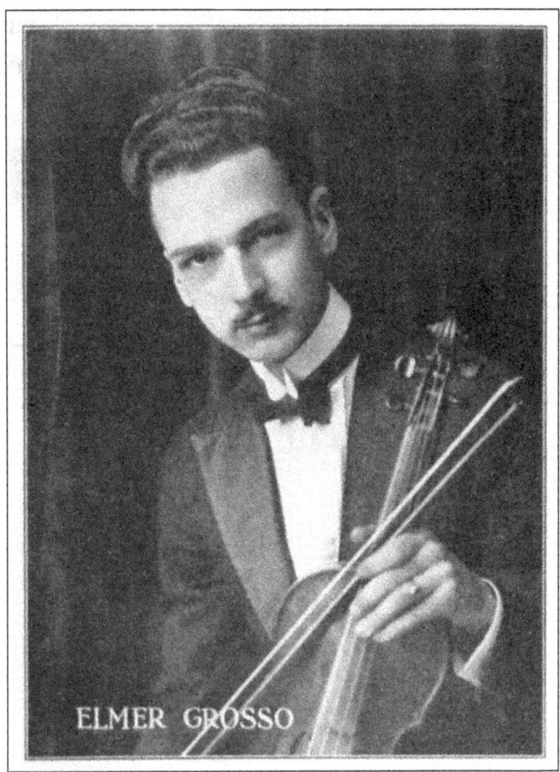

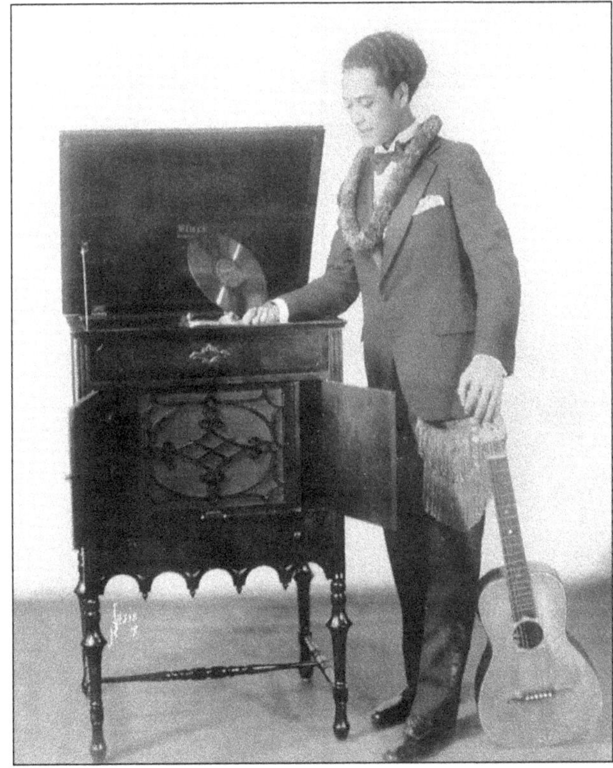

Hawaiian steel guitarist Sam Ku West recorded dozens of sides for Gennett in both the New York City and Richmond studios between 1927 and 1928. He died in 1930 at the age of 23, just as his career began to flourish. In this photograph, West poses with one of his Gennett Electrobeam releases next to a Starr phonograph. (Les Cook and Malcolm Rockwell.)

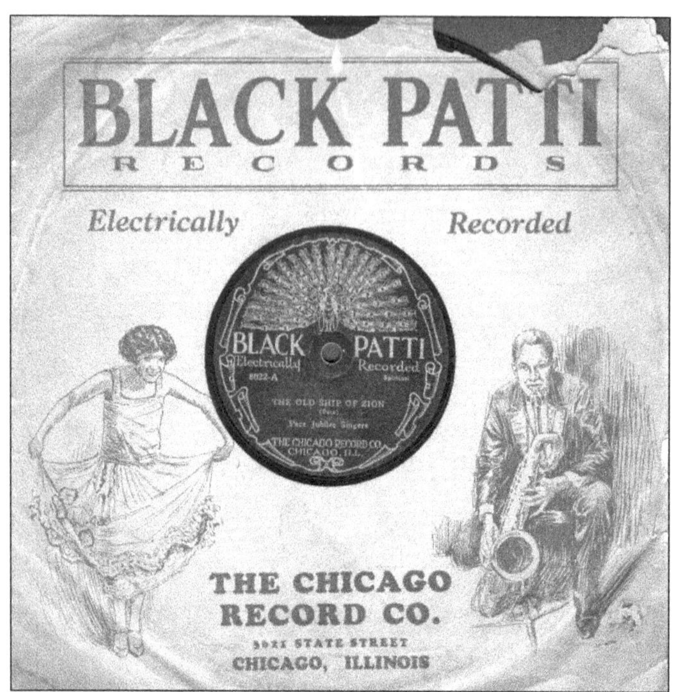

J. Mayo Williams led the Chicago Record Company and its label, Black Patti, in 1927, the only year it was in business. The label took its name from 19th-century African American opera singer Sissieretta "Black Patti" Jones. Despite its brief existence and lack of sales, Black Patti managed to release some of the finest and most desired race and spiritual records. Gennett was a silent partner in the label. Black Patti also used Starr Piano's pressing plant and studios. Many of Black Patti's sides also ended up on a Gennett or Champion issue. (LGI.)

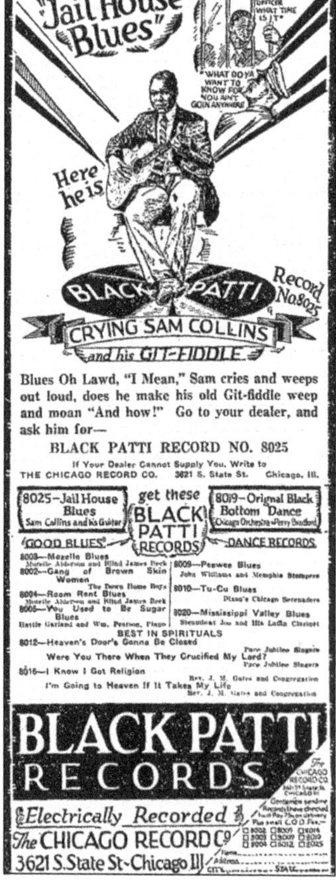

Cryin' Sam Collins and his git-fiddle (guitar) recorded some of the greatest blues sides in the Richmond studio. Black Patti, Champion, Electrobeam, and several other subsidiary labels released Collins's 1927 recordings. "Yellow Dog Blues," "The Jailhouse Blues," and "Do That Thing" are among the finest prewar blues records. Sadly, Gennett rejected the majority of Collins's recordings from his December 1927 session. (CBD.)

Black Patti released over 50 records in its one year of operation, including great blues and spiritual recordings by the Pace Jubilee Singers, Long "Cleve" Reed and Little Harvey Hull, Mozelle Alderson and Blind James Beck, and Hattie Garland. Additionally, Black Patti released sides by two white artists, hillbilly crooner Vernon Dalhart and WLS staff organist Ralph Waldo Emerson. (CBD.)

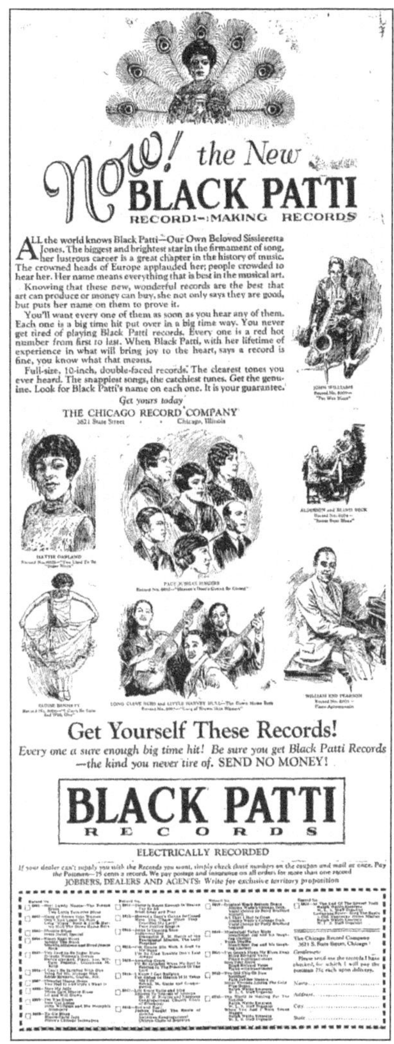

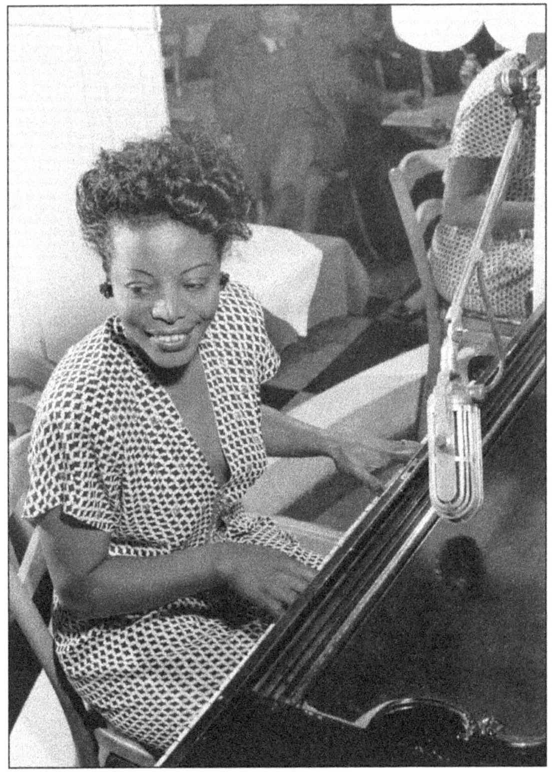

John Williams and His Memphis Stompers recorded for Black Patti. Their recordings featured the singing of Williams's wife, Mary Lou. After several years singing with big bands, Mary Lou Williams, "The First Lady of Jazz Piano," collaborated and mentored many of the young bebop artists, including Thelonious Monk and Dizzy Gillespie. (William P. Gottlieb Collection, Library of Congress.)

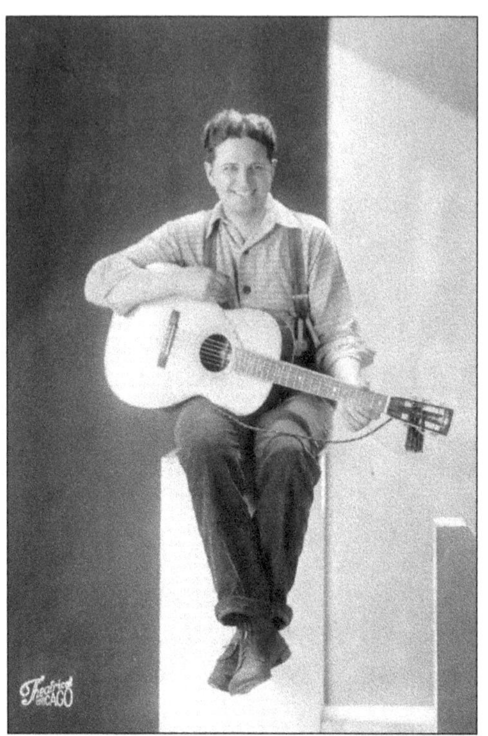

Bradley Kincaid, one of country music's first stars, began recording in 1927 for the Gennett and Champion labels. He recorded over 50 sides in the Richmond studio. Kincaid was a balladeer and star of the *National Barn Dance*, a popular radio program that predated the *Grand Ole Opry,* on WLS-AM in Chicago. In addition to his best-selling records, Kincaid released a very popular and influential songbook, *My Favorite Mountain Ballads and Old Time Songs*, in 1928. (Berea College Special Collections and Archive.)

The Maple City Four was another WLS radio act to record for Gennett in its Chicago and Richmond studios. The vocal quartet and comedic ensemble consisted of vocalists Art Janes, Fritz Meissner, Al Rice, and Pat Petterson. The quartet also appears in several westerns with Gene Autry and Roy Rodgers, including *Git Along Little Dogies* and *Under Western Skies.* (Berea College Special Collections and Archive.)

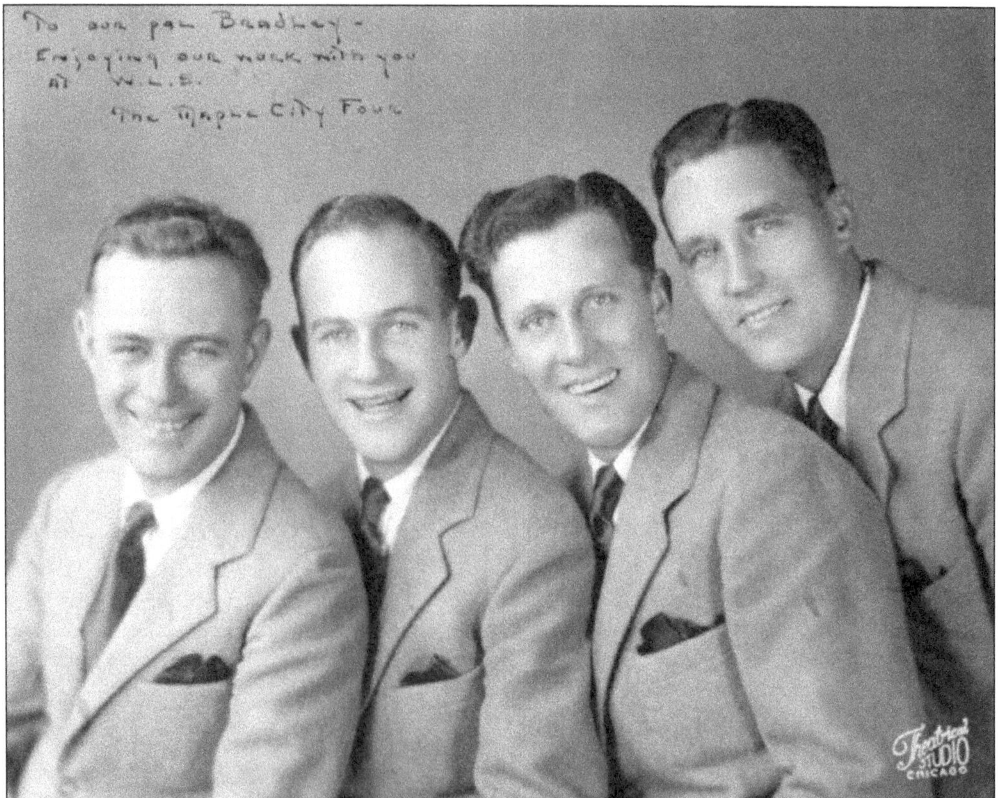

Luther W. Ossenbrink, the Arkansas Woodchopper, was a star on the WLS *National Barn Dance* and recorded approximately 20 sides for Gennett and Champion in 1929 and 1930. He remained as a regular on the *National Barn Dance* through the 1950s, recorded for Conquerer and Columbia, and released a popular songbook entitled *The Arkansas Woodchopper's Worlds Greatest Collection of Cowboy Songs with Yodel Arrangements*. (Berea College Special Collections and Archive.)

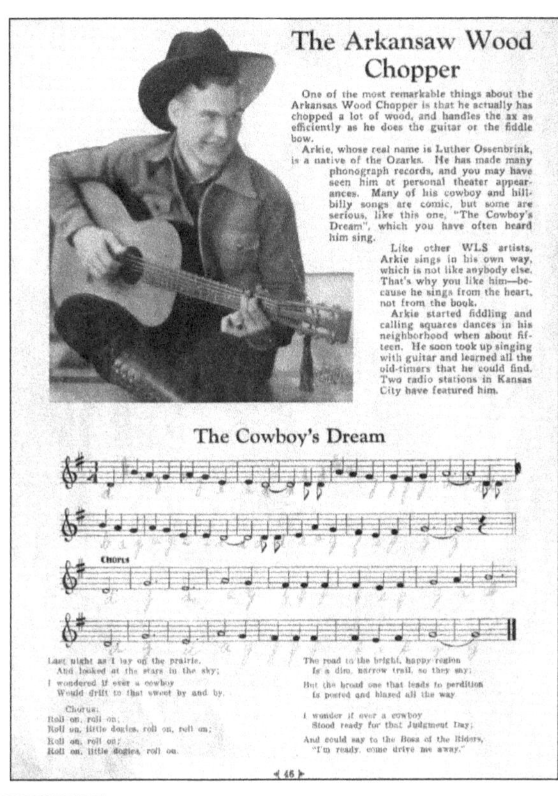

The Arkansaw Wood Chopper

One of the most remarkable things about the Arkansas Wood Chopper is that he actually has chopped a lot of wood, and handles the ax as efficiently as he does the guitar or the fiddle bow.

Arkie, whose real name is Luther Ossenbrink, is a native of the Ozarks. He has made many phonograph records, and you may have seen him at personal theater appearances. Many of his cowboy and hill-billy songs are comic, but some are serious, like this one, "The Cowboy's Dream", which you have often heard him sing.

Like other WLS artists, Arkie sings in his own way, which is not like anybody else. That's why you like him—because he sings from the heart, not from the book.

Arkie started fiddling and calling squares dances in his neighborhood when about fifteen. He soon took up singing with guitar and learned all the old-timers that he could find. Two radio stations in Kansas City have featured him.

The Cowboy's Dream

Chorus

Last night as I lay on the prairie,
And looked at the stars in the sky;
I wondered if ever a cowboy
Would drift to that sweet by and by.

Chorus:
Roll on, roll on;
Roll on, little dogies, roll on, roll on;
Roll on, roll on;
Roll on, little dogies, roll on.

The road to the bright, happy region
Is a dim, narrow trail, so they say;
But the broad one that leads to perdition
Is posted and blazed all the way

I wonder if ever a cowboy
Stood ready for that Judgment Day;
And could say to the Boss of the Riders,
"I'm ready, come drive me away."

‹ 46 ›

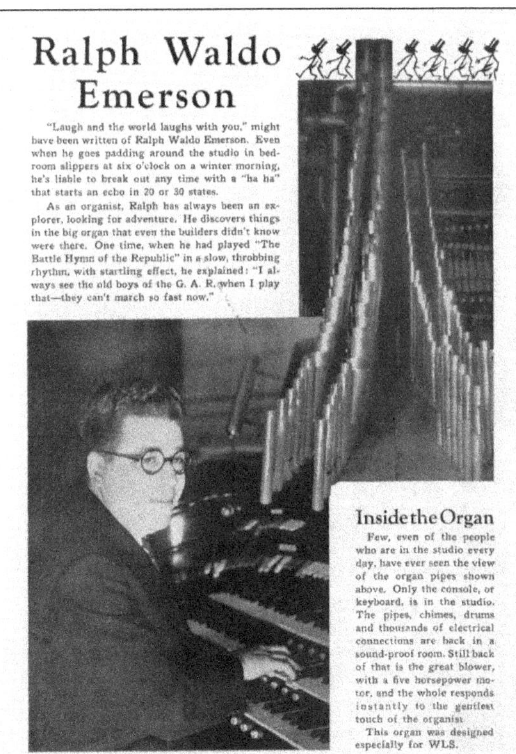

Ralph Waldo Emerson

"Laugh and the world laughs with you," might have been written of Ralph Waldo Emerson. Even when he goes padding around the studio in bedroom slippers at six o'clock on a winter morning, he's liable to break out any time with a "ha ha" that starts an echo in 20 or 30 states.

As an organist, Ralph has always been an explorer, looking for adventure. He discovers things in the big organ that even the builders didn't know were there. One time, when he had played "The Battle Hymn of the Republic" in a slow, throbbing rhythm, with startling effect, he explained: "I always see the old boys of the G. A. R. when I play that—they can't march so fast now."

Inside the Organ

Few, even of the people who are in the studio every day, have ever seen the view of the organ pipes shown above. Only the console, or keyboard, is in the studio. The pipes, chimes, drums and thousands of electrical connections are back in a sound-proof room. Still back of that is the great blower, with a five horsepower motor, and the whole responds instantly to the gentlest touch of the organist.

This organ was designed especially for WLS.

Eleven

Ralph Waldo Emerson served as WLS's staff organist and played the specially designed pipe organ on most of the shows in the 1920s. In addition to recording 10 sides that appeared on Gennett, Gennett Rayo, Black Patti, Central Church Chorus, and several other subsidiary labels, Emerson also served as the house organist at Chicago Stadium. (Berea College Special Collections and Archive.)

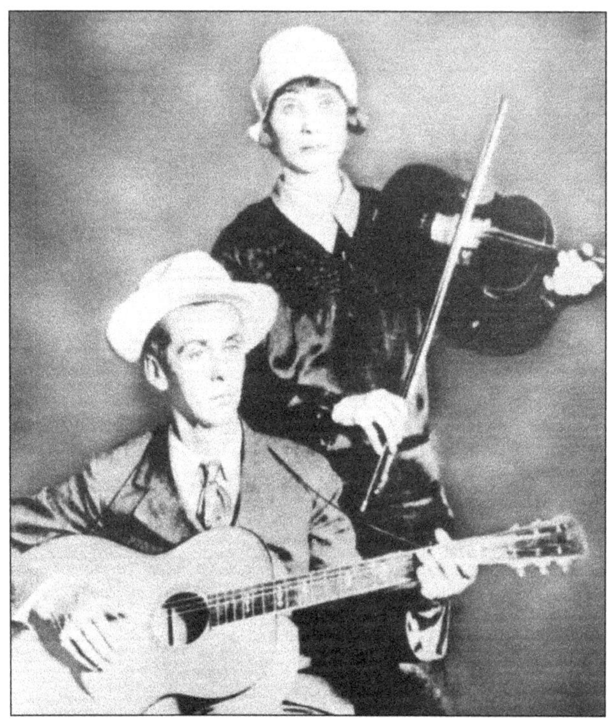

Like Doc Roberts, Ernest "Pop" Stoneman was both a great hillbilly artist and a talent scout. While Stoneman is best known as one of the artists at Victor's 1927 Bristol Sessions, he recorded over 50 sides with Gennett and Champion under his own name, with his wife, Hattie Stoneman, and with Frank Jenkins and His Pilot Mountaineers, the Grayson County Railsplitters, and the Virginia Mountain Boomers. Stoneman and his family were mainstays on the folk circuit until his death in 1968. Pop Stoneman is one of four artists inducted into both the Country Music Hall of Fame and the Gennett Walk of Fame. Hattie is in the Gennett Walk of Fame. (LGI.)

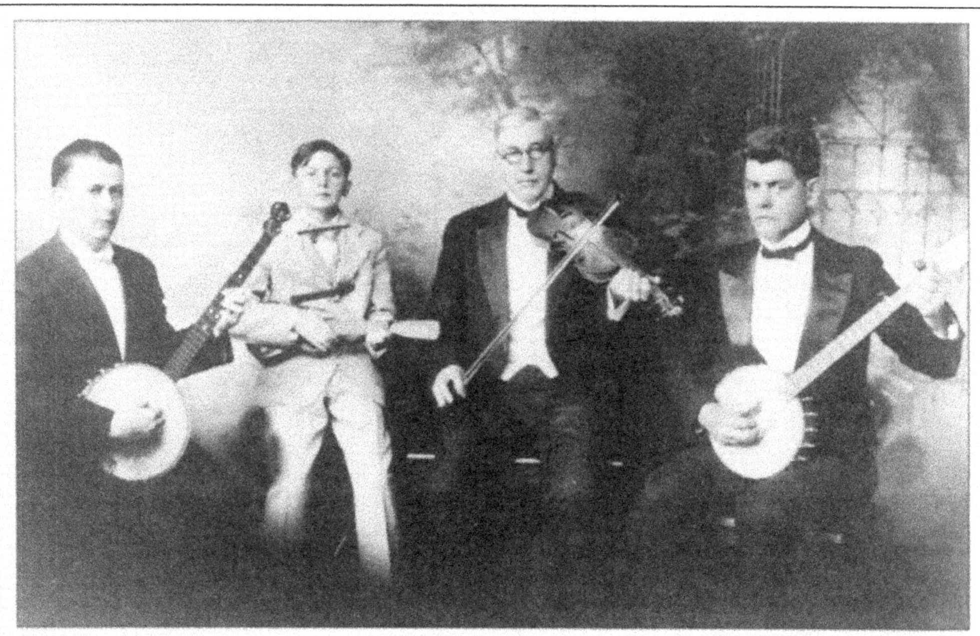

Da Costa Woltz's Southern Broadcasters, 1927: Woltz, Price Goodson, Ben Jarrell, Frank Jenkins. (Author's collection)

Even though Da Costa Waltz's Southern Broadcasters was only in the studio for three days in May 1927, the group recorded some of the finest and virtuosic old-time string sides ever. The band consisted of, from left to right, Da Costa Woltz (banjo), 12-year-old Price Goodson (harmonica, ukulele, and vocals), Ben Jarrell (fiddle and vocals), and Frank Jenkins (banjo). (Tony Russell.)

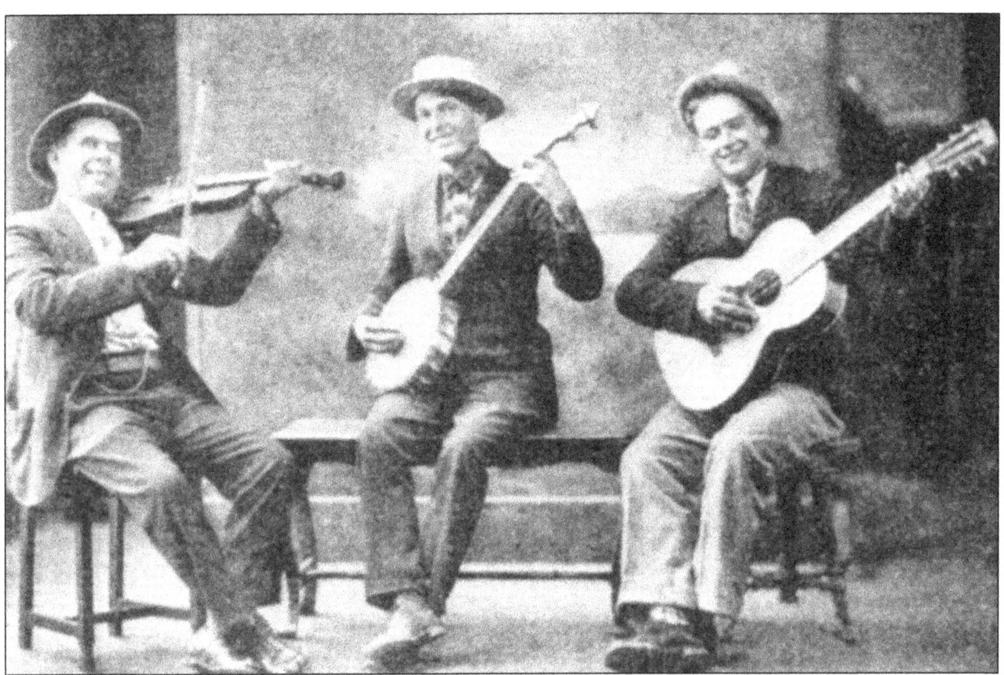

Taylor's Kentucky Boys, named after their manager and Gennett talent scout Dennis Taylor, recorded in 1927. The group was racially integrated and consisted of Marion Underwood (banjo), Willie Young (guitar), and Jim Booker (fiddle). However, the photograph shows a white musician, probably Dennis Taylor, posing with a fiddle as a stand-in for African American fiddler Jim Booker. (Yazoo Records.)

Richard "Dick" Burnett (banjo), blinded from a shotgun blast while being robbed, and his young collaborator, Leonard Rutherford (fiddle), were a popular duo in Kentucky before Dennis Taylor discovered them in 1928. Together and separately, Rutherford and Burnett recorded over two dozen sides that also feature Byrd Moore (vocal and guitar) and John Foster (vocal and guitar). The Leonard Rutherford and John Foster recording of "Six Months Ain't Long" on Champion 15750 sold over 28,000 copies at the dawn of the Great Depression. (Yazoo Records.)

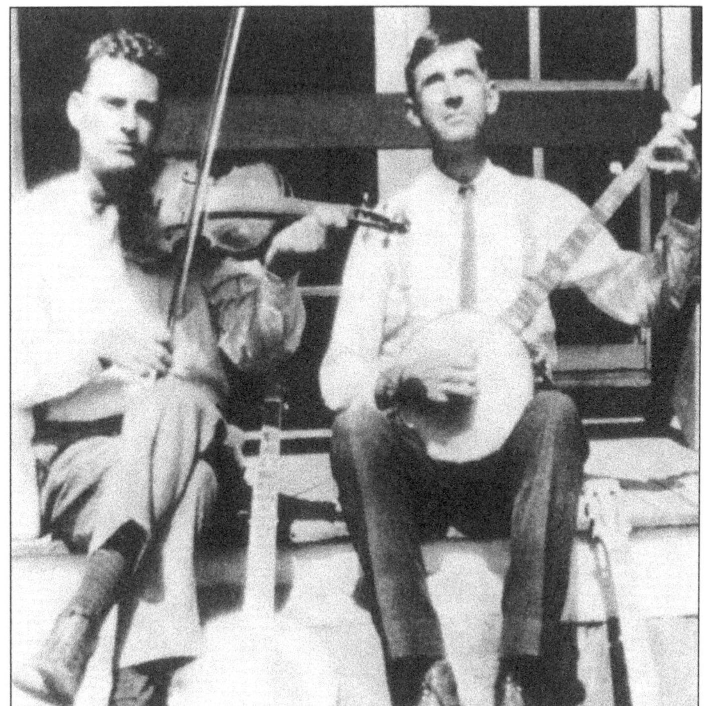

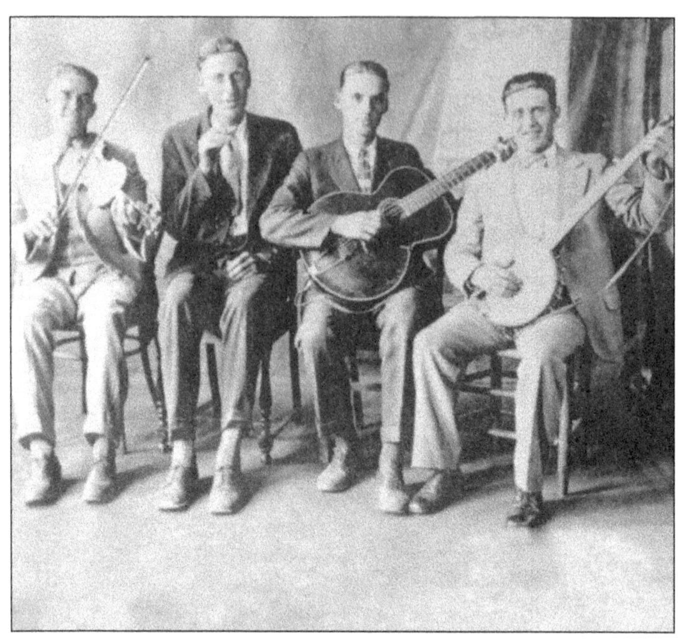

Paul Miles and the Red Fox Chasers recorded over two dozen sides for Gennett in 1928 and 1929. The group consisted of, from left to right, Guy Brooks (vocal and fiddle), Bob Cranford (vocal and harmonica), A.P. Thompson (vocal and guitar), and Paul Miles (vocal and banjo). In addition to string band music, the group recorded gospel quartet and bootlegging sketch comedy records for Gennett. Their releases on Gennett's discount label, Champion Records, tended to sell a few thousand copies in the post–stock market crash economy. (CBD.)

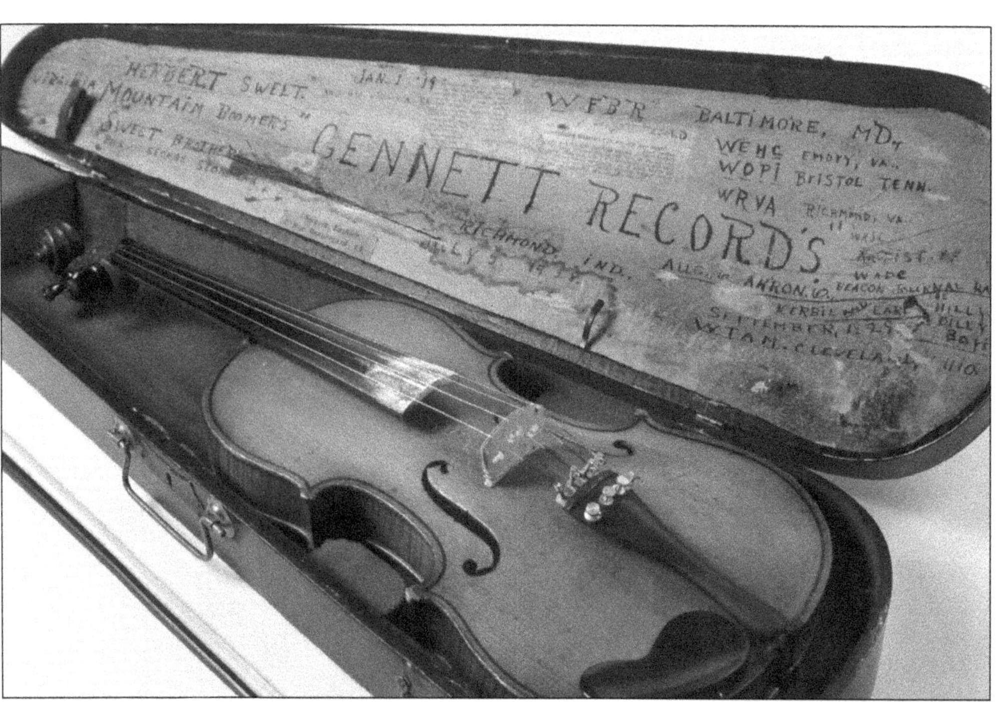

This photograph shows Herbert Sweet's fiddle and bow with his inscribed case. Even though Herbert and his brother Earl (banjo) only recorded a few sides with Gennett in July 1928 with Ernest Stoneman, he still noted it prominently in his fiddle case, which also documents the many towns and radio stations where he performed. (Ruth Roe and Herbert Sweet Collection at the Birthplace of Country Music Museum, photograph by Hannah Holmes.)

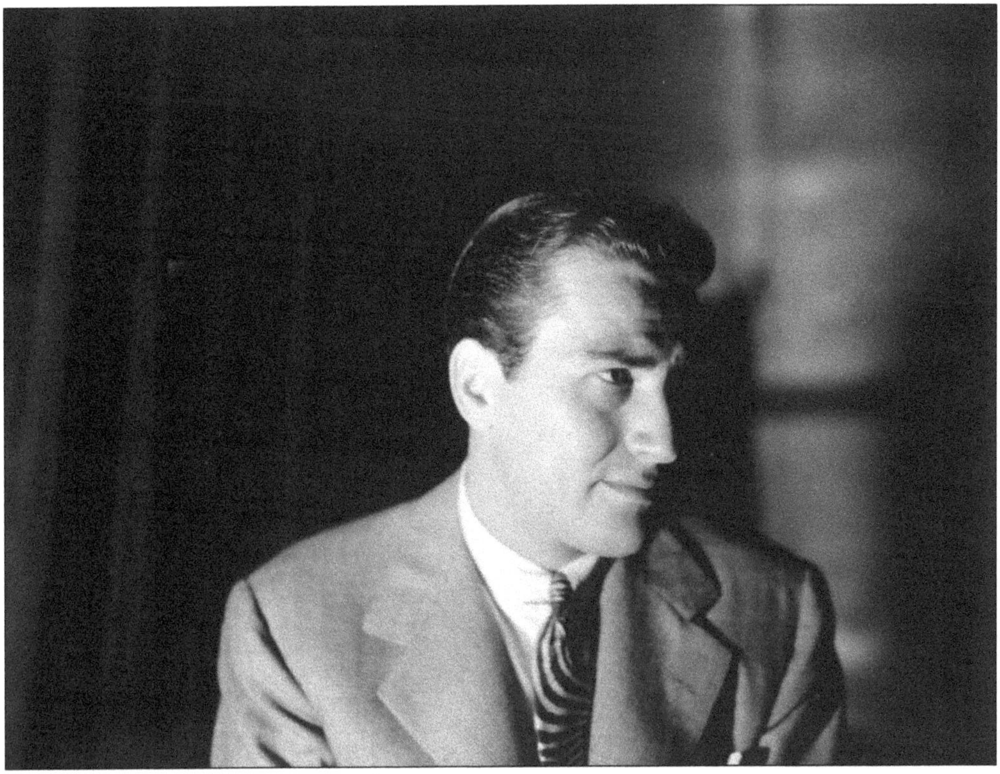

Two prominent 20th-century recording artists made their first recordings in Gennett's Richmond studio, only to have their efforts rejected and lost forever. Artie Shaw (above), the legendary jazz clarinetist, bandleader, and composer, recorded four sides as a member of Joe Cantor and His Orchestra. In addition to playing either the alto saxophone or clarinet, Shaw appears as a vocalist on "Heartbroken and Lonely." Burl Ives (right) auditioned for Gennett on July 23, 1929, with a performance of "Behind the Clouds." After recovering from his rejection, Ives popularized the traditional American folk music songbook on his radio show, *The Wayfaring Stranger*, in the 1940s and performed with Woody Guthrie and Pete Seeger. In the 1960s, Ives acted in film and television, which includes his iconic role as the voice of Sam the Snowman in the holiday classic *Rudolph the Red-Nosed Reindeer*. (Both, Library of Congress.)

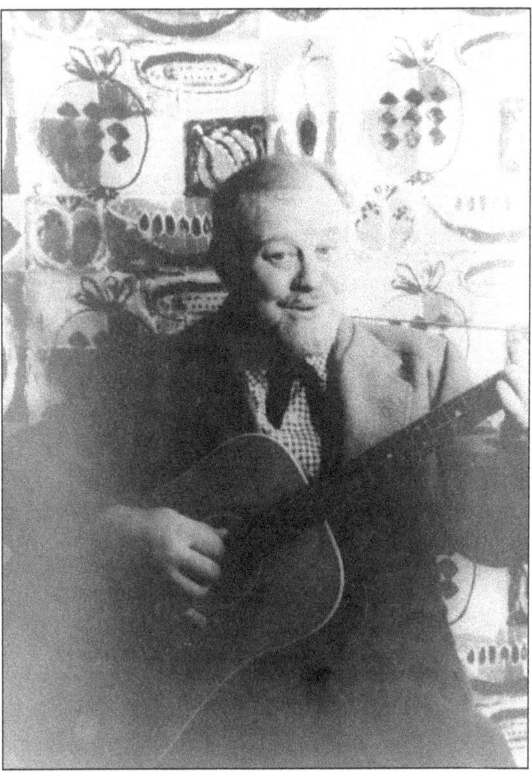

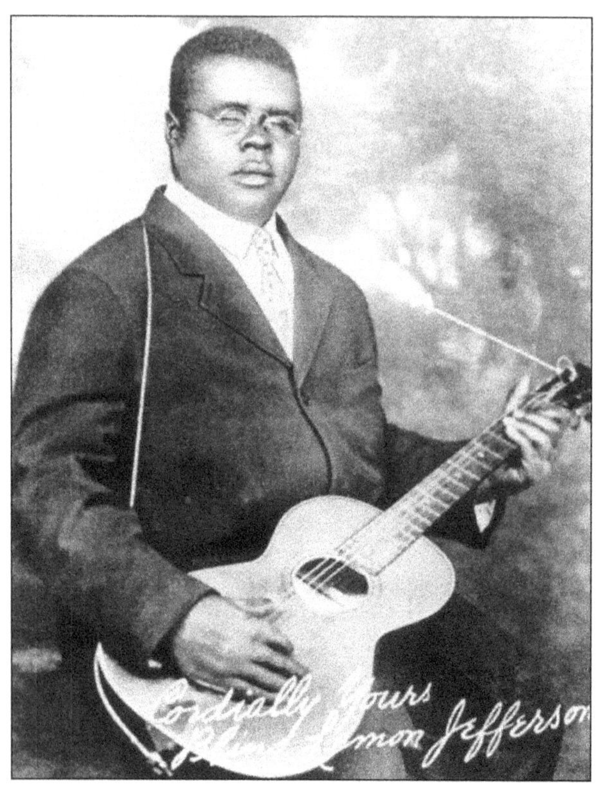

In 1929, as Paramount Records built a recording studio in Grafton, Wisconsin, the label rented Gennett's facility for $40 a side and sent some of its best blues and country artists to Richmond. Blind Lemon Jefferson's 1926 recordings started a trend for the acoustic country-style blues, and his records were amongst its best sellers. His September 24, 1929, session in Richmond yielded 12 new sides. Sadly, these were Jefferson's last recordings, as he died three months later in Chicago. (CBD.)

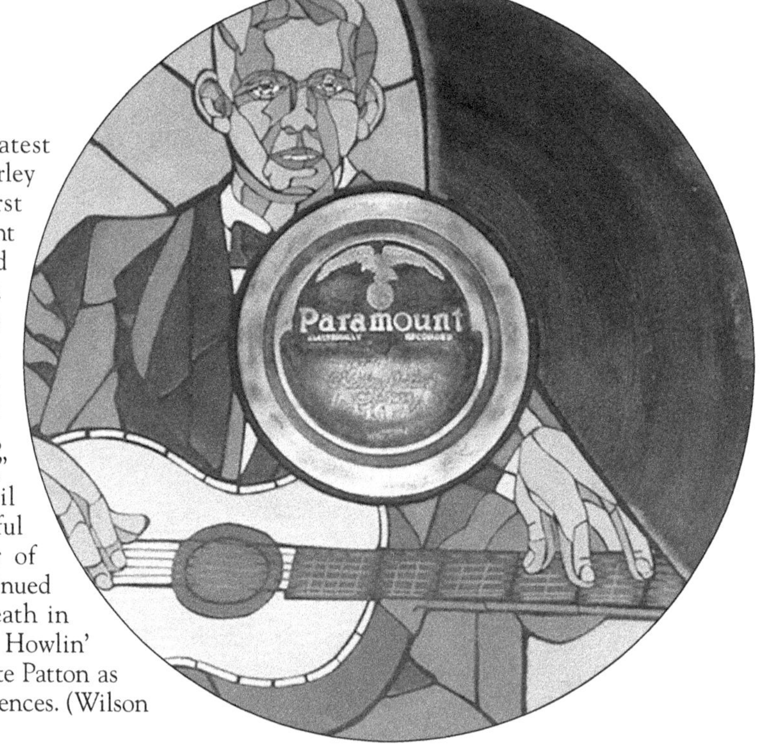

The delta blues' greatest recording artist, Charley Patton, made his first recordings for Paramount in Gennett's Richmond studio on June 14, 1929. During his few hours in Starr Valley, Patton recorded 14 of the most dynamic and influential country blues sides, including "Pony Blues," "Mississippi Boweavil Blues," and "A Spoonful Blues." "The Father of the Delta Blues" continued to record until his death in 1934. Musicians from Howlin' Wolf to Jack White cite Patton as one of their main influences. (Wilson Custom Tile.)

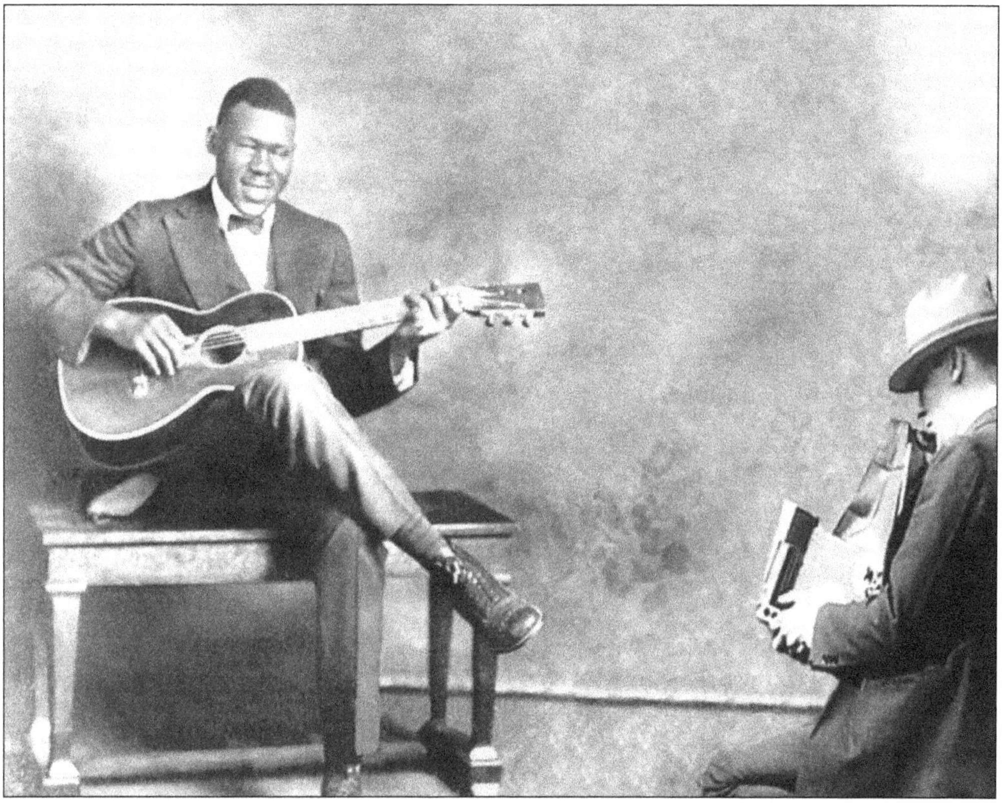

Arthur "Blind" Blake was another of Paramount's top artists who recorded at Gennett in 1929. Blake's music was equal parts ragtime and blues, which made his recordings more up-tempo and danceable. Some of his landmark Paramount recordings waxed in Richmond include "Diddie Wa Diddie" and "Georgia Bound." (CBD.)

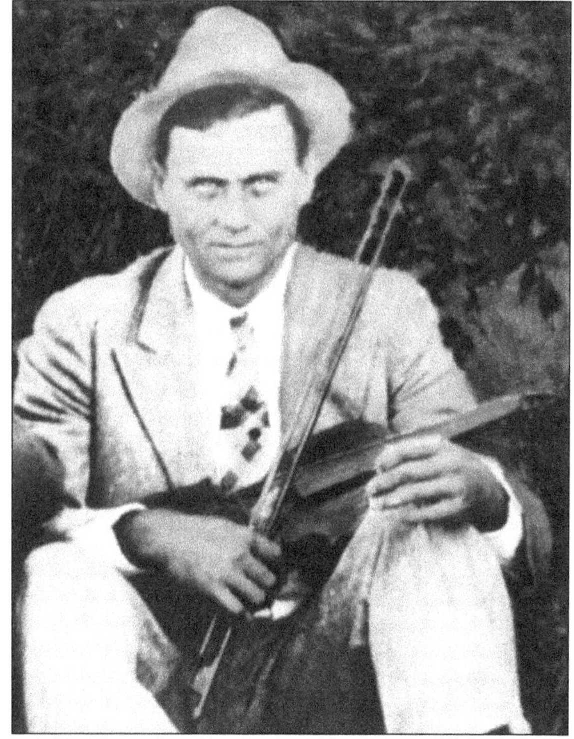

Paramount also sent some of its roster to Gennett's New York City studio in 1929. One of the finest fiddlers of this era, Wilmer Watts, and his band, the Lonely Eagles, recorded there on October 29. They waxed 16 sides, 14 of which Paramount released, including "Been on the Job Too Long" and "Fightin' the War with Spain." (Marshall Wyatt of Old Hat Records.)

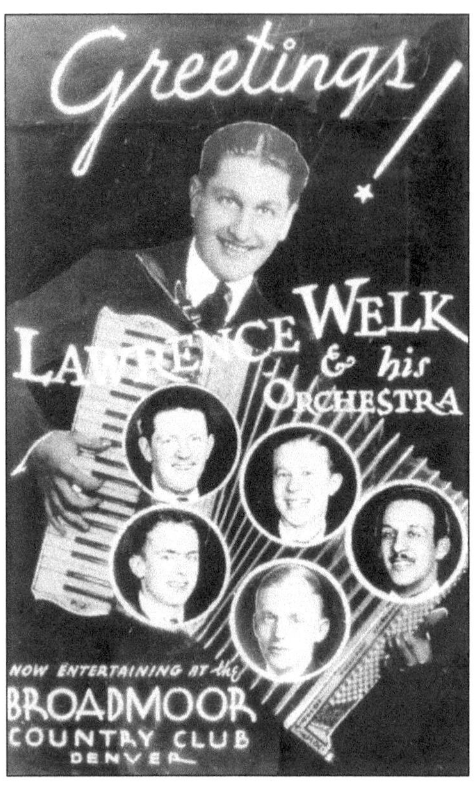

Lawrence Welk brought his Novelty Orchestra to Richmond to make his first sound recordings in 1928. At the time, Welk was a regular on South Dakota radio station WNAX, which resided at the top of the Gurney Seed and Nursery building. Three of Welk's sides were issued on Gennett and on a custom label for Gurney. He later starred on the *Lawrence Welk Show*, one of the longest-running and most popular shows in television history. (Morrisson-Reeves Library.)

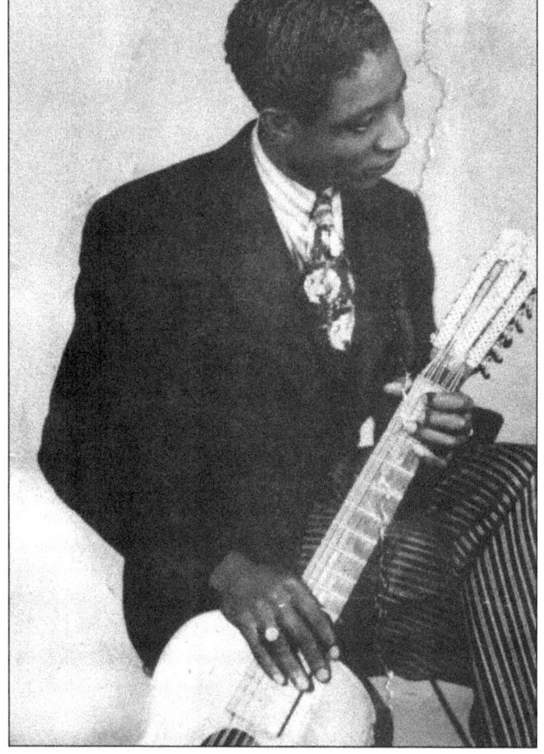

Lonnie Johnson was a groundbreaking jazz and blues guitar player. His 1928 guitar duets with Eddie Lang set the standard for jazz guitar players. Johnson and Jimmy Blythe recorded eight sides, six of which Gennett released, in Chicago on December 13 and 14, 1927. Johnson later recorded with Louis Armstrong, Duke Ellington, and Tommy Dorsey. He actively recorded and toured until his death in 1970. (CBD.)

Four

Depression Blues

1930–1969

EXECUTIVE OFFICERS: HARRY GENNETT, Pres. CLARENCE GENNETT, Treas. FRED GENNETT, Secy.

THE STARR PIANO CO *Sales Corporation*
THE STARR COMPANY
STARR, RICHMOND, TRAYSER, REMINGTON PIANOS
GENNETT & CHAMPION RECORDS
"STARR FREEZE" ELECTRIC REFRIGERATION
ELECTRICAL TRANSCRIPTIONS FOR RADIO BROADCASTING
FACTORIES
RICHMOND, IND., U. S. A.

September 2nd, 1931

Mr. Doc Roberts
Richmond, Kentucky
Route #1

Dear Sir:

Answering yours of the 1st, the writer will do all he can with reference to your royalty check. However, the record business is very poor and collections are very slow.

We hope to be able to send your check in the very near future.

Very truly yours,

STARR PIANO CO SALES CORPORATION
Gennett Record Division

By. L A Butt
L. A. Butt

LAB:IMH

Like many record companies, Gennett suffered from the perfect storm of calamities that developed in the late 1920s and early 1930s. Between the rise of radio and an economy about to transition to the Great Depression after the 1929 stock market crash, Gennett Records scaled back its output to only sound effect records and leased its manufacturing and pressing facilities to outside firms. However, before Gennett completely left the music industry, it recorded a few more great artists for its discount label, Champion Records. This letter to Doc Roberts from Lee Butt, the head of the recording division, affirms the dismal state of the music business, and the letterhead shows the beginning of the Gennett family's move into the refrigeration business. (Berea College Special Collections and Archive.)

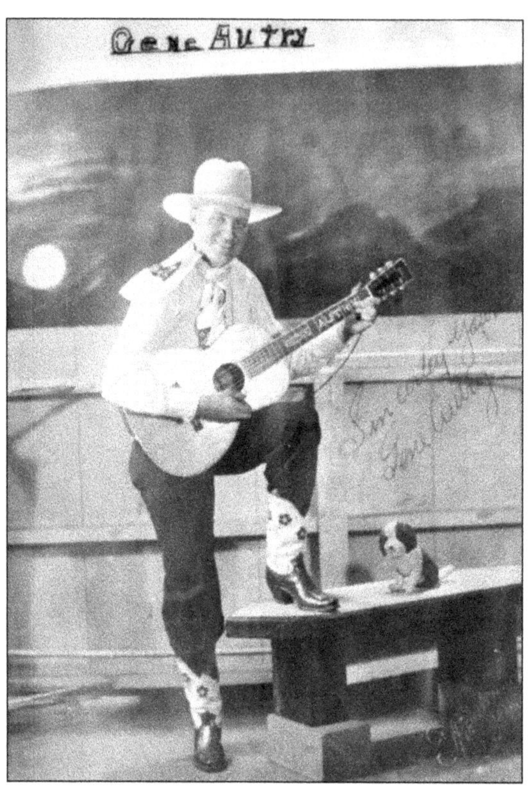

Gene Autry recorded almost 50 sides for Gennett between 1930 and 1931. In 1934, Autry began appearing in Westerns and on television, including in his own *Gene Autry Show*. He quickly became a star and top-selling recording artist of both cowboy and holiday songs. Additionally, Autry owned several radio and television stations, as well as the California Angels, a major-league baseball team. (Berea College Special Collections and Archive.)

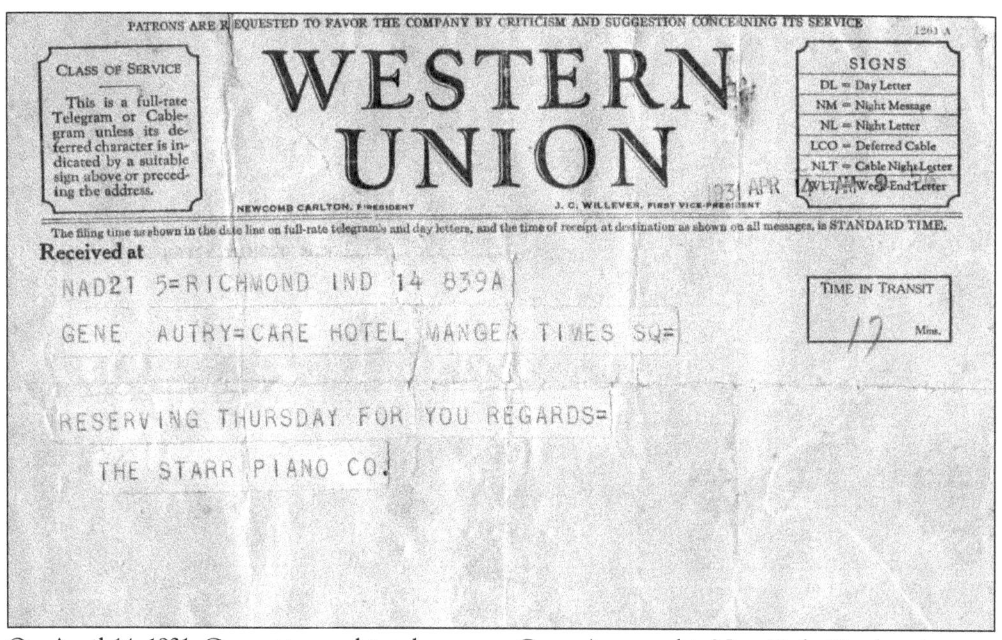

PATRONS ARE REQUESTED TO FAVOR THE COMPANY BY CRITICISM AND SUGGESTION CONCERNING ITS SERVICE

CLASS OF SERVICE

This is a full-rate Telegram or Cablegram unless its deferred character is indicated by a suitable sign above or preceding the address.

WESTERN UNION

NEWCOMB CARLTON, PRESIDENT — J. C. WILLEVER, FIRST VICE-PRESIDENT

SIGNS

DL = Day Letter
NM = Night Message
NL = Night Letter
LCO = Deferred Cable
NLT = Cable Night Letter
WLT = Week End Letter

1931 APR

The filing time as shown in the date line on full-rate telegrams and day letters, and the time of receipt at destination as shown on all messages, is STANDARD TIME.

Received at

NAD21 5=RICHMOND IND 14 839A

GENE AUTRY=CARE HOTEL MANGER TIMES SQ=

RESERVING THURSDAY FOR YOU REGARDS=

THE STARR PIANO CO.

TIME IN TRANSIT 17 Mins.

On April 14, 1931, Gennett sent this telegram to Gene Autry at his New York City hotel room. It confirmed what would be his final recording date with Gennett two days later in Richmond. Gennett's country music/discount label, Champion, released each one of these recordings. Autry named his famous horse Champion after the label that gave him one of his first breaks in show business. (CBD.)

Uncle Dave Macon, one of the first members of WSM's *Grand Ole Opry*, started recording and performing after he turned 50. Along with Sam and Kirk McGee, Macon traveled to Richmond for sessions with Gennett's Champion subsidiary on August 14 and 15, 1934. Macon is one of four artists inducted into both the Country Music Hall of Fame and the Gennett Walk of Fame. (Starr-Gennett Foundation.)

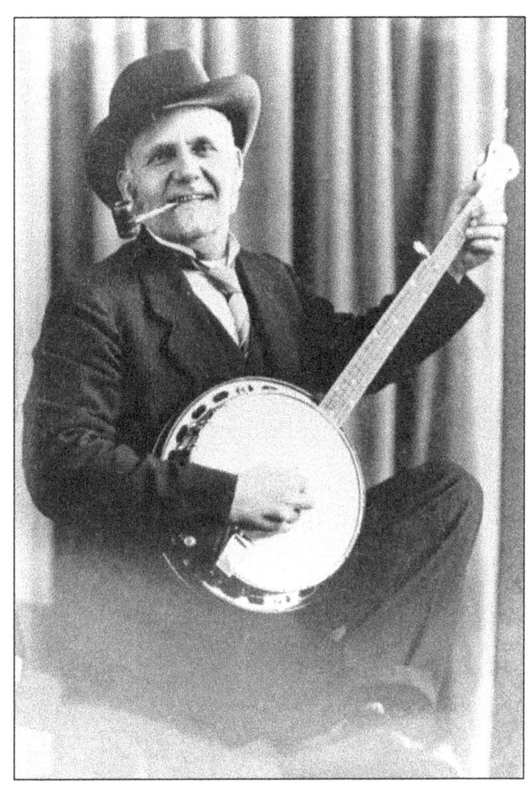

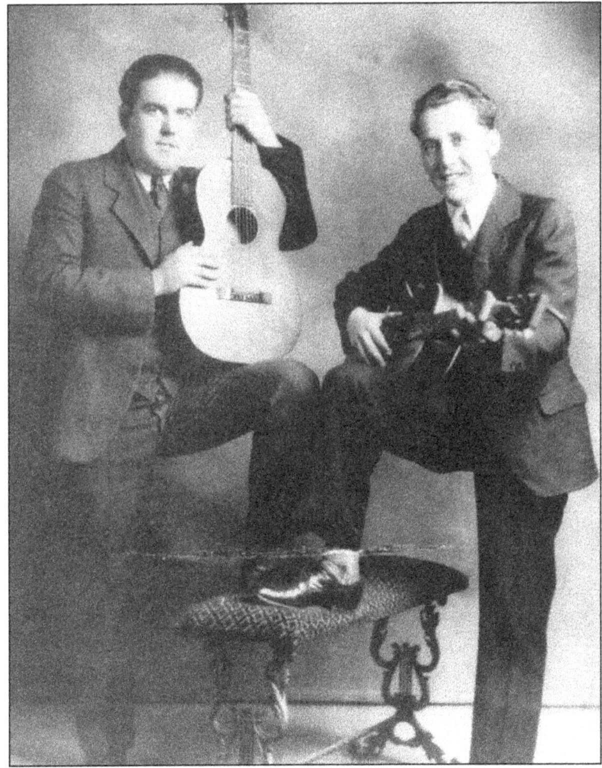

Cliff Carlisle (right) began his recording career with Gennett in 1930, after he made a name for himself on the Louisville radio station WLAP. Carlisle, with his characteristic yodel and influential steel guitar playing, joined guitarist Wilbur Ball (left) for many of his Gennett recording dates. Carlisle and Ball soon caught the attention of country music star Jimmie Rodgers, who asked them to join him on a recording date in 1931. (Tony Russell.)

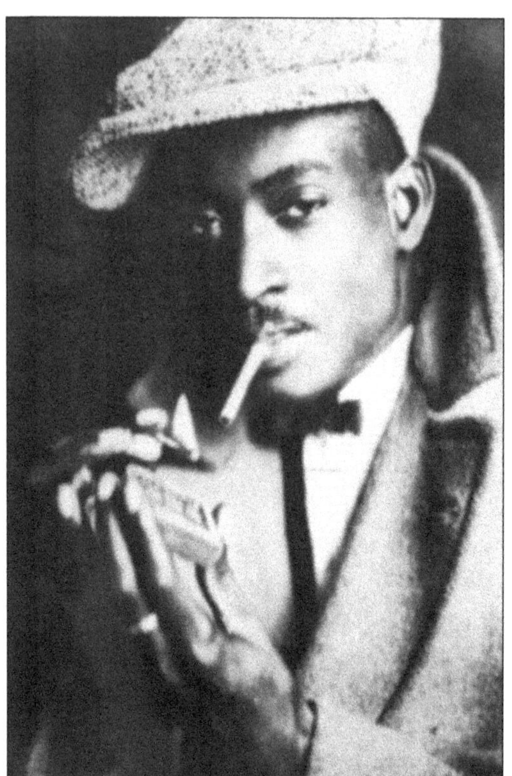

Thomas A. Dorsey, also known as "Georgia Tom," was an in demand collaborator in the Chicago blues scene before he traveled to Richmond on July 8, 1929, and recorded eight sides. He returned to Richmond twice in 1930, first with Scrapper Blackwell and then with Jane Lucas and Big Bill Broonzy. Dorsey is best known for his later work in the development of gospel music. He composed the gospel standard "Precious Lord Take My Hand" and collaborated with Mahalia Jackson. (CBD.)

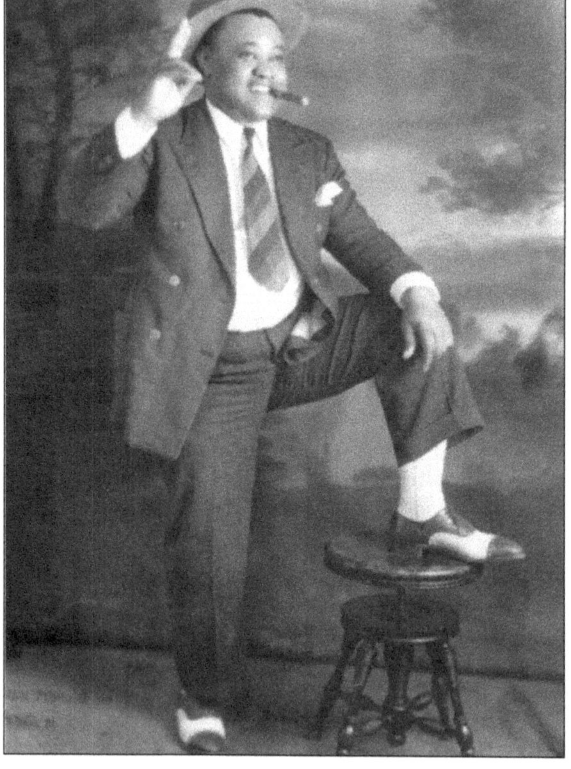

Pianist Roosevelt Sykes recorded over 25 sides for Champion and Paramount in the Richmond studio as both a featured artist and sideman between 1929 and 1932. Sykes composed the lyrics and recorded his signature song, the soon-to-be blues standard "44 Blues," for Okeh in 1929. The "Honeydripper" enjoyed success during the 1960s blues revival and passed away in 1983. (CBD.)

William "Big Bill" Broonzy was one of the key figures in the transition of acoustic country blues to electric urban blues. Broonzy was one of the most recorded blues artists of the prewar era and played guitar on over 30 sides made in Richmond. John Hammond invited Broonzy to perform and represent country blues for his legendary 1939 Carnegie Hall concert "From Spirituals to Swing." Broonzy remained an active recording and performing artist until his death in 1958. (CBD.)

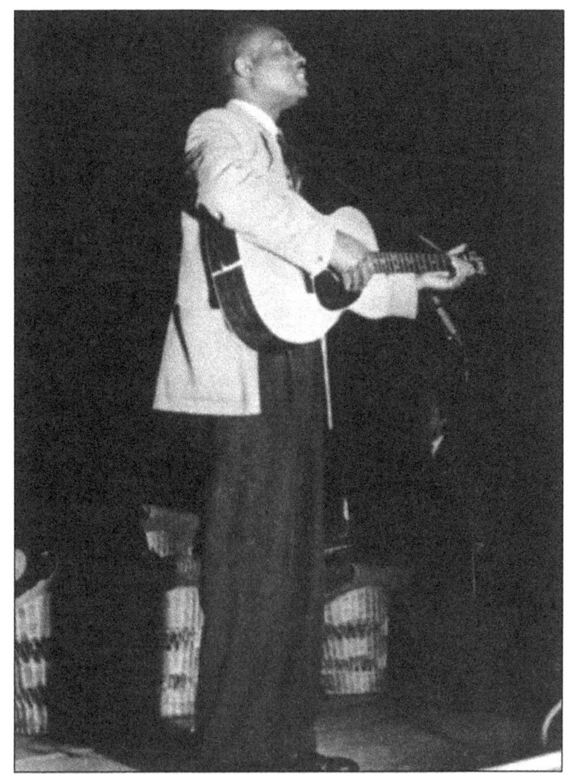

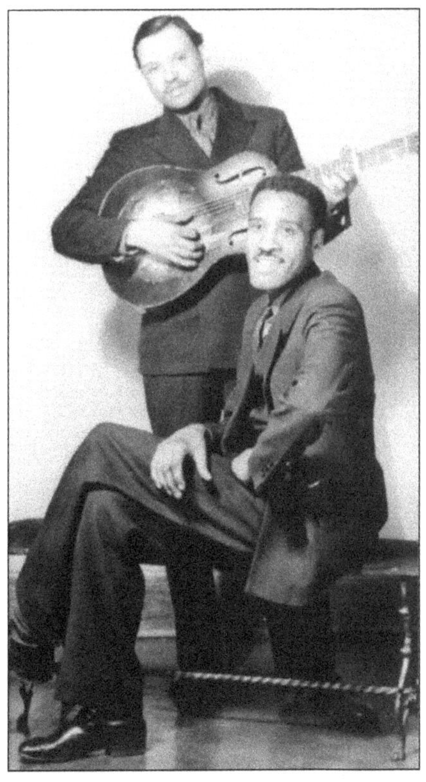

Pianist Leroy Carr and guitarist Scrapper Blackwell recorded their guitar, piano, and vocal blues at Gennett's Richmond studio in 1930 and 1931. Together, they recorded more than 100 sides, seven of which were from their Richmond sessions. Blackwell played in an interesting style that bordered blues and jazz. He recorded both as a featured artist and sideman on many sessions at Gennett, including sides with Georgia Tom. Blackwell did not record after the 1930s until Duncan Scheidt located him in 1962 and he released new material on 77 Records. (CBD.)

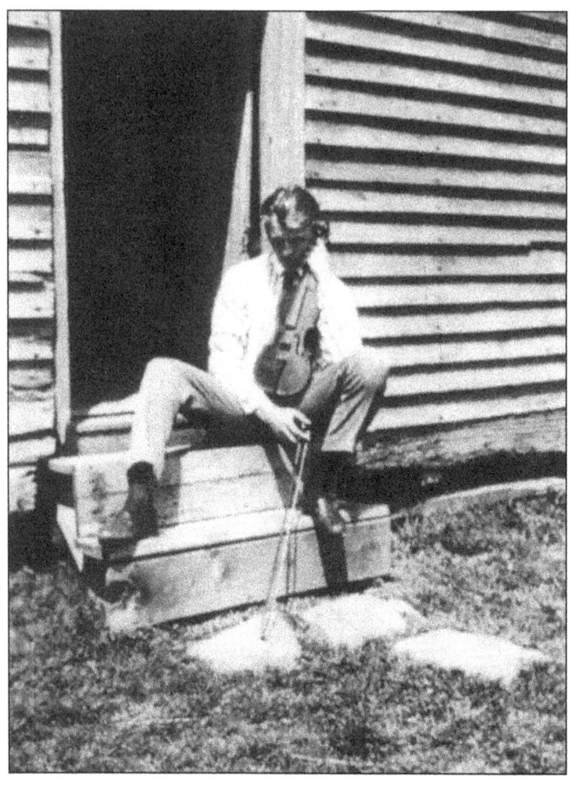

Ted Gossett's String Band recorded nine sides in Richmond on September 16, 1930, that are considered by many aficionados as some of the best and most dynamic string band music of the era. The band consisted of Earl Nossinger (guitar), Enos Gossett (guitar), Pete Woods (banjo), and Ted Gossett (fiddle). (Yazoo Records.)

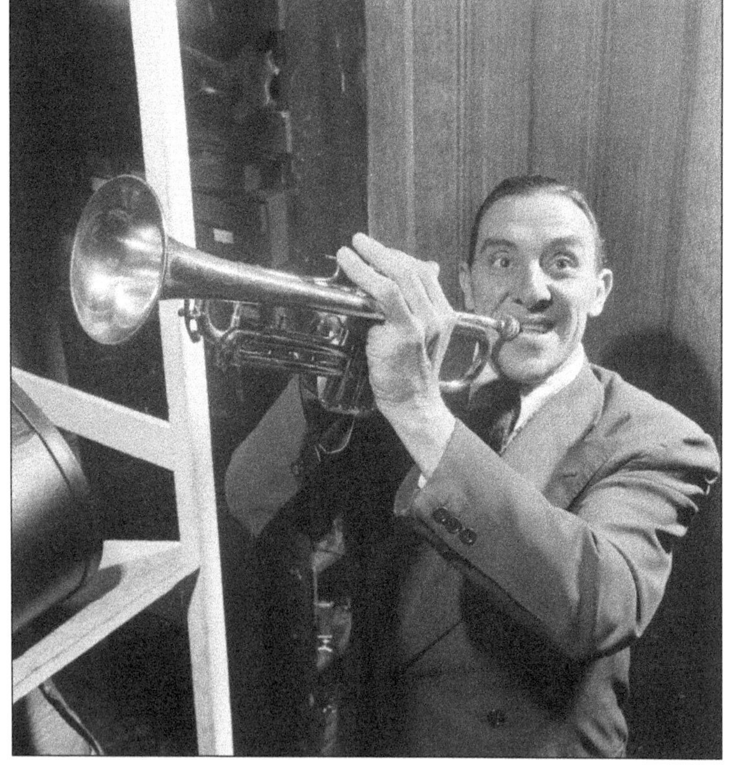

Joe Manone lost his right arm in a streetcar accident at the age of eight, thus the nickname "Wingy." Louis Armstrong and Bix Beiderbecke's recordings influenced Manone, who first recorded in 1924. Manone and his orchestra recorded eight sides over two sessions in August and September 1930. In the 1940s, Manone appeared in films, including several with Bing Crosby. He also regularly performed in Las Vegas and at jazz festivals through the late 1970s. (William P. Gottlieb Collection, Library of Congress.)

In 1935, Jack Kapp leased several Gennett masters and the name "Champion Records" for his Decca label. In addition to reissuing several of Gennett's classic sides, Decca also recorded new material, including several sides by Tex Ritter, for the heavily discounted Champion label. Ritter's recitation of "The Deck of Cards" landed on the Top 10 in 1948. Ritter was also the father of actor John Ritter. (Berea College Special Collections and Archive.)

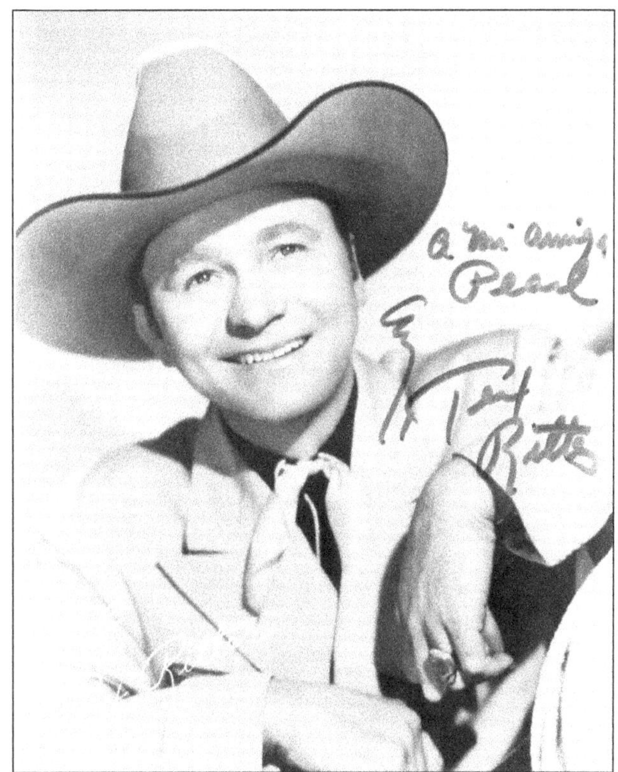

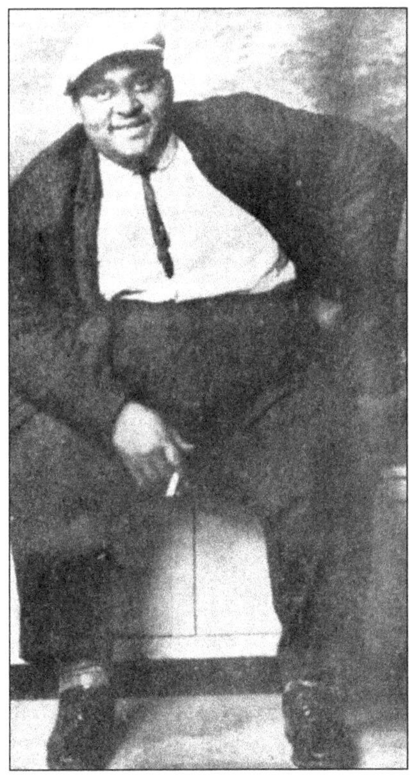

Charles "Cow Cow" Davenport was a veteran of the vaudeville circuit by the time he recorded his boogie-woogie and blues piano in the 1920s. He waxed hundreds of sides in the 1920s and 1930s for multiple record labels. Gennett rejected his first six recordings with Dora Carr on May 25, 1925. However, Gennett asked him to return to Richmond for several productive sessions in 1929 and 1930, many with Ivy Smith. (Center for Popular Music.)

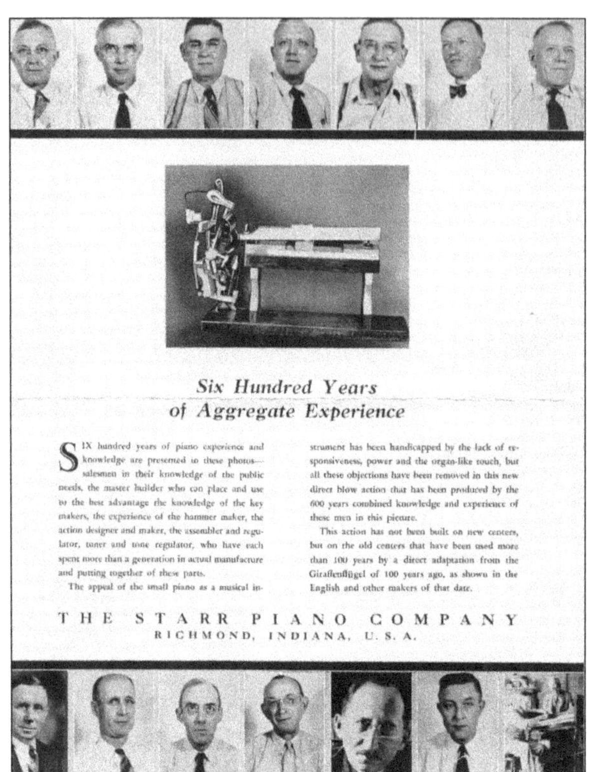

In addition to advertising the features and styles of pianos, Starr Piano highlighted the craftsmanship and experience behind each and every piano manufactured in Richmond. This 1930s advertisement underscores and puts a face to the men and their aggregate experience behind each piano created by Starr. These men, including Harry Gennett Sr. and the Kauper brothers, possessed "six hundred years of piano experience and knowledge." Unfortunately, the piano company went out of business in 1952. (LGI.)

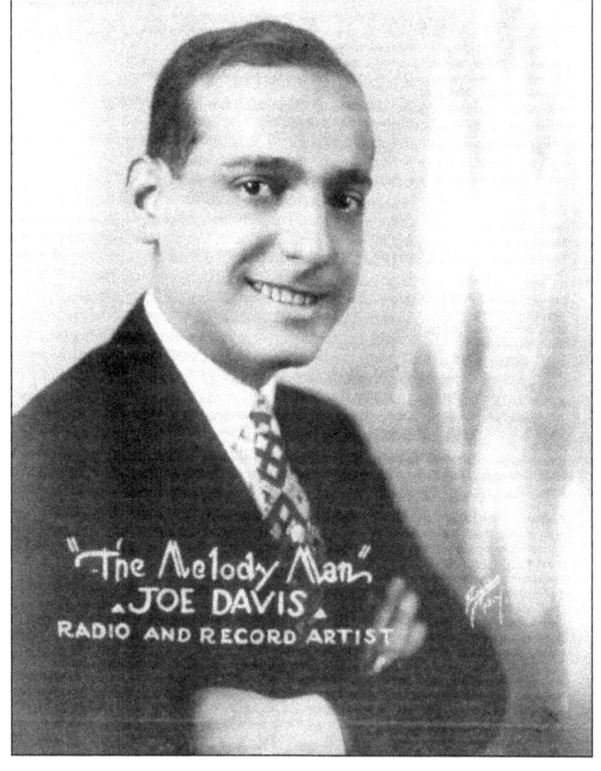

Joe Davis was a recording artist, publisher, and talent scout in the 1920s. In 1942, Davis founded Beacon Records, which developed several subsidiary labels. On September 23, 1944, Davis placed an advertisement in *Billboard* that announced the relaunch of Gennett Records. Davis licensed the Gennett name from Harry Gennett Sr., pressed his records in Richmond, and released new material by the 5 Red Caps, Gabriel Brown, and Savannah Churchill on a newly designed label. The relaunch only lasted a little over a year. (Starr-Gennett Foundation.)

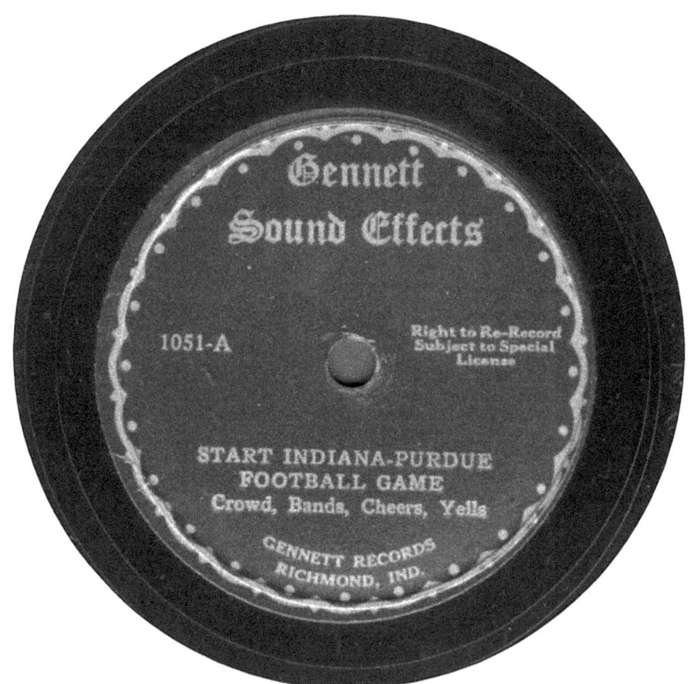

In 1928, the introduction of "talking" pictures led to the demand from theater owners for background music and sound effects to make hold-over silent pictures more impressive and desirable to theater customers. Gennett Records, Victor, and Columbia produced this mood or orchestral background music and sound effects. Gennett Record's library of these sound effects was the White Label 0100 Series. The theater demand slowed in 1929, and Gennett Records was the only company that continued the sound effects business. Radio stations, movie producers, and, later, schools purchased the records. The sound effects recording business was the longest-lived line of Gennett Records. Gennett Sound Effects 1051 was recorded during the Indiana-Purdue football game in Bloomington, Indiana, in the early 1930s. Side A showcases the band playing "The Star-Spangled Banner," the band marching on the field, yells, cheers, and crowd noises. Side B is the crowd after a touchdown and the band playing the "Gang's All Here," "Comin' Round the Mountain," and "Old Oaken Bucket" with cheers and yells. (Both, LGI.)

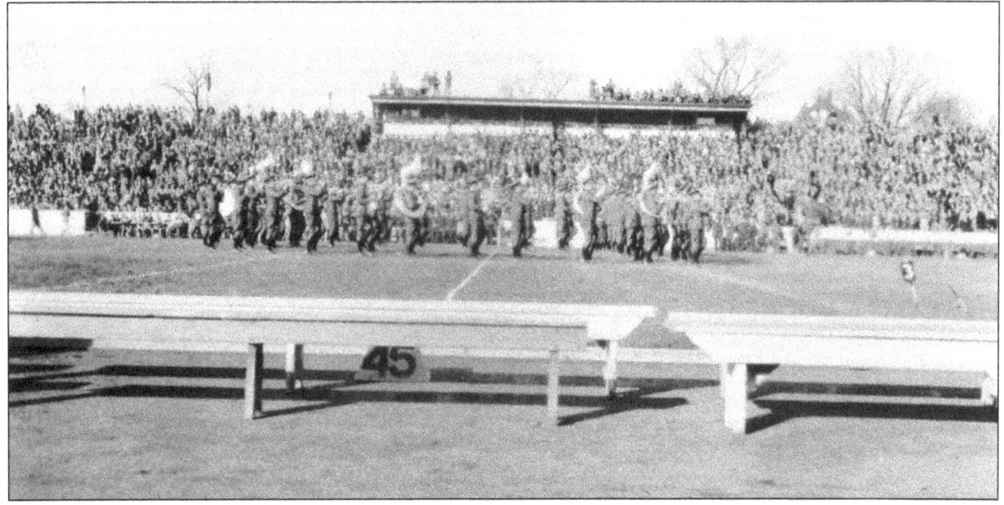

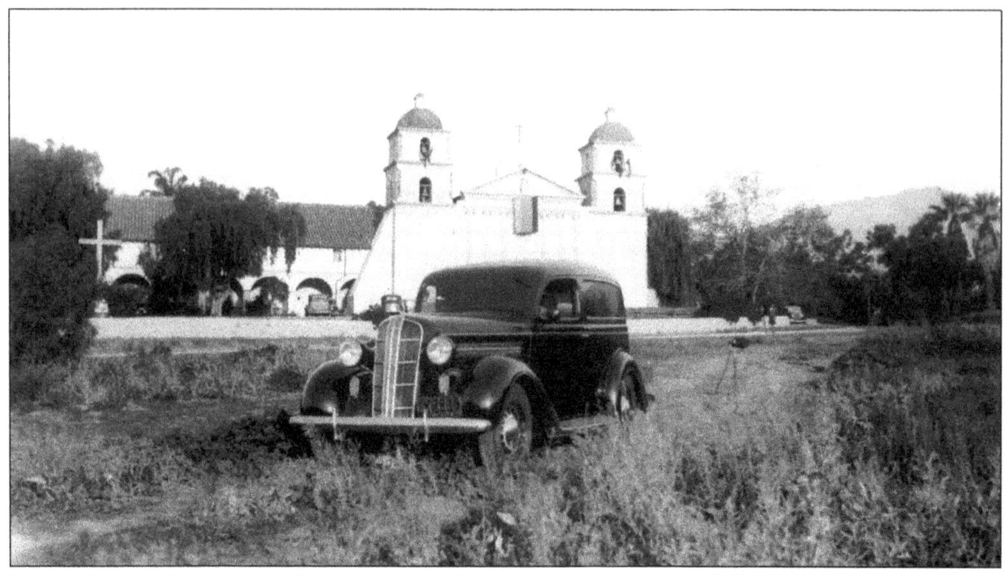

Harry Gennett Jr. (1906–1957) was one of the pioneers in the sound effects field. His interest in sound effects began between 1928 and 1929 when movies shifted away from silent films to talkies. Robert T. Conner worked with Gennett to record many of the sound effects recordings. Gennett Jr. and Conner set aside a wood shed in the Starr Piano complex as their sound effects laboratory. In 1930, Gennett assembled the first "portable" recording unit designed to obtain sound effects from life and in isolated locations. The complete library of sound effects, including Gennett Electrical Transcription Effects, Gennett Sound Effects, Speedy Q, and Syncro Sounds Effects, was 375 records. Specialty series included Skating Rink Service and Chapel Transcriptions. The 1929 Studebaker truck contained over a ton of equipment. Speedy Q Sound Effect 7815 was a recording of the Santa Barbara Mission bells in Santa Barbara, California. (Both, LGI.)

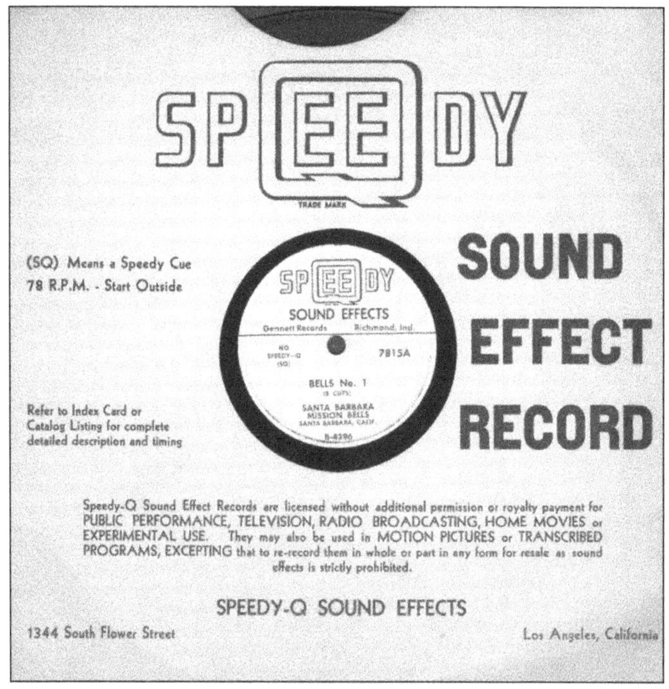

Gennett Records built the first commercial mobile unit using the acetate disk method of recording. The first recording trip was from Richmond, Indiana, to Los Angeles, California. This advertisement appears in the October 20, 1933, Gennett Electrical Transcription Effects catalog: "Transcription, effects, sales talks, etc. can now be made in the office or plant of any advertiser. Incorporate this added touch of realism in your programs and sales plans." (LGI.)

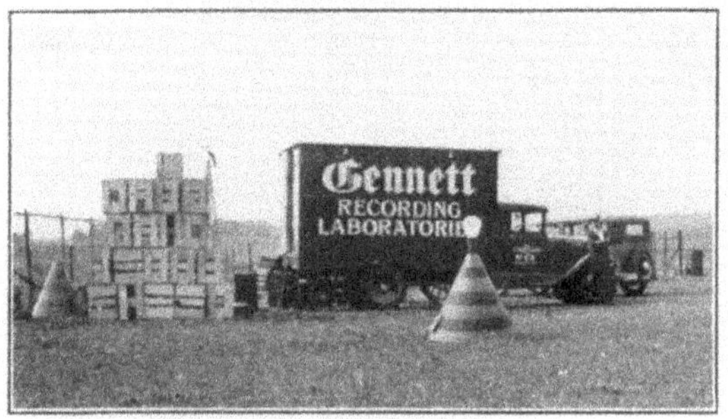

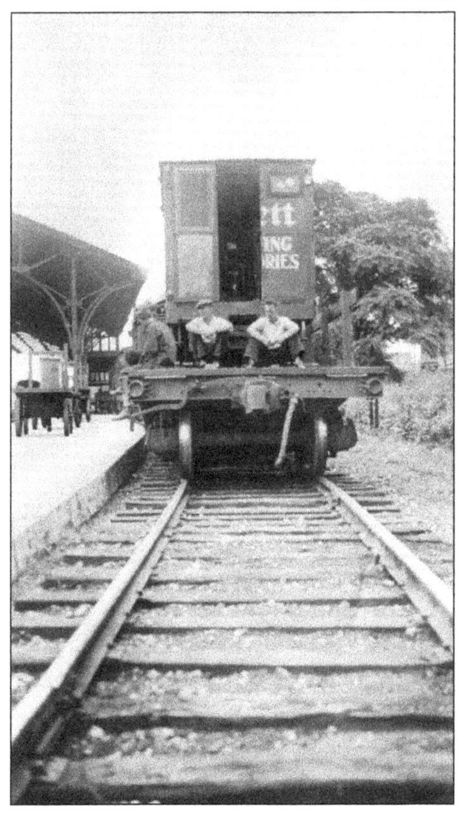

The Gennett Recording Laboratory was loaded on a railcar of the Penn Railroad in Richmond, Indiana, in 1934. Harry Gennett Jr. said, "An effect is only effective when it blends in and does not distract." Gennett responded to a request for a recording of a single cricket in the key of G by simply varying the turntable speed. The sound effect of "Old Lil" trumpeting for a loaf of bread was used in many jungle movies of that era. (LGI.)

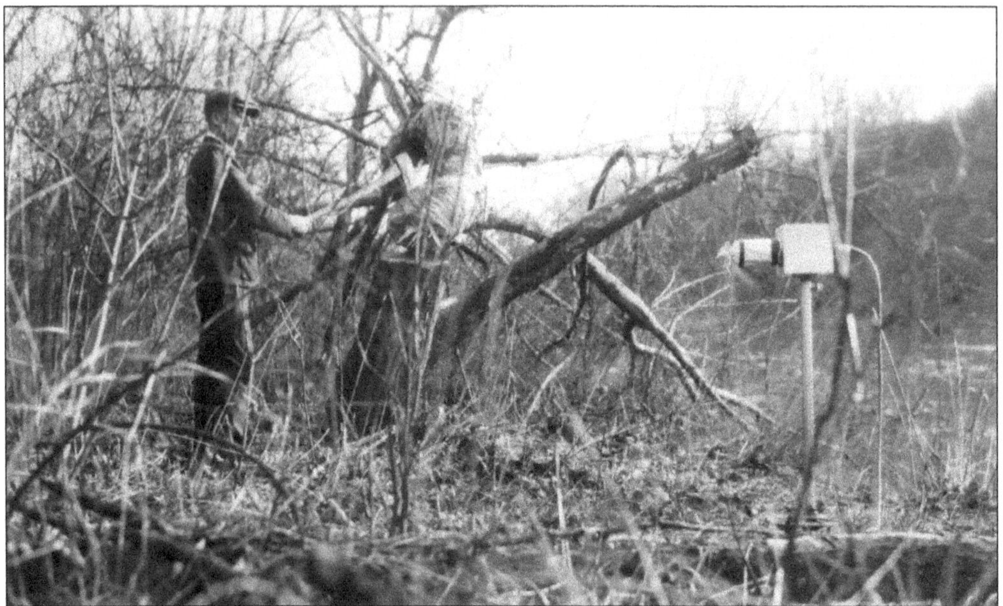

Harry Gennett Jr. is pictured chopping wood with an axe for Gennett Sound Effects 1054A. Lobo wolves were recorded on a pitch-black night near Kane, Pennsylvania, when a siren set them off howling. Many nights, Gennett and Robert Conner stayed on location and slept in the sound truck to get the best sound effect possible. (LGI.)

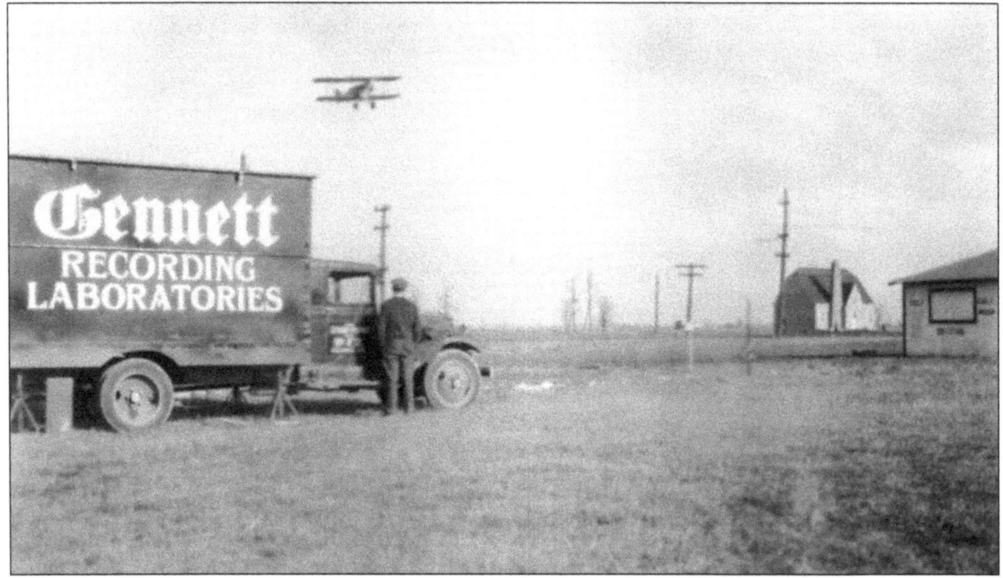

Harry Gennett Jr. is pictured recording a single engine biplane at Boston Airport, near Richmond, Indiana, in 1933. The most famous record catalog number is 1008-B. "Automobile Continuously Running" was recorded in Richmond on February 5, 1931. Another well-recognized effect in the Speedy Q catalog was the Los Angeles harbor foghorn recorded in 1940 and used for the famous B.O. Lifebuoy commercial. Gennett's hobby of photography resulted in great documentation of many of the recordings. (LGI.)

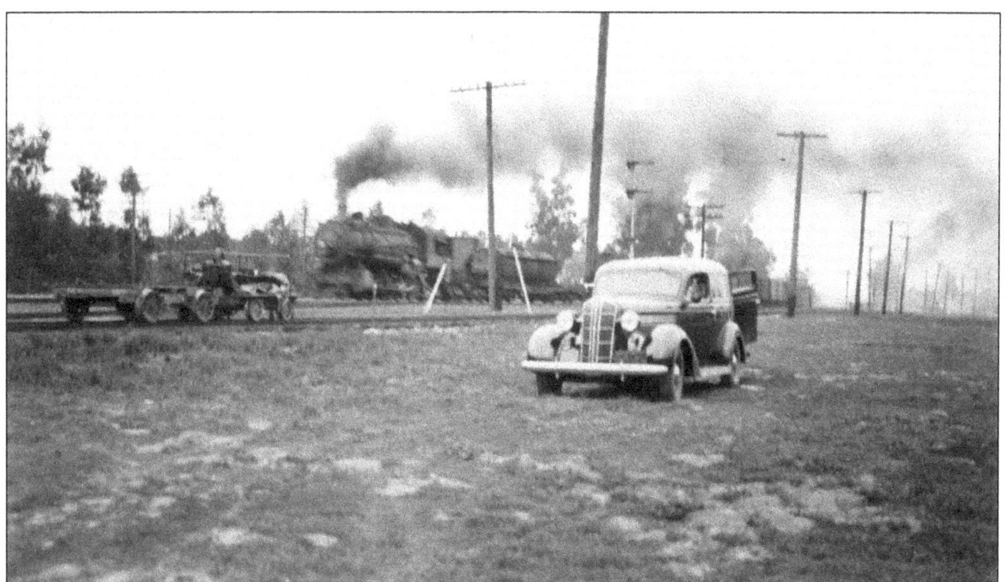

The sound effects catalogs featured many recordings of trains. It may have been because Harry Gennett Jr. was a model-train enthusiast. A recording was made of the Burlington Zephyr entering the station at Galesburg, Illinois, with its diesel motors roaring and its triangle clanging. Near a central Nebraska town, the sound truck parked all night by a long, straight stretch of Union Pacific track where the streamliners whistled almost continuously and attained very high speeds. (LGI.)

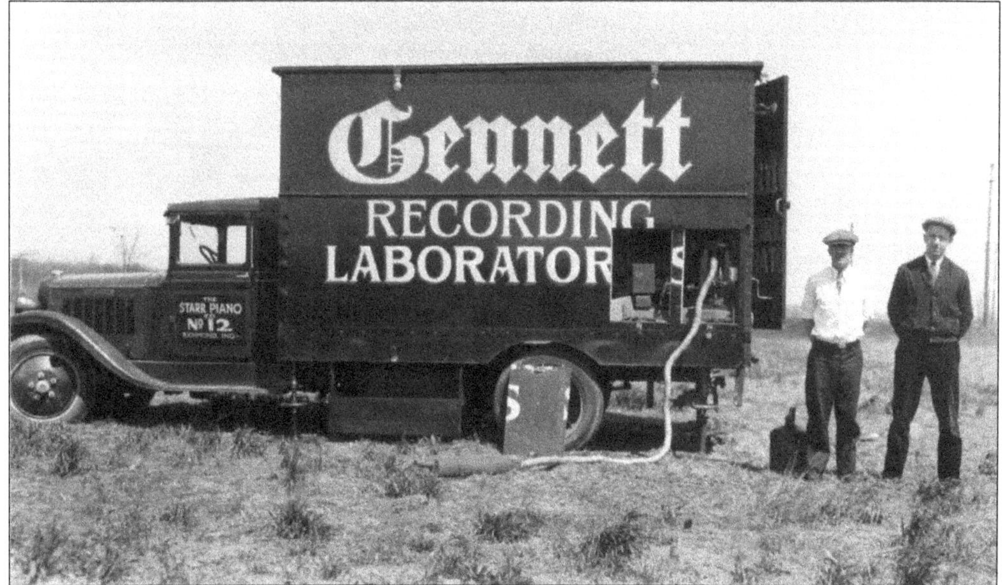

Harry Gennett Jr. is on the right with Robert Conner in 1933. Conner became the plant manager of the Starr Piano buildings and manager of equipment leased to Decca in 1935. Gennett remained in the sound effect business. After Starr Piano closed in 1952, he sold sound effects through a mail-order business. When Gennett died in 1957, his wife, Florence, continued selling sound effects until she sold the business in 1964 to David Gold. (LGI.)

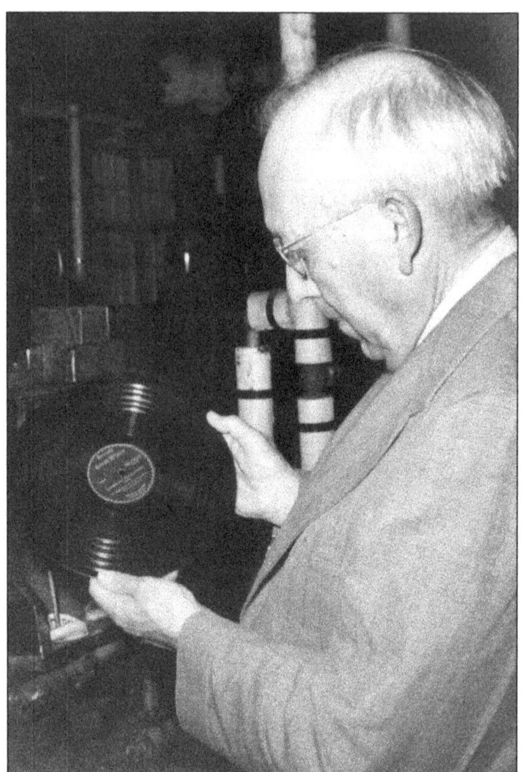

While the record label and recording studio ceased operation by the middle of the 1930s, the pressing plant remained an active business through the 1960s. In addition to pressing the various sound effect releases, in 1935, the Gennett family leased the pressing facility to Decca Records. Here, Harry Gennett Sr. inspects one of the freshly pressed Gennett Sound Effects releases. (LGI.)

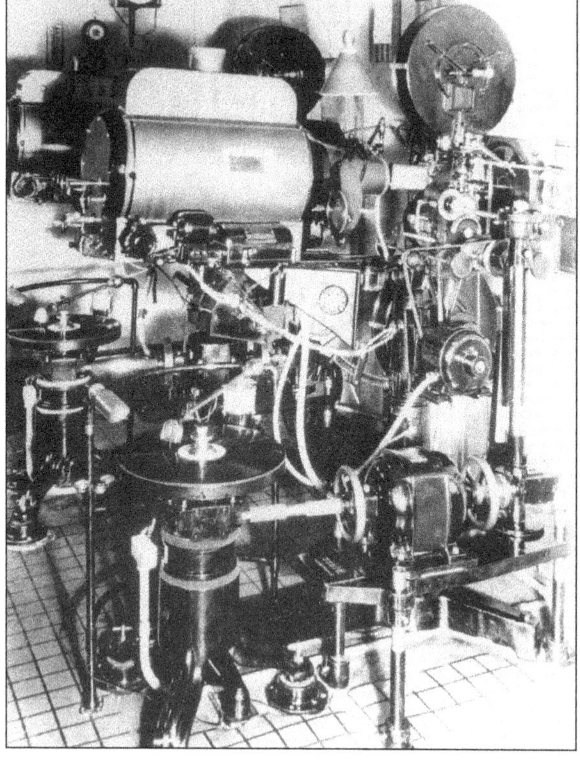

Gennett's sound effects discs were sold largely to radio and television stations, as well as to movie studios for synchronous and nonsynchronous playing. Before movie studios inserted a strip of sound into their films in the 1930s, a transcription player, like the one pictured here and manufactured by Starr Piano, was synched to the projector so the audience could hear sound and music. (Starr-Gennett Foundation.)

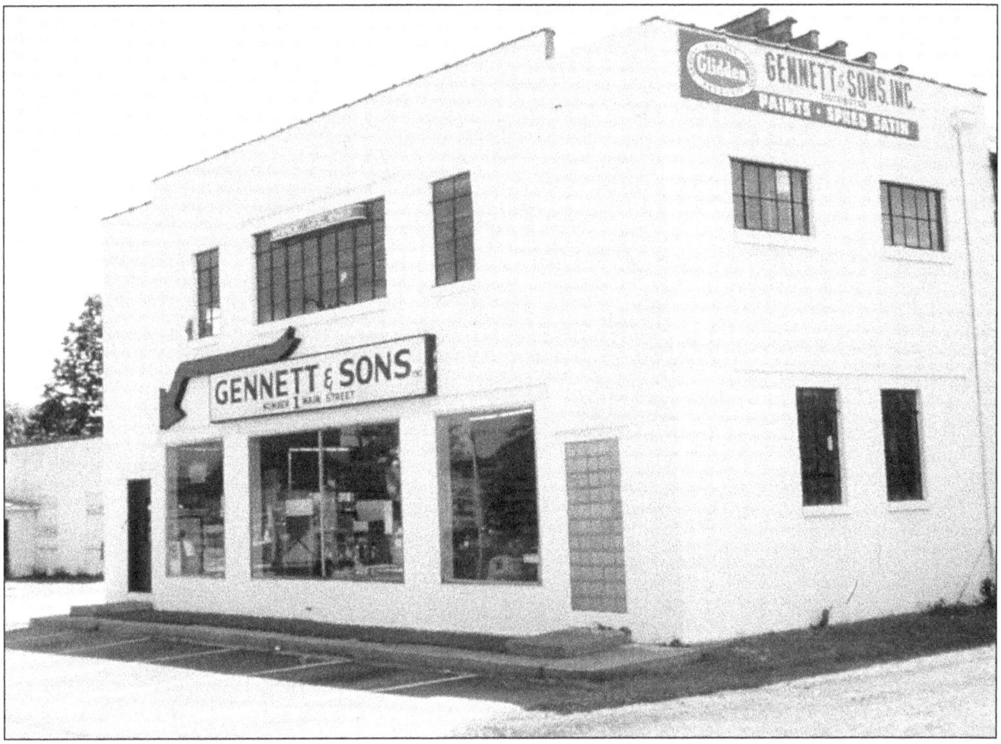

In January 1931, Starr Piano began manufacturing Starr Freeze electric refrigerator equipment. Distribution stores were opened in Richmond, Cleveland, Nashville, Birmingham, and, in 1934, Los Angeles. When the Starr Freeze was discontinued, the profitable parts' stores called the Refrigeration Supplies Distributor, or "RSD," were kept open. The Richmond RSD was always named Gennett & Sons. When Henry Gennett's estate was settled in 1936, children Harry Gennett and Rose Gennett Martin inherited the Pacific Division RSD stores and Clarence and Fred Gennett inherited the others, including the Richmond store. In 1937, Fred (below, right) was president. Gennett & Sons had three businesses. Manufacturing stainless steel hotel and hospital carts was run by Fred's son Richard. Another son, Henry, was in charge of the wholesale business, which was mostly replacement parts for refrigeration, heating, and air-conditioning. Fred ran a travel business called Richmond Travel Bureau, the only travel business in town. Gennett & Sons closed in 1984. (Both, Mike Gennett.)

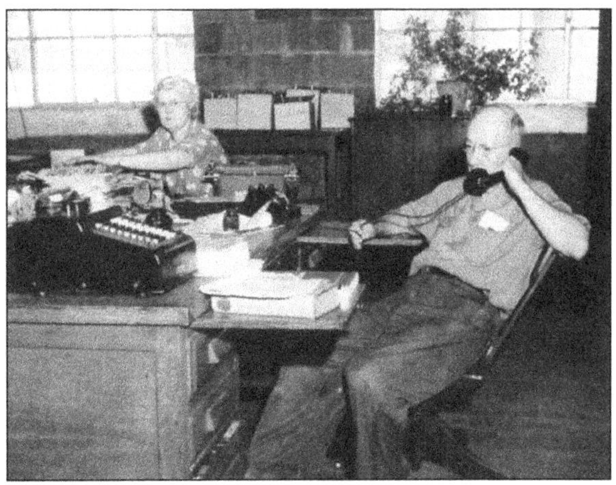

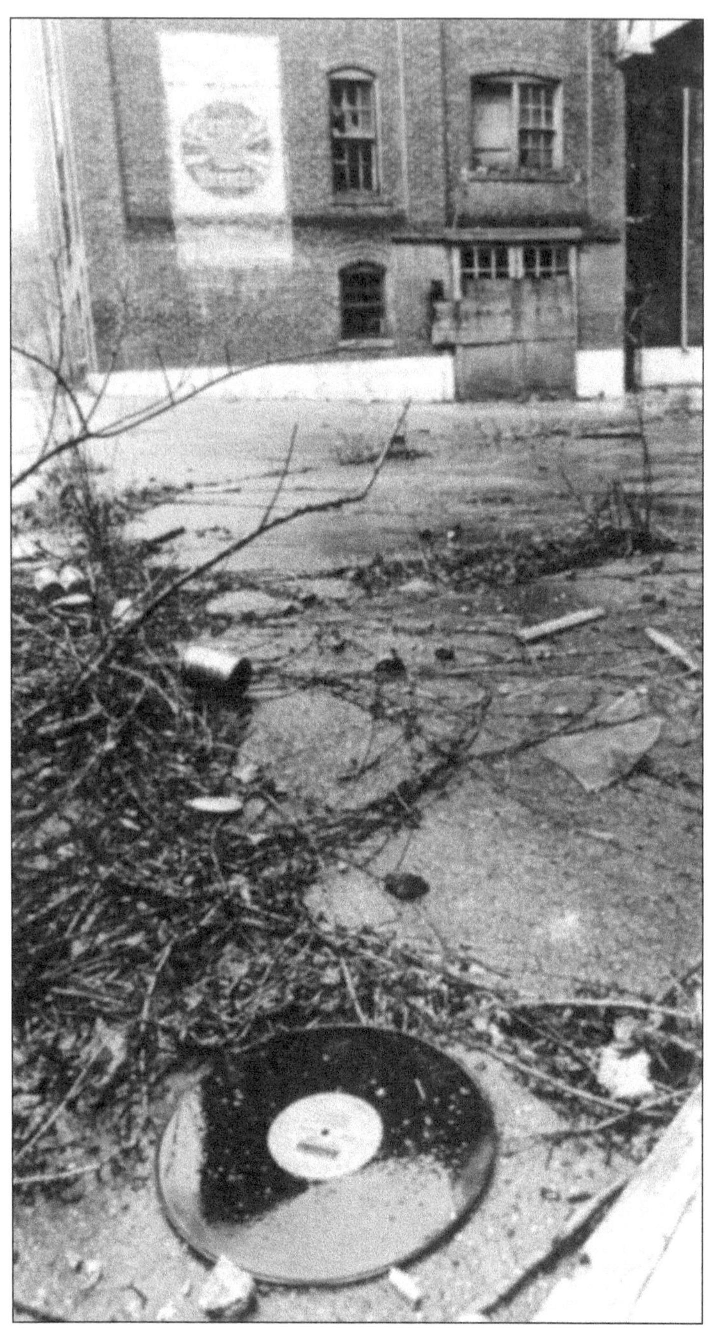

After 1969, Starr Valley was vacant and subject to neglect, deterioration, and vandalism. Over the next three decades, while many Richmond residents wrestled with how to repurpose or preserve the buildings, many ended up beyond repair. This picture taken by Steve Kroger appears in the April 9, 1978, *Pal-Item* newspaper. In the early 1980s, Al Gentry and Bill Delk formed the Starr Gennett Preservation Fund. Henry Gennett Martin and his wife, Laurel, attended the first Richmond Jazz Festival in 1985, sponsored by the Starr Gennett Preservation Fund. Laurel Martin joined the preservation fund and was very actively involved as a representative of the Gennett family. (*Palladium-Item.*)

Five

Once There Was Music Here 1970–2016

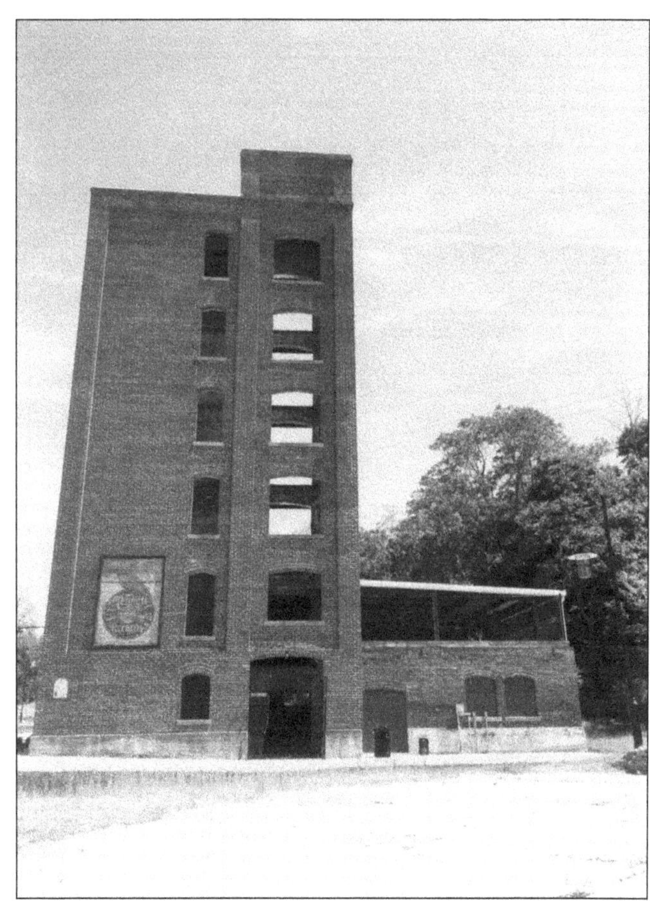

There have been many changes in Starr Valley through the years. The story began with a single four-story building and continued with the growth to over 37 buildings with 3 million square feet covering 35 acres. Time has taken its toll, and the story now returns to a single Starr building, but the legacy of the music continues strongly. (LGI.)

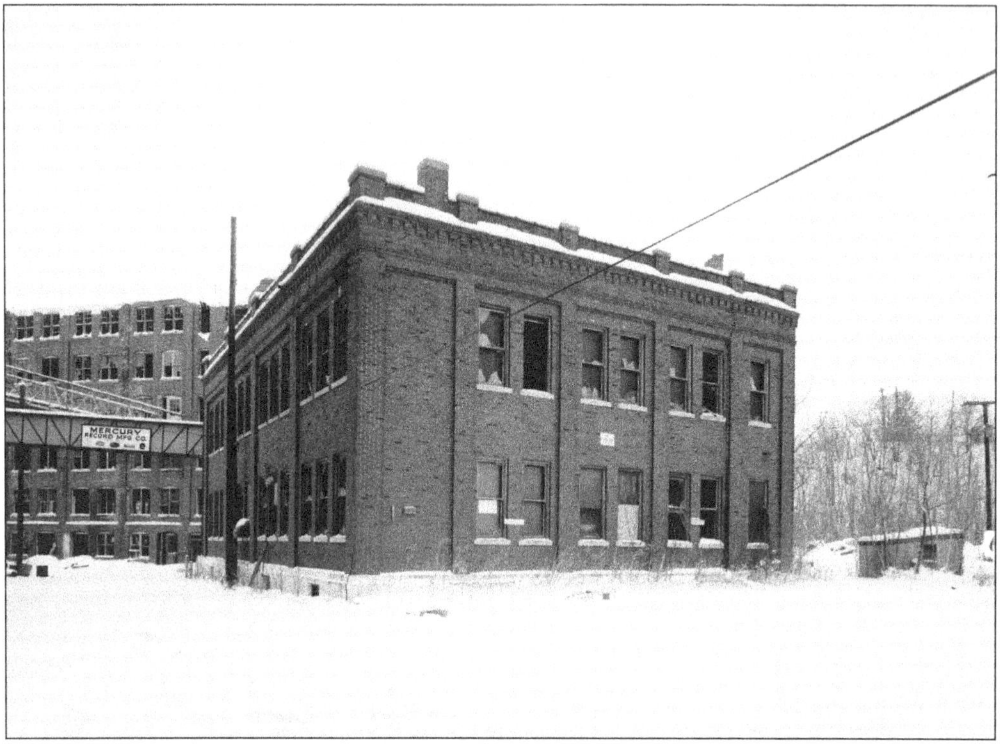

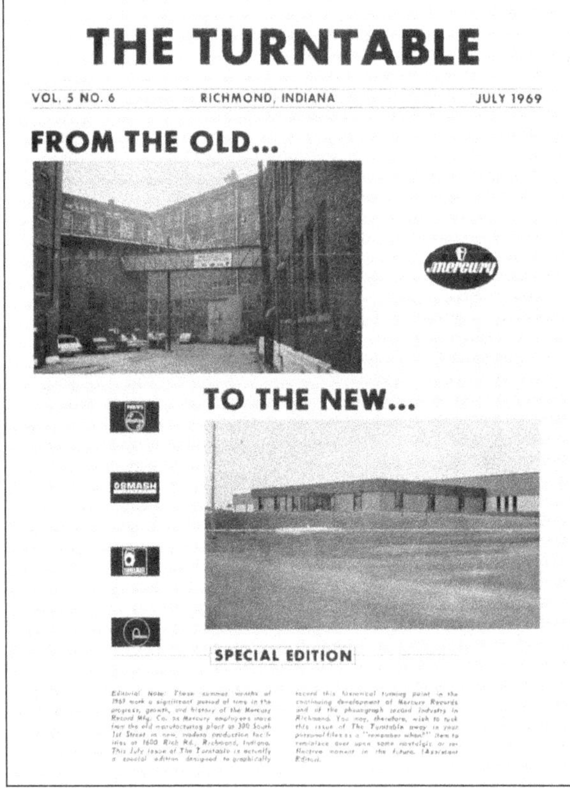

THE TURNTABLE

VOL. 5 NO. 6 RICHMOND, INDIANA JULY 1969

FROM THE OLD...

TO THE NEW...

SPECIAL EDITION

Editorial Note: These summer months of 1969 mark a significant period of time in the progress, growth, and history of the Mercury Record Mfg. Co. as Mercury employees move from the old manufacturing plant at 300 South 1st Street to new, modern production facilities at 1600 Rich Rd., Richmond, Indiana. This July issue of The Turntable is actually a special edition designed to graphically record this historical turning point in the continuing development of Mercury Records and of the phonograph record industry in Richmond. You may, therefore, wish to tuck this issue of The Turntable away in your personal files as a "remember when?" item to reminisce over upon some nostalgic or reflective moment in the future. (Assistant Editor).

In 1935, Starr Piano sold its Champion label and master recordings to Decca, which leased the factory and office space from Starr. When Starr Piano closed in 1952, Decca purchased the record presses. In 1957, Decca closed and was sold to National Record Pressings (NRP). During the next three years, NRP became one of the largest record-pressing plants in the United States. Consolidated Electronics Industries Corp. bought NRP in 1961 and, in 1966, combined its pressing and printing enterprises to form Mercury Record Manufacturing Company. Mercury moved in 1969 from Starr Valley to a new plant at 1600 Rich Road and changed its name to Philips Recording Company. (Both, Morrisson-Reeves Library.)

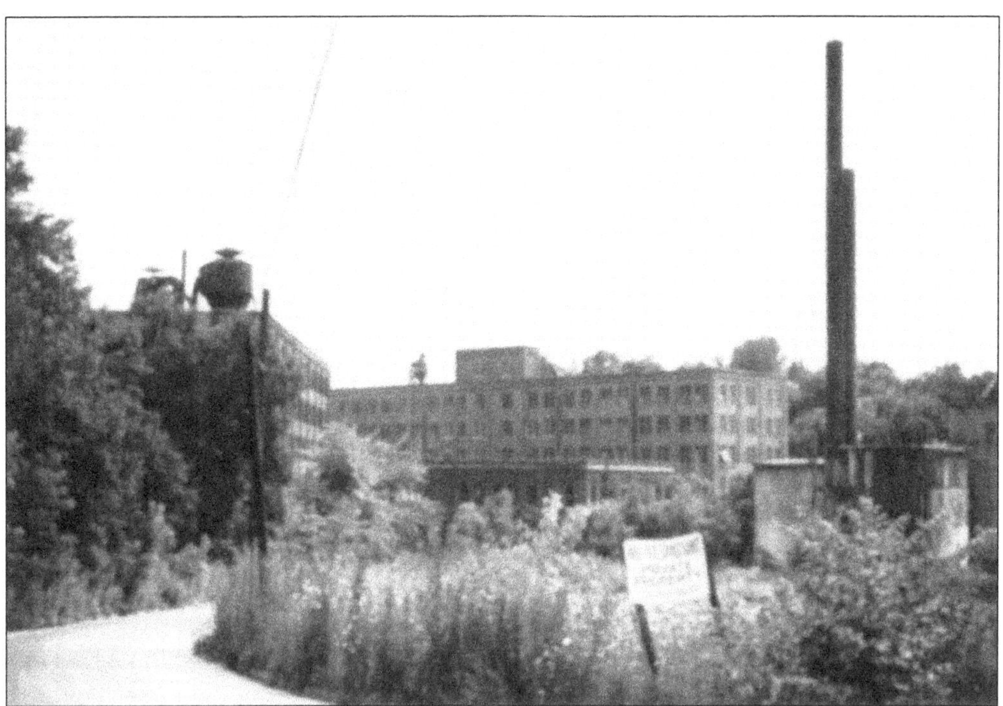

After Mercury Records moved out of Starr Valley in 1969, the once vibrant industrial complex became dormant. The abandoned buildings became subject to deterioration from neglect, infestation, and vandalism. In 1976, Harry Alpert of the J. Solotken Company auctioned Starr Valley to the highest bidder, Frank Robinson, for $84,000. Only two of the structures, the administration and warehouse buildings, qualified for the National Register of Historic Places. Robinson decided to demolish the remaining buildings. Before the destruction occurred, the Historic American Engineering Record (HAER) took several photographs of the abandoned buildings in Starr Valley in the 1970s. The HAER "focused less on the building fabric and more on the machinery and processes within, although structures of distinctly industrial character were recorded." (Above, Starr-Gennett Foundation; right, Library of Congress, Historic American Engineering Record.)

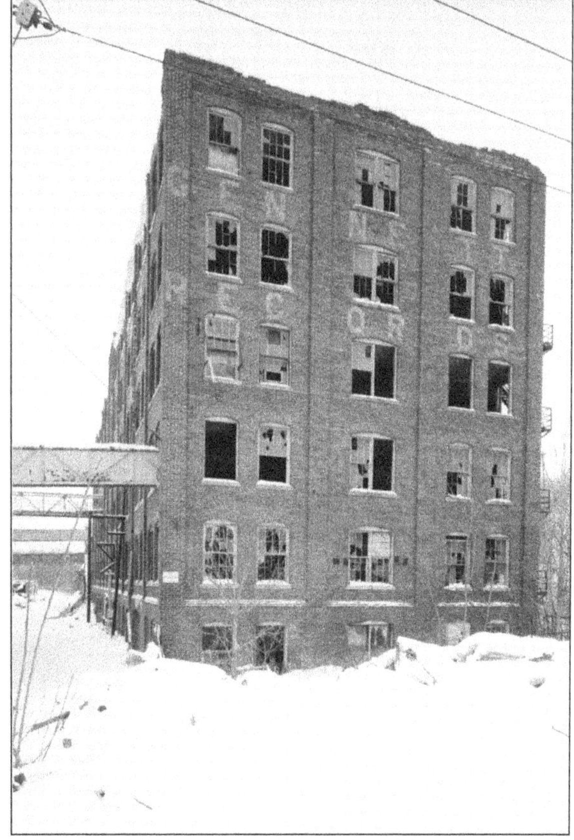

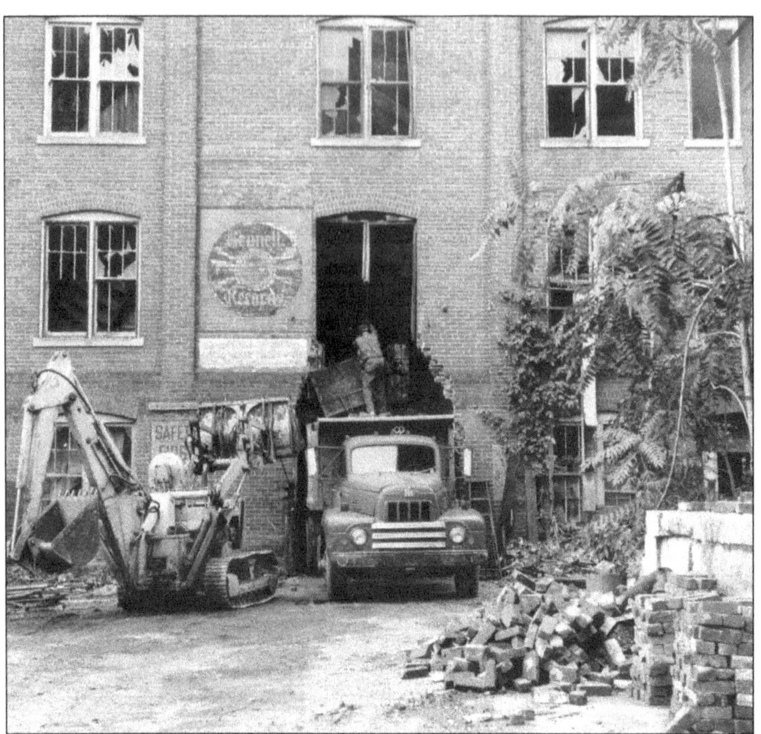

The 1979 photograph above shows one of the buildings being readied for partial demolition from six stories to three. Frank Robinson said that jazz enthusiasts from other states were still continuing to visit what was left of the Starr plant in search of souvenirs or keepsakes. In September 1993, a fire, probably started by vagrants, gutted what was left of that Starr Piano building, but the faded Gennett sign on the tower of the building was not damaged. In the main structure of the building, only the steel beams remained standing above the rubble. Amazingly, this building was restored. Today the "logo" building is being used for concerts and public events. The photograph at right was taken by Dick Rogers for the *Pal-Item* newspaper. (Both, Stephanie Gennett Beach.)

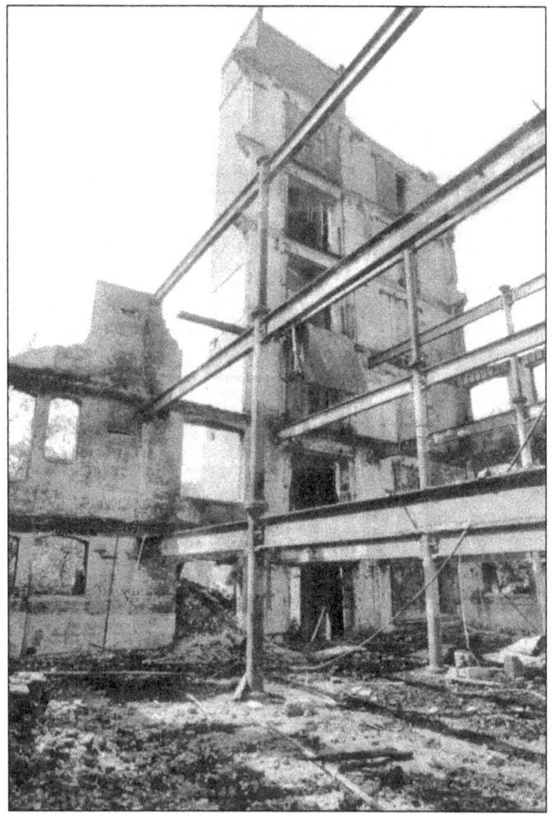

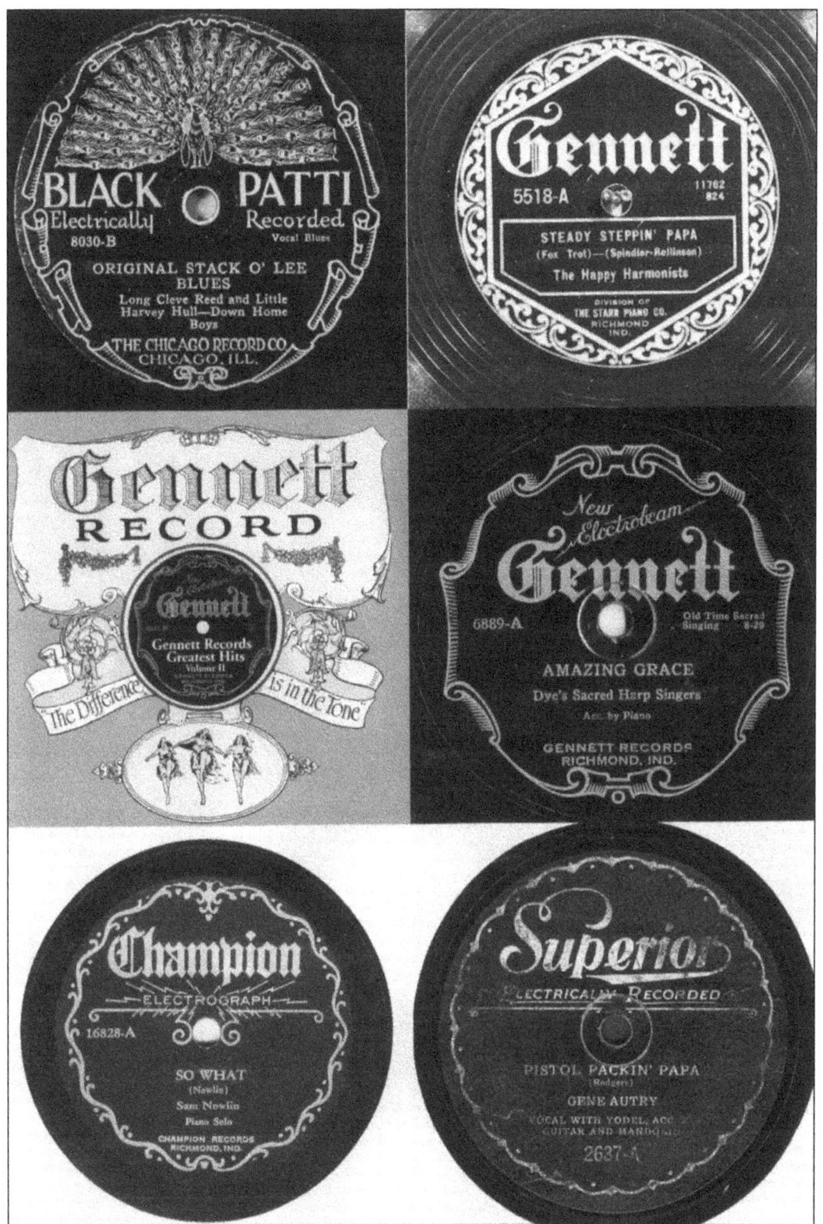

Collecting Gennett Records and the many related labels today is much more than a hobby. The collectors who started years ago say "it's still fun but more expensive and harder to find the rarer records." There is only one known copy of Black Patti 8030, "Original Stack O' Blues." Joe Bussard found it and 14 other mint Black Pattis hidden under a bed in 1966. Roger Misiewicz provided the Electrobeam Dye's Sacred Harp Singers scan. Sacred Harp music, started in the late 1700s in New England, was an idiosyncratic system of musical notation identifying the notes by shape, usually in three- or four-part harmony. Sacred Harp 6889 was recorded in the Richmond studio. Sherwin Dunner provided the Gennett label scan by the Happy Harmonists, with Hoagy Carmichael on the piano. The Starr-Gennett Foundation has reissued many of Gennett's greatest hits on several CDs. Pete Whelan provided the green label scan of Champion 16828, one of the last Champions issued in the 16000 Series. Gene Autry recorded Superior 2637 in 1931. (LGI.)

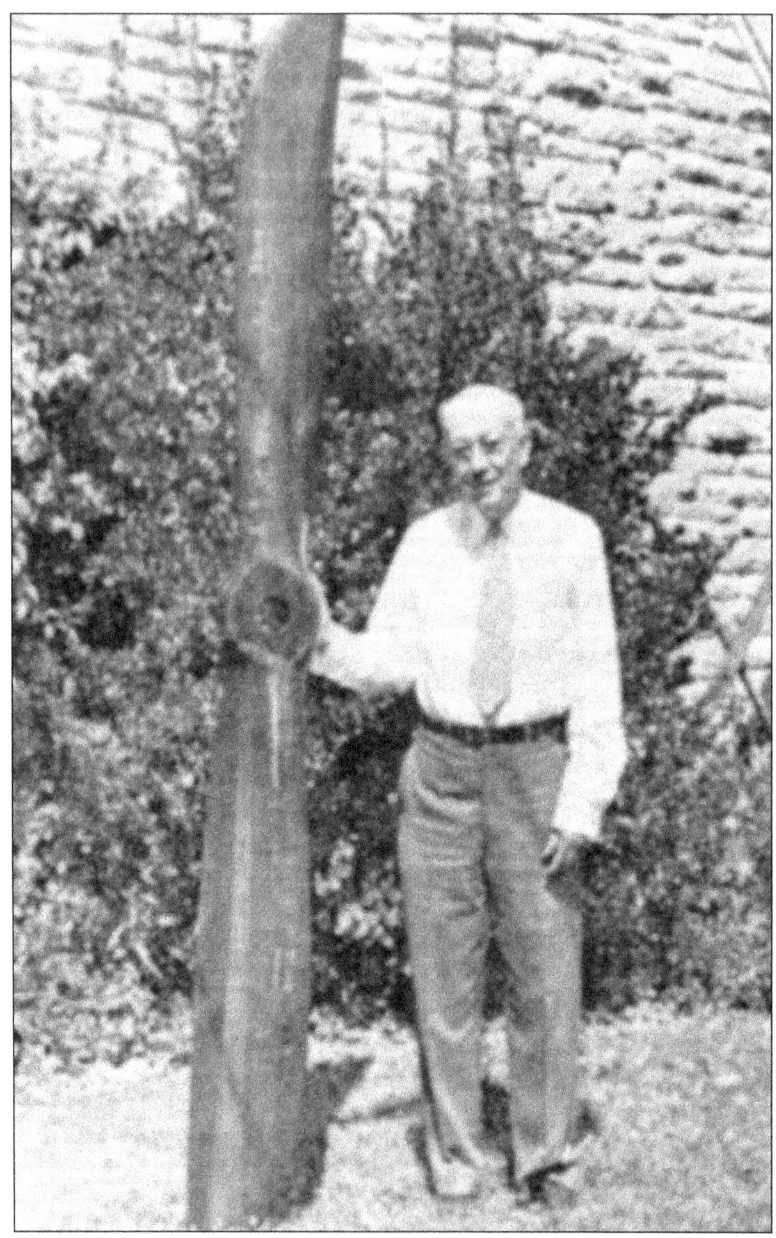

During World War I, companies like Starr Piano were forced to stop production of normal peacetime goods. From April 1917 through October 1918, Starr manufactured all of the wooden replacement and experimental parts in the country's lighter-than-air program. Eight-foot-long wooden propellers like the one Fred Gennett is holding were made of cherry, walnut, and mahogany. "Starr" appears in gold on both ends. A 1917 *Pal-Item* article states that because "some of the materials used to make a player piano are also utilized in balloon construction," Starr was chosen to make the valves for the barrage balloons used by the United States Signal Corps for aerial observation. In the 1940s, Starr Piano made billy clubs to quiet a strike at a local factory. No such labor disputes ever occurred at Starr Piano since most of its craftsmen considered themselves employed for life. During World War II, the factory made caskets and shell casings. (Wayne County Historical Museum.)

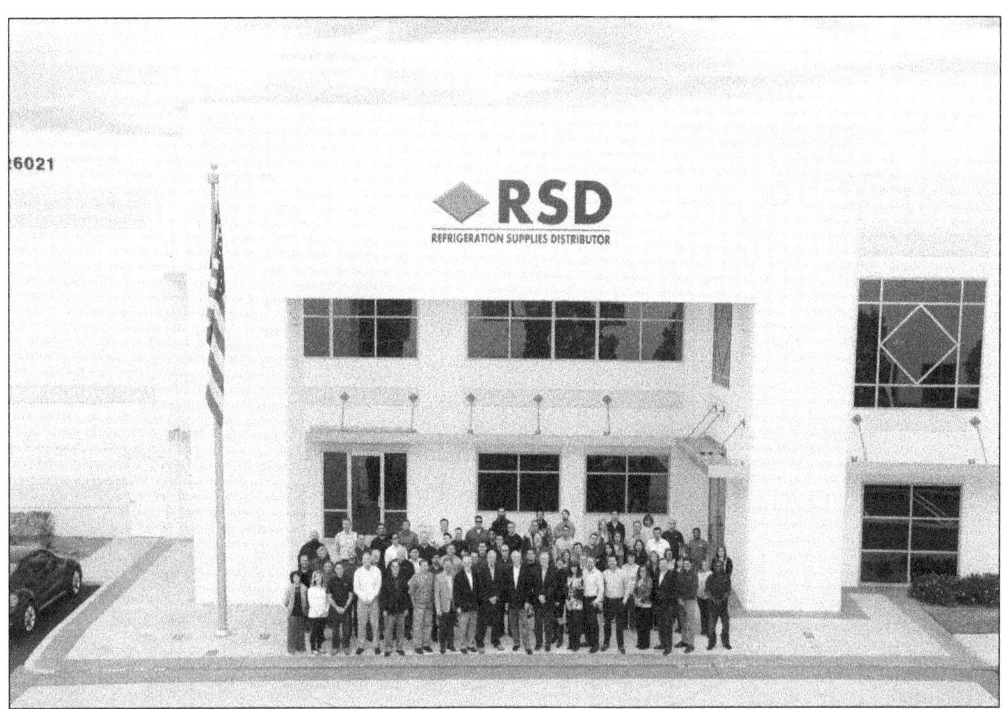

In 1936, Alice Lumsden Gennett, her daughter Rose, and family moved to Los Angeles. Alice assumed the presidency of the Pacific Division of Starr Piano, which included a retail Starr Piano store, various real estate, and four refrigeration (RSD) supplies branches. Rose became president in 1945, and in 1951, Henry was appointed as a board director. In 1952, the piano store and inventory were sold. Henry saw opportunities for growth in the emerging postwar industry of refrigeration and took night classes to learn the principles of refrigeration. Soon, he crossed state lines and opened the fifth RSD branch in Las Vegas, then another in Phoenix. He became president in 1969. In 1978, the Starr Piano Company RSD officially became Refrigeration Supplies Distributor. By 1992, when Henry stepped down and his son Brian Henry Martin became president, there were 36 branches. Today, Brian has expanded RSD to 75 branches in 10 states with 550 employees. Rose Gennett Martin celebrated her 93rd birthday with her son Henry Gennett Martin. (Above, Brian Henry Martin; below, Laurel Martin.)

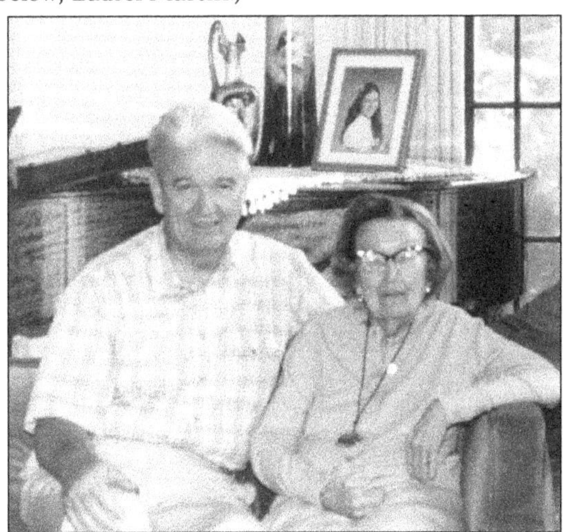

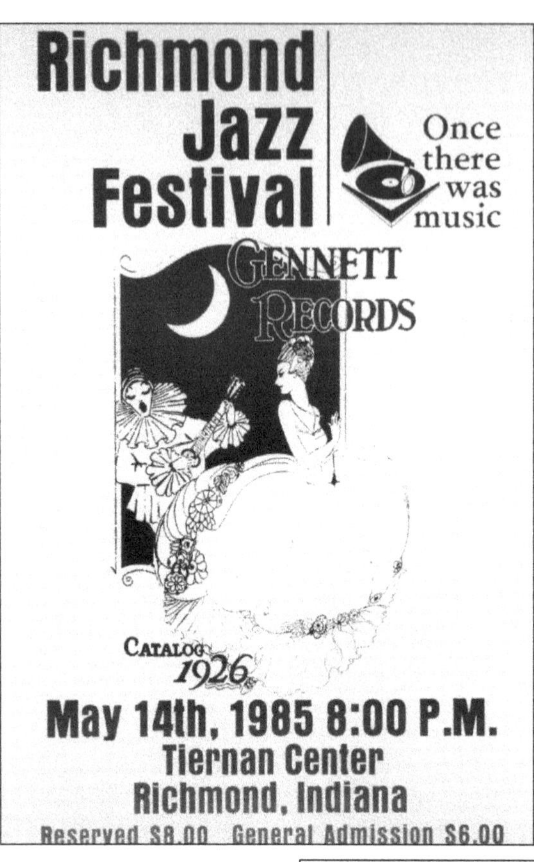

The first and second Richmond Jazz Festivals were sponsored by the Whitewater Valley Gorge Park Committee of the Richmond Area Chamber of Commerce and benefited the Starr Gennett Preservation Fund of the Wayne County, Indiana, Foundation, Inc. A reception for former Starr-Gennett employees was held before each concert. (LGI.)

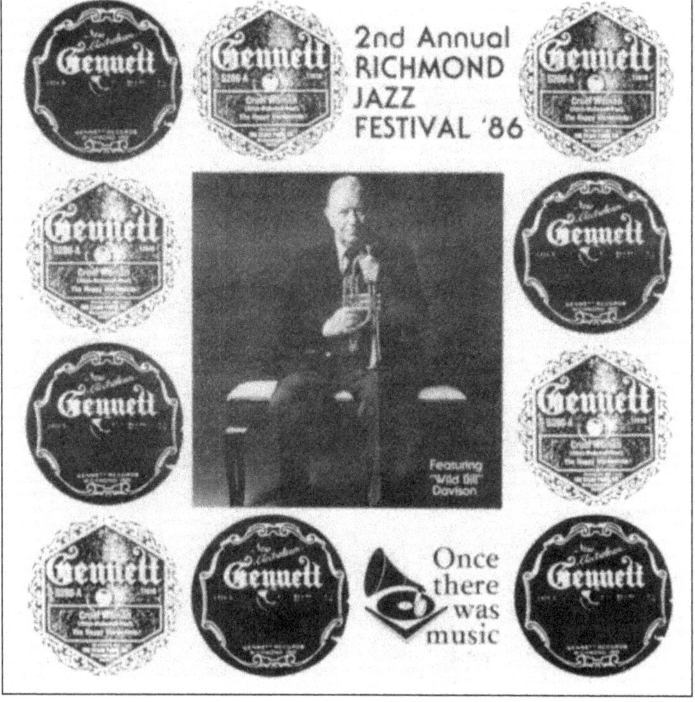

Cornetist "Wild" Bill Davison recorded nine sides, though Gennett only released four of them, with the Chubb Steinberg Orchestra at the Richmond studio in 1925. Sixty-one years later, Davison headlined the Second Annual Richmond Jazz Festival, which raised awareness and funds for the preservation and recognition of Richmond's musical history. Davison was a celebrated trumpeter with Eddie Condon in the 1940s and continued recording and touring until his death in 1990. (Starr-Gennett Foundation.)

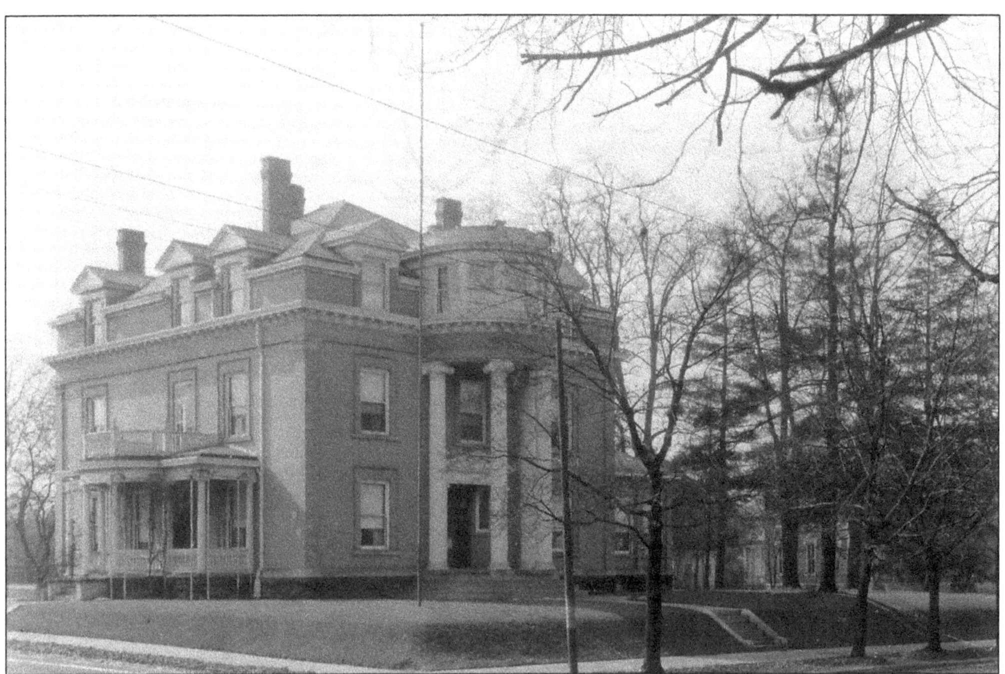

Henry and Alice Gennett's Colonial Revival–style home, pictured here in the 1900s, was built in 1898. The 10,000-square-foot home is constructed of yellow ceramic brick with an Indiana limestone foundation and monumental, semicircular entry portico. It has eight fireplaces and beautifully carved woodwork. Henry Gennett died in 1922, but it was not until 1936 when wife Alice, daughter Rose, and her family moved to Los Angeles. The home was sold at auction in 1938 and turned into 12 apartments, four on each floor, becoming the Shelley Apartments. In 1982, the home was saved from demolition by Wayne Vincent, president of World Life and Accident Association. After three years of renovation, it opened as headquarters for World Life. Vincent is responsible for the home being listed in the National Register of Historic Places. It continued as offices until 2006, when Bob and Donna Geddes purchased the home and began a complete restoration, returning the first floor to 99 percent of its original design and having public events there. The third floor was their residence. In 2016, the home was sold but will remain as a residence. (Above, Mike Gennett; below, LGI.)

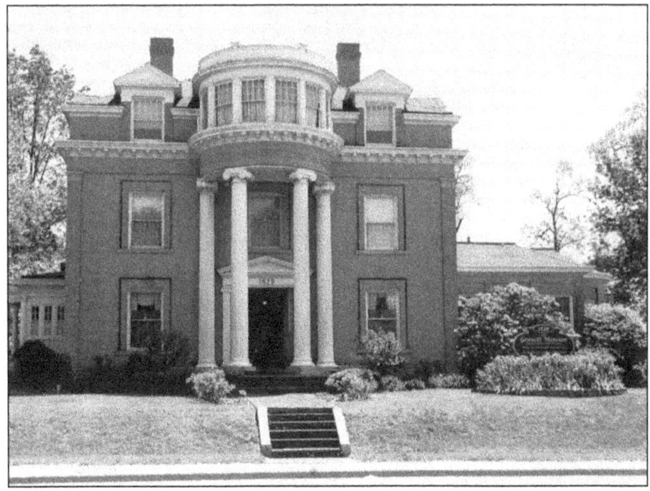

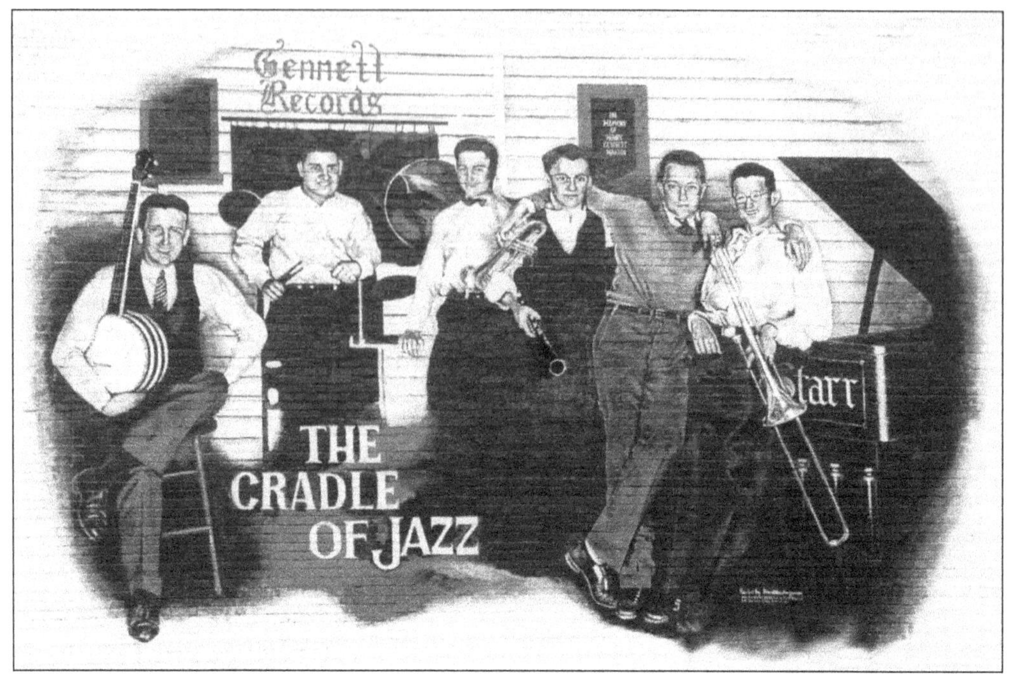

The Cradle of Recorded Jazz was the first of many Starr-Gennett–related murals painted in Richmond. This mural is Pam Bliss Ferguson's rendition of a 1925 photograph of Bix Beiderbecke and his Rhythm Jugglers. Band members depicted are, from left to right, Howdy Quicksell, Tommy Gargano, Paul Mertz, Don Murray, Bix Beiderbecke, and Tommy Dorsey. The mural was dedicated in memory of Henry Gennett Martin by his wife, Laurel Martin. (LGI.)

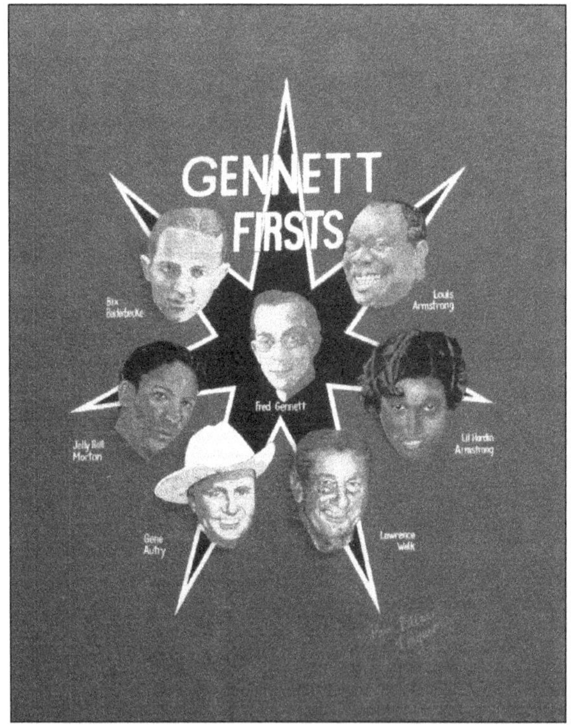

The mural *Gennett Firsts* is on the A.H. Bartel building. Fred Gennett, at center, was the manager of Gennett Records. The first recording session by King Oliver and his Creole Jazz Band was in 1923 and included Louis Armstrong's first recorded cornet solo. Jelly Roll Morton was on the piano with the New Orleans Rhythm Kings on the first documented joint recording of black and white jazz musicians in a studio. Hoagy Carmichael's first composition was recorded at Gennett. (Bob Jacobsen.)

The first Gennett Records Walk of Fame celebration and induction occurred in Whitewater Gorge Municipal Park, also known as Starr Valley, on September 8, 2007. The Starr-Gennett Foundation's National Advisory Board selected the first 11 accomplished artists honored with medallions. Wilson Custom Tile of Omaha, Nebraska, designed and created each mosaic tile and bronze medallion. Over 50 descendants of Henry Gennett attended the ceremony. There were representatives from the families of each of Henry's four children—Harry, Clarence, Fred, and Rose. (Starr-Gennett Foundation.)

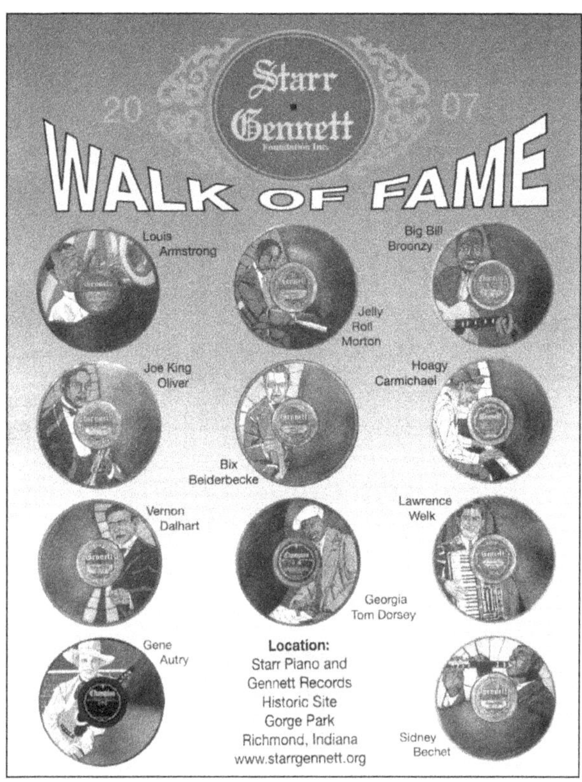

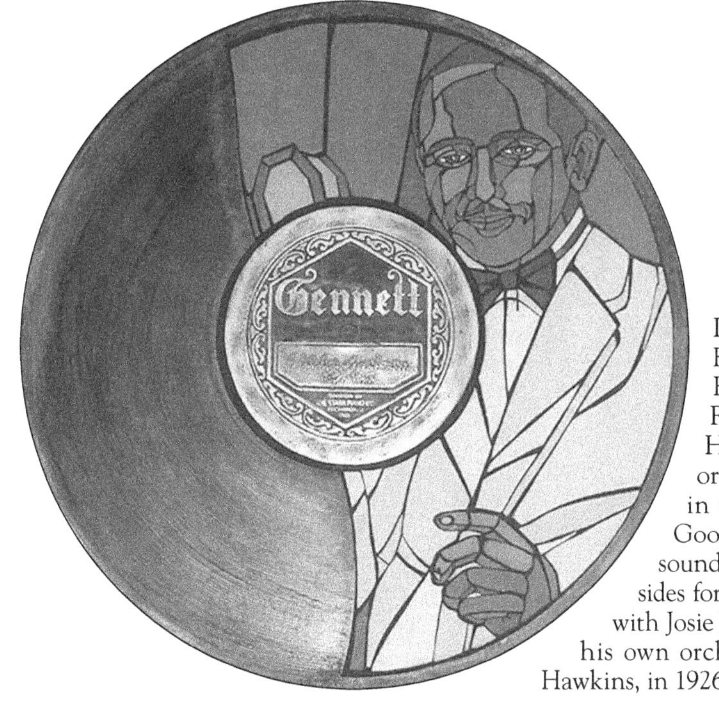

In 2008, the Starr-Gennett Foundation inducted Fletcher Henderson into the Gennett Records Walk of Fame. Henderson was a prolific orchestra leader and arranger in the 1920s and with Benny Goodman created the swing-era sound. He recorded over a dozen sides for Gennett in New York City with Josie Miles in 1923 and 1924 and his own orchestra, featuring Coleman Hawkins, in 1926. (Wilson Custom Tile.)

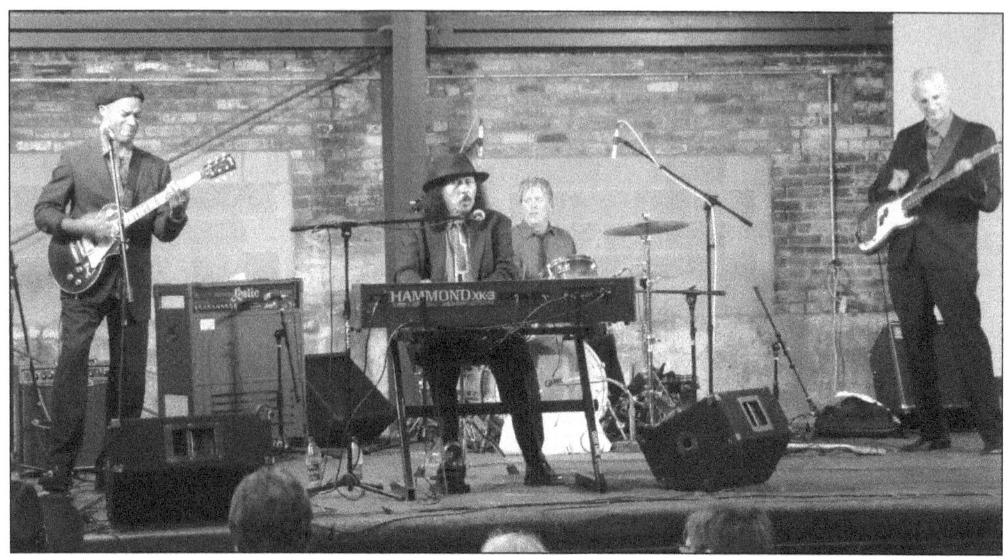

In 1997, the Starr Gennett Preservation Fund was presented by chairman Laurel Martin to the Richmond Park Board, which changed the name to the Starr-Gennett Foundation. The not-for-profit organization's mission is to "preserve and promote the legacy of the Starr Piano Company and its Gennett Records Division." The foundation is located at 33 South Seventh Street, Richmond, Indiana, 47374. One very successful project has been the installation of the Gennett Records Walk of Fame. There are currently 34 medallions in the walk, honoring many well-known Gennett recording artists. At the 2010 Walk of Fame Festival, "Deacon" Jones, a Grammy-winning Richmond native, performed at a concert in the "logo" building in Starr Valley. The foundation has also promoted a school program for local second- and third-grade children to educate them about the history of the music recorded at Gennett Records. Below, some children surround the Alberta Hunter medallion. (Above, LGI; below, Bob Jacobsen.)

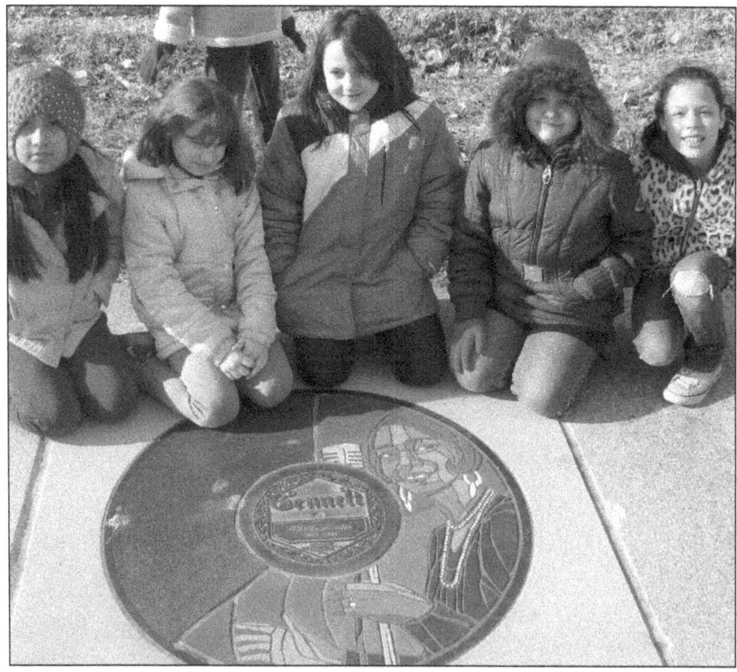

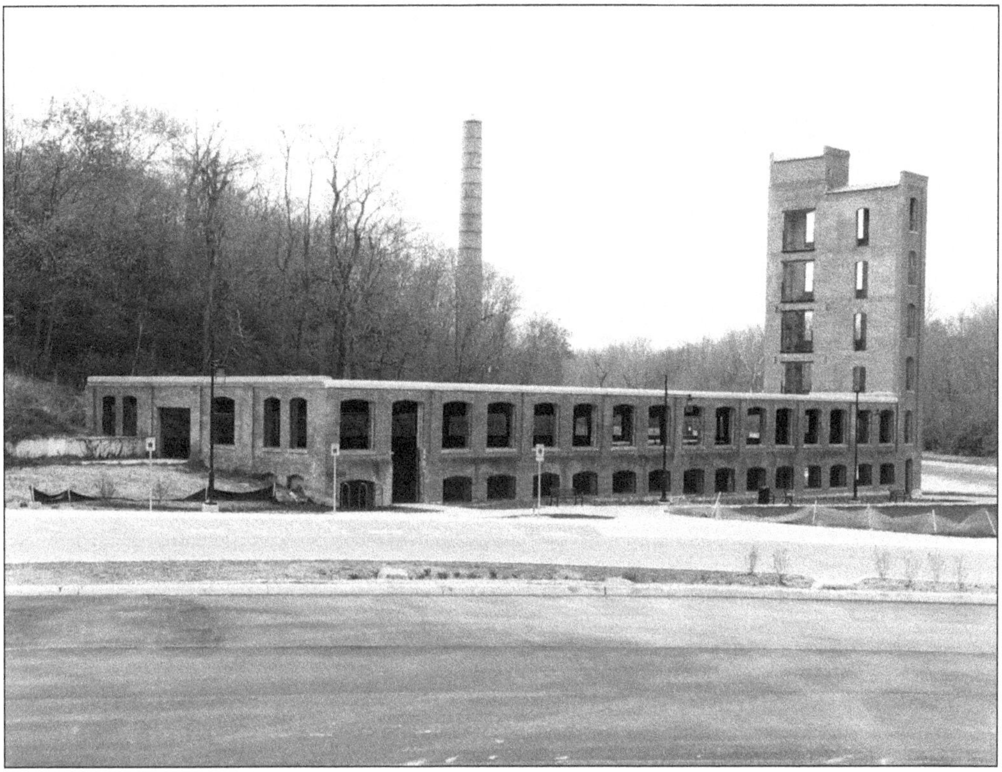

The "logo" building and the smokestack are the only reminders of the once booming Starr Piano complex. In the 1980s, the owner partially demolished the six-story building to three stories. A fire in 1983 further gutted it. The City of Richmond received the building in the early 1990s. Funding to stabilize and restore the "logo" building to its present two-story condition came from Build Indiana funds. Concerts, weddings, proms, and school field trips are among events now held there. The "logo" building and Starr Valley are stops along the Whitewater River Gorge Trail. In 2016, the Whitewater Gorge Alliance was formed to enhance and promote the Whitewater River gorge. The next step for the City of Richmond is to secure funding to connect the gorge trail to the Cardinal Greenway, a rails-to-trails spanning five counties in east-central Indiana. The photograph at right features a view across Starr Valley from the Louis Armstrong medallion, which marks the location of the famous Gennett recording studio beside the railroad spur. "Once there was music." (Both, LGI.)

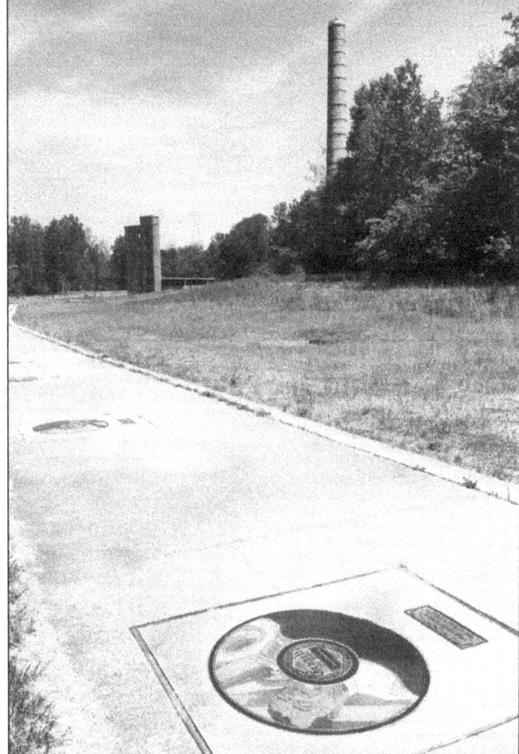

Bibliography

Dixon, Robert M.W., John Godrich, and Howard Rye. *Blues and Gospel Records, 1890–1943*. New York: Oxford University Press, 1997.

Kay, George W. "Those Fabulous Gennetts!" *Record Changer*, June 1953.

Kennedy, Rick. *Jelly Roll, Bix, and Hoagy: Gennett Records and the Rise of America's Musical Grassroots*. Bloomington: Indiana University Press, 2013.

Kenney, William Howland. *Chicago Jazz: A Cultural History, 1904–1930*. New York: Oxford University Press, 1993.

Marco, Guy A., and Frank Andrews. *Encyclopedia of Recorded Sound in the United States*. New York: Garland Publishing, 1993.

Miller, Karl Hagstrom. *Segregating Sound: Inventing Folk and Pop Music in the Age of Jim Crow*. Durham, NC: Duke University Press, 2010.

Pictorial History of the City of Richmond, Indiana, 1806–1906, Dolby's Centennial Souvenir. Richmond, IN: Nicholson Printing & Mfg. Company, 1906.

Russell, Tony. *Country Music Originals: The Legends and the Lost*. New York: Oxford University Press, 2007.

Russell, Tony, and Bob Pinson. *Country Music Records: A Discography, 1921–1942*. New York: Oxford University Press, 2004.

Rust, Brian. *Jazz Records, 1897–1942*. New York: Arlington House Publishers, 1978.

Schiedt, Duncan. *The Jazz State of Indiana*. Pittsboro, IN: Duncan P. Schiedt, 1977.

Sutton, Allan. *Race Records and the American Recording Industry, 1919–1945*. Denver: Mainspring Press, 2016.

Tomlan, Mary Raddant, and Michael A. Tomlan. *Richmond, Indiana: Its Physical Development and Aesthetic Heritage to 1920*. Indianapolis: Indiana Historical Society, 2003.

Tuuk, Alex Van Der. *Paramount's Rise and Fall: A History of the Wisconsin Chair Company and Its Recording Activities*. Denver: Mainspring Press, 2003.

Ward, Gertrude. *Richmond: A Pictorial History*. St. Louis: G. Bradley Publishing, 1994.

Wolfe, Charles K. *Classic Country: Legends of Country Music*. New York: Routledge Press, 2001.

———. *Kentucky Country*. Lexington: University of Kentucky Press, 1996.

SELECTED INDEX

www.ingramcontent.com/pod-product-compliance
Lightning Source LLC
LaVergne TN
LVHW060625110826
845147LV00015B/939